Anne Bourne
29 River Street
Woodstock, Vermont 05091

D1712966

The
Long Light
of
Those Days

To Nan Bourne,

I hope you find much to
enjoy in this attempted
recovery operation.

With all best wishes,

Bruce Coffin

9/1/07

The
Long Light
of
Those Days

RECOLLECTIONS
OF
A VERMONT VILLAGE
AT
MID-CENTURY

Bruce Coffin

The Elm Tree Press
Woodstock • Vermont

Published by The Elm Tree Press, an imprint of
The Woodstock Historical Society, Woodstock, Vermont 05091
www.woodstockhistsoc.org

Library of Congress Cataloging-in-Publication Data
Coffin, Bruce, 1942-
The long light of those days: recollections of a Vermont village at mid-century/
Bruce Coffin.
p.cm.
ISBN 0-9767729-0-6
1. Woodstock (Vt.)--Social life and customs--20th century. 2. Coffin, Bruce, 1942--
Childhood and youth. 3. Woodstock (Vt.)--Biography. 4. Woodstock (Vt.)--
Description and travel. I. Title.
F59.W8C64 2005
974.3'65--dc22
2005011835

10 9 8 7 6 5 4 3 2

Jacket Design by Charlotte Strick

Book Design by Wayne Thompson

Typesetting by Wendy Chamberlin

Printed in the United States of America
By Queen City Printers Inc.
Burlington, Vermont 05402-0756

For my father, WALLACE COFFIN (1907-1983),
and my mother, ARLENE JILLSON COFFIN (1915-2000),
in loving memory.

And for Maria, Lizzie, Jonathan, Howard, and Jane.

And might it not be. . . that we also have appointments to keep in the past, in what has gone before us and is for the most part extinguished, and must go there in search of places and people who have some connection with us on the far side of time. . .?
W. G. SEBALD

Memory is more than a looking back to a time that is no longer; it is a looking out into another kind of time altogether where everything that ever was continues not just to be but to grow and change with the life that is in it still.
FREDERICK BUECHNER

Chapters

Acknowledgments

A book of this sort is by its very nature a kind of collaboration. In the course of writing it, I have consulted a number of people whom I would like to recognize for their assistance. Among them were a great many who were able to supply me with factual information or confirm various vague recollections: Ed Bacon, Anna Biathrow, Bobo Birsky, Paul Bourdon, Ed Brehaut, Ralph Coffin, Sara Dana, Fred Doubleday, Charlie DuBeau, Helen Dunn, Don Eaton, Erwin Eddy, Barbara Fleming, Tom Flower, Esther Frost, Howard and Alice Gould, Cecile Hively, Pat Holland, Frankie Houghton, Janet Houghton, Lucy Houghton, Pat Huntington, Paul and Anne Kenefick, Mary Lord, Cathy Ludwig, Jack Moore, Bev Oliver, Jim Paul, Geneva Potwin, Tink Reed, Mary Sharpe, Pam Stephan, Morgan Vail, John Wells, and John Wiggin. Special thanks are due to Marge Vail for her assistance in the Norman Williams Public Library and for her interest in this project, and to George Goodrow for allowing me to peruse photographs at The Woodstock Historical Society and for our ongoing talks about old Woodstock.

I am indebted to Phil Camp, Kevin Forrest, and Kathy Wendling at *The Vermont Standard* for their interest and support.

I wish to express my gratitude to a number of people for their assistance with technical matters and aspects of design: to my friend and colleague Tom Hungerford for his endless patience in organizing and printing out early drafts; to Steve and Laura Volovski for their advice and help in putting together the final drafts; Mathilde Hungerford for suggestions about design; to Abigail Pope and Charlotte Strick for their generous artistic contributions.

I have greatly benefited from the support and encouragement of a number of people who read earlier or later versions of the book: Robert Anderson, Mimi Baird, Paul Bresnick, Ken Colby, John Elder, Janet Gould, Bruce Hartman, Frank Harvey, Edward Hirsch, David Lamb, Linda Nye, Tom Powers, Bill Roorbach, and Liz VanHoose. I am grateful to Susan DiSesa for her confidence in a wider potential readership than I had anticipated and for her ordering of the chapters, to Bill Henderson of Pushcart Press for his belief in the book and his important advice on matters of publication, and to Cary Goldstein for his assistance with publicity. Above all, I owe a special debt to the people of The Elm Tree Press: first of all to the late Peter Jennison for his initiative and expertise as well as his leadership in the early stages; to Corwin Sharp for his administrative role in bringing the manuscript to book form; to Wayne Thompson, the designer of the book; to Wendy Chamberlin for her work as typesetter; and finally to Chris Lloyd, production supervisor; and Carl Taylor, fellow-member of the production team, for all their invaluable contributions.

I want to thank Steve Jenkins and, again, Tom Hungerford for our many discussions, in the course of which some of the reflections in the opening chapter were shaped and refined.

I am especially grateful to my old friend Dave Doubleday for his interest, but most of all for our many years of reminiscence about the old days.

Lastly, my deepest gratitude is reserved for my family. I owe a great deal to my father, who, though he died before I began working on this book, was a sustaining presence throughout the years of its creation. To my wife, Maria, I am indebted for everything, but especially for her interest in old Woodstock and her patience in listening to my endless monologues about what it was all like back then. I am more grateful than I can say to my children Lizzie and Jonathan, who gave me the extraordinary experience of being a father and, in so doing, helped me to recover my own childhood; it is for them, primarily, that this book is written. I owe special thanks to my sister Jane, whose belief in my efforts was an ongoing source of inspiration and whose sensitivity to the written word made her a kind of tuning fork for the writing and revision of its chapters. I am most deeply grateful to my twin brother Howard for all of his efforts on behalf of this book, including his support and encouragement from start to finish and his editorial suggestions, but mostly for living with me twice, and then some, the years which it was my task to recall. Finally, to my mother I am indebted, first of all, for hours and years of conversations and reflections on times gone by, informed always by her unique sense of compassionate wonder, but also for her insight and understanding as my first and perhaps my best reader.

Memory and the Flight of Time

*Strange forces are at work in this process
of unpacking memory, forces that we,
in our turn, may want to unpack.*

STEPHEN OWEN

This book grew out of my years in Woodstock, which have been all the years of my life. Or, to be more exact, as I have actually spent only one full year there since graduating from Woodstock High School in 1960, it grew out of my sense that wherever I happened to be residing, in America or abroad, a part of me continued to live very fully and vividly in the Woodstock in which I grew up. Woodstock is, as anyone who has as much as visited it briefly knows, a place that is hard to forget. Located in the foothills of the Green Mountains slightly south and east of central Vermont, it lies in a valley where the Ottauquechee River and the Kedron Brook wander beneath summer-green and winter-white hills that flame into red and gold for a few brief and remarkable days every autumn. Today, the village, in its setting of great natural beauty, appears much the same as it has for a very long time. Settled about the time the American Revolution was heating up, Woodstock by the 1790s had lost the traces of its frontier beginnings and, as the shire town of Windsor County, it was on the way to becoming an important banking and manufacturing town and a center for the practice of law. Its general air of gentility and prosperity date from this time when a generation of prominent doctors and lawyers and merchants were building the most impressive of those homes which today give

1

much of the village its position on the National Register of Historic Places. With its white clapboard and brick houses set upon a little maze of tree-shaded streets and its remarkable collection of stately early nineteenth-century homes which surround the elliptical village green and line Elm Street, it has long deserved its reputation as one of the half dozen most beautiful villages in America.

Today I suppose everyone knows about Woodstock, Vermont. A functional farm village in my childhood in the 40s and 50s as it had been in my parents' and grandparents' early years, this town of some 3,500 people is now advertised far and wide, and it attracts people from all over the world. It has become a tourist destination. Most of the farms have given up the ghost, the hardware and grocery stores have largely become galleries and souvenir shops, and the old inn was long ago demolished for a larger accommodation. If the old houses are now peopled with wealthy newcomers we don't know and the businesses are owned by people we sometimes cannot understand, at least things *look* much as they did. For the most part, the old buildings have not been leveled and replaced, concrete and steel have not filled most of the open spaces. There's not one fast food emporium in town. Thus, though Woodstock has certainly changed, it still retains something of the appearance, if not the character, of the place it was in my childhood, now some fifty years past. As though to honor this sense of continuity, each year as spring becomes summer in Vermont, hundreds of people return to Woodstock for a high school reunion. A little after noon on what is usually the second Saturday in June, they gather on and around the village green to watch a parade of floats, to reminisce about times gone by, and to compare notes on the present. For more than half a century, this annual reunion, known as Alumni Day, has continued to attract graduates from more than seventy years of high school classes and has played its part in bringing people together and keeping alive the memory of the village as it was in their time.

It is this sense of preservation in the midst of change that has kept me coming back to Woodstock time and time again every year of my life and has made me decide to keep ownership of the old family home. During my visits and periods of seasonal residence there, I would grow accustomed to the alterations in the village only to discover that once I had resettled in Ireland or England or New Jersey or Connecticut, the old Woodstock of the 1940–1950s would slowly replace the new one in my memory. In fact, it would so insistently reestablish itself that upon returning home I would expect to see houses and gas stations where there was open land, and open land where there were long established buildings, and trees that had been gone for years would seem to be missing from their locations along the streets. I would find myself astonished once again by the absence of places whose disappearance I had, so I thought, long since come to accept. And I began to realize that, however I might assume an ability to adapt and to accommodate myself to change, the Woodstock of my childhood and youth had survived and was continuing to live in me a curiously unchanged and timeless existence. The chapters which follow are an attempt to make some record of that existence and to give some form to my recollections. Their writing occupied me during summer vacations and school holidays over the better part of a decade. But if this project had a long gestation and was a long time in the making, the idea for it can be dated precisely. It came to me one winter afternoon on top of Mt. Tom at about 4 PM on New Years Day of 1984. I had skied up the mountain road to be next to the great wooden star on one of the days of Christmas when its lights come on to shine above the village throughout the night. It was almost a year since the death of my father, and as I was standing at the star's base, looking down onto the snow-covered rooftops and lawns and streets of Woodstock, I suddenly realized that I was surveying the place which entirely contained his life. Watching the barren and silent

3

woods darkening under the mountain's lengthening shadow, I was struck anew by the realization that the names by which my family and I continued to identify the houses and stores of Woodstock were the names of people who no longer lived or worked there and who had, in many cases, long since vanished. I could imagine a time when my children would gain enough familiarity with contemporary Woodstock to be baffled at hearing my brother and sister and me, in apparent ignorance of all current store fronts and street signs and occupants, referring to a defunct art gallery by Tribou Park as the Amsden house after the name of my old high school superintendent and his family, and to a building containing a furniture store and restaurant as the Elm Tree Press, a print shop; and orienting ourselves by such anachronisms as the Electric Company and Sterling's Drugstore, the former now a jewelry store, the latter, I am happy to say, still a pharmacy.

As I began considering these two Woodstocks, the town full of strangers who at that moment were lighting their lamps against the oncoming winter night, and the old, familiar town that maintained itself in the memories of a dwindling number of long-time residents, I suddenly felt the need to recover the older and, to me, the more real Woodstock. I wanted, in other words, to restore the Woodstock I had first known, where the houses were largely homes and not real estate investments, and where the commercial buildings were seen as places for stores serving the basic needs of the community and its outlying farming districts rather than as so many square feet of retail space for profiting from the consumer demands of transients and tourists. I wanted to put it back just the way it had been before I grew up and went away, before it all changed.

That's as it seemed to me twenty years ago there on Mt. Tom, at the beginning of a new year. The task, which then began to take shape at that moment, would be one of recollection and recovery, and though I had no idea how I would set about it, I felt as though

it was something that I would have to do, something I was supposed to do. As I considered how to begin, I began wondering
about the timing of it all, about why the memories that I had always had of my childhood and youth had lately begun to take on a
kind of clarity and vividness, even a sort of urgency, almost as
though they were directives. I wondered at the flood of memories
that at this time in my life so often arrived unannounced to fill the
present with so many fully realized moments and experiences from
the past, and I recalled something that the neurologist Oliver Sacks
had written on the subject: "[The disposition to recollect] comes
only with changes and separations in life — separations from people,
from places, from events and situations.... It is, thus, discontinuities,
the great discontinuities in life, that we seek to bridge, or recon-
cile, or integrate, by recollection.... Discontinuity and nostalgia are
most profound if, in growing up, we leave or lose a place where we
were born and spent our childhood, if we become expatriates or
exiles, if the place, or the life, we were brought up in is changed
beyond recognition or destroyed. All of us, finally, are exiles from
the past." His suggestion here is that a sort of crucial point of
tolerance exists, beyond which memory becomes inspiration. It is
as though by some law of conservation, as the things in our lives
which we assumed to be constant and unchanging alter or disappear, we find ourselves engaged in recreating them in memory.

But by the time I finally got down to work three years later, the
mounting sense of urgency that had forced me to begin writing had
suggested another answer. Even without a sense of loss and exile,
until we have reached a certain age and passed through certain for-
mative experiences, much of our past is not retrievable because it
is simply not available to us in any immediate or vivid way. We
need to feel the fulcrum to have shifted so that the years of life
behind us are in all likelihood greater in number than the years to
come; we need to find ourselves in that curious middle position

5

with our children on one side of us and our parents still there on the other and to feel our own identity thus strangely enhanced. We need to stand astonished at the disparate length of our own childhood, which seemed to have lasted an eternity, and that of our children, which, regrettably, seemed to have lasted no time at all, in order to gain access to our early years, to find them suddenly visible and intelligible and standing across from us in a sometimes blinding clarity. Or maybe life simply has to calm down, allowing us to discover some repose on the other side of the demands of youth and courtship, the tasks of beginning life on our own and starting our own families, before we can receive those intimations from our life as we first experienced it. And then, as Marcel Proust explains, we begin to hear something that has always been with us, something that "never ceased but was not audible until life grew quiet like those distant convent bells which are drowned in the noise of the daytime and sound out again in the evening." It is as though sometime around middle age we discover our past as a new and well-furnished addition to our lives. In dimension it occupies very much the same place the future once occupied, and its horizons stretch away to an uncertain and distant vanishing point similar to the one at which the future once pointed. Whatever the case, as I set about this task of recovery, I began to discover my childhood years beckoning to me with something like the same sense of openness and possibility that had once belonged to the future, and my future seemed very much to depend on my success in answering that summons. I had been more than forty years out, and the great adventure now seemed to lie in making the journey homeward.

To put it another way, the idea of trying to recover a period of my childhood and youth had to wait for its time. That time arrived when I had reached that age at which, as though by some natural process, memory begins working to compensate us spiritually for the growing distance which the passing of time puts between us

6

and our early years. In that sense, memory is something that happens to us without our intention or even our consent, and not something that we consciously activate or control. That is the distinction between involuntary and voluntary, or purposive, memory, and any exercise in extended recollection is inspired and sustained by the deliverances of involuntary memory. It is certainly to such deliverances and the charge they carry that I owe my most complete and vivid memories of the Woodstock of my childhood and youth. For instance, a few years ago at the house of a friend in Woodbury, Connecticut, my first taste of raw rhubarb in more than forty years suddenly returned me to the back lawn and gardens of the house in Woodstock at 8 Pleasant Street where I lived as a child. Our landlady, Bessie Thomas, a very warm and proper gray-haired lady who had been the high school principal in my mother's day, grew a patch of rhubarb at the edge of her garden, and my brother and I were allowed to pick some of it. Just over the wall on the property of the aloof Mrs. Fisk, was another patch to which we helped ourselves. We often picked stalks and broke them in half and sucked out the juice, and I remember that we used to have contests to see who could bite off a piece and chew it up with the least trace of a sour face, and sometimes we took the stalks up to the house and dipped the ends in sugar to make them more palatable. At any rate, when, in the summer of 1994, I tasted rhubarb again for the first time since those far off days, it was as though that pungent taste and stringy texture suddenly unlocked doors to a stored richness of sense and association, and I could see, in my mind, the space between the stones in the Fisks' wall where we'd find a toehold to climb over and could feel on the palms of my hands the warmth of the stones which lay along the top of the wall and absorbed the sunshine, and I could hear the rumble and squeak of the wheelbarrow of our neighbor Elba Buckman, a retired postal employee, as he rolled it down the lawn to his garden in the adjacent property. And, perhaps most poignantly, I caught once again the fresh, earthy scent of gill-over-the-ground, the little blue flowering weed that grew so abundantly in among the grass of the lawns and with which our play so often brought us into contact. As we crawled along the edge of the fence in games of cowboys and indians or burrowed our way into high grass in games of hide and seek or lay sprawled on the lawn in games of football or in wrestling matches, it seems that we were always, consciously or unconsciously, breathing in the fragrance of gill-over-the-ground.

That all this richness of detail was suddenly returned to me after so many years simply by the taste of raw rhubarb suggests the wealth of past experience stored behind the senses and thus available to us through the most ordinary means of contact with the world. In the words of Proust, "The smell and taste of things remain poised a long time like souls, ready to remind us, waiting and hoping for their moment, amid the ruins of all the rest; and bear unfaltering in the tiny and impalpable drop of their essence, the vast structure of recollection." When the moment arrives, as it does in any experience of involuntary memory, it is accompanied by a feeling of astonishment that so much can be called back by so little. In fact, it is largely in acknowledgment of this sense of plenitude that involuntary memory has perhaps been best defined, by Esther Salaman, as "memory of experience which comes unexpectedly, suddenly, and brings back a past moment accompanied by strong emotions, so that a 'then' becomes a 'now'"; that is, the past moment is so fully returned to us that it dominates and actually obscures the present moment in which it arrives. Such was the case on another occasion when I was miles and years away from Woodstock. I was stepping onto a train in London's Paddington Station when suddenly a peculiar, unidentifiable scent carried me back to Ferguson's Stables, as we used to call that grand old late Victorian carriage and horse barn on Court Street, situated behind, and belonging to, the Woodstock Inn, and I experienced it just as I had known it before it was destroyed by fire in April of 1963. From the brightness of a summer afternoon in the early 1950s, I once again walked through the open, wide doors and felt my eyes adjust to the darkness of the carriage room, and I began to pick out the old carriages and buggies parked in the shadows along the walls. Even more clearly, I recalled the yard along the south end of the building with Roy Hudson's blacksmith wagon next to the fence under a straggling clump of willows. And I could again cross that yard and walk up the ramp leading into the stables and feel the pressure in my arch of the fine-ground sawdust that covered the floor and shifted with every step I took along the wide aisle between the stalls. Then came the muffled drumming of the horses as they were led out or in, and the strangely fragrant blend of sawdust and horse manure, and I saw the forms of horses as they became visible in the soft light that struggled through the spidery, cobwebbed back windows of the stalls. Through the glass in the low door of the tack room, I even caught a forgotten but entirely familiar glimpse of Oliver Ferguson, the gray-haired, raspy-voiced, energetic proprietor, slumped down in a chair with his legs extended straight before him, his lined face with its horn-rimmed glasses and dangling cigarette turned slightly toward Ruth Keck, Fergie's assistant, who was standing at a desk facing the door in her red and black wool logger shirt and dungarees, talking in a loud and assertive voice. All of this was borne in upon me from my boyhood experiences of that place by the sense of smell, perhaps the most ethereal and most evocative of the senses, and for the first hour or so of that train journey into Oxfordshire, during which involuntary memory had made a past moment become a present one, a *then* become a *now*, I was oblivious to the interior of the train and to the scenery flashing past the windows.

Times like this when, suddenly and unexpectedly, the present

9

moment is deluged in reminiscence suggest that it is a fact of the life of memory that, initially, it seeks us and not we it. Such occurrences convince us that the past has some continuing existence somewhere to which it sometimes summons us as witness, as beholder. For their duration, these occasions simply ask that we surrender to their disclosures and receive them just as they are, and we consent to do so because they bring to us, absolutely undiminished by the passage of years, something that we had lost. That something may be a place that no longer exists, or it may be the lost quality of childhood innocence and wonder which once shaped our vision of the world. For what is recovered in these moments is never just the sum total of so much empirical data, but rather a fusion or synthesis of sensual detail, an ideal image dominated by feeling and an overwhelming sense of ourselves as belonging to that long passed world with its people in its place and time. Whether it is in our sense of awe at the peculiar radiance of those memories, or in our sense of gratitude for the serenity which they seem to bring, they make us feel as though our lives have, at once, been both illuminated and enlarged.

But if these experiences of involuntary memory are freely given, there is also something curiously imperative about them. In receiving what they send us, we may feel we are being called upon to give testimony to the clarity of the transmissions and to give them our heartfelt assent, to become so fully mindful of them as to recognize their place in what they show us to be the developing story of our life. In a word, memory asks for recollection. Recollection is *our* activity, our conscious contribution to what we have received. By virtue of it, we acknowledge and consecrate what memory has given us; we give full life and form and meaning to those moments which, unsummoned and unannounced, light their way into our immediate experience, and in so doing, we create for ourselves a past. Thus does recollection shape the deliverances of memory into the stories from whence we derive that curiously ongoing sense of our life in the places where, over time, we have come to know ourselves.

My labors at recollection took many forms. For some ten years I spent most of my school vacations trying to complement involuntary memories with my own voluntary ones; trying, that is, to prod memory into yielding up what I trusted it to have stored; and then, in some cases, seeking confirmation of what it gave me. When I was not reminiscing with my mother and brother and sister and a few old friends, and occasionally questioning various Woodstock natives, I was cloistered in the basement of the Norman Williams Public Library, poring over old issues of *The Vermont Standard,* and through its pages settling back into the village as it used to be. And I spent hours, as I always have, simply walking around Woodstock, experiencing in a more deliberately conscious way old neighborhoods and old fields of play and of association. In doing so, I became more aware of how fully I had appreciated all that I had back then, of how much I had loved certain places in the village simply for what they were — the first patches of bare ground in the spring on Billings Hill, the deserted buildings and fields of the old Woodstock Country School on Church Hill, all of Mt. Tom, the banks of the Ottauquechee River, Linden Hill and its view of the Woodstock Inn tower — and had sometimes sought them out by myself for no other reason than to be there. Even in what might seem the heedless comings and goings of my childhood ways, I was at least fitfully aware that the patches of shade on the sidewalks and the streets were coming from the magnificent elm trees fanning out above me, and no sense of familiarity ever dulled the red leaves and the gold of another October and the brilliance of autumn light on white clapboard, or excluded me from the silent communion of streetlights and falling snow. And on these walks I began to understand more clearly something I had felt for many years: that in the place one calls home, the place of one's child-hood, there are no *things* as such, no objects standing detached and neutral over against ourselves equipped with five senses and a mind and conceived of simply as a subject. The details of home are not so much things as icons; that is, they are seen not so much with the eyes as with the heart. Particular, familiar places all have their lingering association with some aspect of the world as first experi-enced there, so that any hometown is a kind of psychic map: The base of that great maple still carries a promise of spring and an assurance of friendship; on the front steps of that house glimpsed from the gate, jealousy still resides; hilarity continues to resound from that grassy bank sloping toward the road; infatuation is felt in that stretch of pickets along that white fence; wistfulness still calls to us from that big rock at the edge of the river. I still some-times receive signals of the shock that precedes grief from the park-ing meter on Elm Street that I happened to be touching when I learned of the death of a first cousin in an automobile accident. Thus even the most seemingly inanimate places and details are found to have interi-ors which can resonate with the stored life that is in them still. At almost any place in Woodstock, I found, the doorway could swing open into those years for which I was searching.

In a way, there is nothing very surprising in any of this, as any-one will find who begins looking for what used to be. We natu-rally spend most of our lives poised between two times: we inhabit the present, arise each morning in it, go to bed in it, do our shop-ping in it, but we live in the past, for that is the place in which our inner lives are rooted and nourished, and it is all that we really know. It was simply one of the features of my work at recollection that it taught me how much of my experience takes place on the threshold, as it were, between what I came to think of as the two Woodstocks. For example, when the clock in the basement of the library would tell me it was closing time, I'd leave and inevitably go through some peculiar moments of disorientation and re-entry outside on the front steps. Looking out across the lawn to the park and down toward the square in the late afternoon, I'd feel something like mild culture shock at being projected so suddenly from the Woodstock of forty years ago, where I had been living all day, into the present-day Woodstock in which I resided and functioned and worked for part of each year. Those moments were made all the more strange and compelling by the visual similarities and dissimilarities between the two places. The continually unfamiliar sight of the new covered bridge in the place of its historic iron predecessor on that section of Mountain Avenue which, until recently, was Union Street, and the equally unfamiliar spectacle of the great volume of traffic streaming through the streets would bring on a feeling of estrangement. Then this sensation would be immediately allayed by the reassuring presence, in all seasons, of the great pine trees rising from behind the White Cupboard and by the same old expressions on the faces of the houses on the Green, and behind them, the perennial and unchanging backdrop of Mt. Tom. Setting out for home, I'd experience the same kind of double consciousness as I walked sometimes along Central Street past old, familiar blocks housing unfamiliar businesses, and sometimes along the old route of Elm Street and Pleasant Street. I felt curiously suspended between two worlds, the contingent world of the past, to which I belonged and in which I was consenting to live as fully as possible, and the immediate world of the present, which served both to recall and to obscure the contours of what had once been there in its place. And I kept thinking of something an old schoolmate of mine said to me once: "Isn't it strange how everything has changed and how nothing has really changed at all."

Stated in another way, in any attempt to recover something of what has been, we come up against two of the great diagnostic facts of life: mutability and the persistence of memory. No sooner are we astonished at how quickly the years of our life pass and how far we have journeyed from our childhood, than we stand amazed at how indelible are the colors and forms of those distant times, so indelible, in fact, that they seem to bleed through the successive layers of years and experience superimposed upon them. This proved to be the case, in a double sense, in a remarkable moment a few years ago when I was talking with a friend of mine, Don Eaton, who recalled a strange incident from our early days together in grade school, an incident he had never told me about. One night when the two of us were going to the movies, Jim Fountain, the affable but no-nonsense proprietor of the Town Hall Theatre in those days, detained Don as he was taking his ticket. I evidently went on ahead, no doubt fearing that we were in trouble and being issued a warning (for we were much given to horsing around in the movie theatre), and feeling relieved not to have been singled out. I was not to know for a very long time what transpired between the two of them. As Don told it, he remembered Jim pointing at me as I went on ahead to choose our seats, and saying to him, "You see your pal there? He'll always look to you the way he looks now. When you both grow old, and you think of him, this is how you'll remember him." Since those words were expressive of sentiments that boys of our age couldn't hope to comprehend, Don, for some forty years, never mentioned them to me. They were meant, I think, to germinate and take root and to be understood when we had reached the age of the man who had uttered them. And what brought them out of the depths of memory and across almost half a century to where we sat that afternoon, on the Eatons' back lawn in Willow Vale, was the recognized truth that we did, in fact, appear to each other in much the same way as we had back then. That is the truth of the persistence of memory, and it is confirmed for me every year in the park on Alumni Day. For when I encounter old friends and schoolmates there, some of them much changed, "come in the gray

14

disguise of years," as Robert Frost puts it, I realize how much I've expected them to be just as I've continued to picture them and always will picture them. And I'm reminded of how firmly fixed, as in some long gallery of portraits, are the people and places of the past, no matter how radically they may have been altered by the passing of time.

The passing of time... that is the other side of the experience, the detractor, the immutable force against which memory seeks to make us mindful of the fullness of life. One summer in the 1980s, when browsing through some boxes of old postcards at a flea market at the high school, I came upon a card made from a black and white photograph, probably taken sometime shortly before 1914. It showed the Wilder house, as we still call it, at 10 Mountain Avenue, in winter. Snow was piled high against the front and back porches, and only partly visible between the snowbanks along the driveway was a young boy bundled up against the cold and holding a snow shovel. The card was sent, miraculously it seemed to me, by one member of the Wilder family to another — by Mrs. Arthur B. Wilder in Woodstock to her son Frederick, in Paris. Mrs. Wilder, who was, I think, then in her fifties, directed her son's attention to the figure of his brother in the photograph and began her brief message by saying, "This picture was taken several years ago when we had the high snowbanks. Notice the size of Junior [Arthur Wilder Jr.] and you will see the flight of time." That card and its simple message have haunted every stage of my efforts at completing this book until it came to seem as though the whole experience of gathering and recording was simply one utterance of astonishment at the passing, indeed, the "flight," of time. Suddenly as my generation in its turn approached and then reached and passed the age of fifty, our talk naturally turned more and more to the subject that used to belong to my parents and grandparents: how many years and how many people seem unaccountably to have disappeared.

15

And in my walks around the village in all seasons, I kept hearing, in all its deceptive simplicity, part of a sentence from the American writer William Maxwell: "But for the passing of time," he wrote, "they might be there now...." In these words he suggests to me that mutability is a sort of accident which, if I had been more attentive, I might actually have glimpsed, and in so doing, have come to domesticate and understand. It came to seem as though the actual process of the aging of a place, as the mind perceives it, were simply a displacement of moments and years and that what stood between the village now and the village then was the arrival and duration and succession of largely unnoticed events — clouds drifting over the court house on an April morning, snow topping the base of the cannon in Tribou Park, a last yellow leaf letting go from a maple on Mountain Avenue, the weathervane on top of the Congregational Church showing black against a summer sunset — events which I might have slowed down by being more mindful of them and answering to them in some way.

Finally, from the time of that winter afternoon on top of Mt. Tom until this book's completion some twelve years later, my work became progressively more shadowed by that sense of closure that haunted the last years of the century. They seemed something like a preparation time for a departure from people of long acquaintance in a time and a place where we have been very much at home. Even people of whom I was only peripherally aware when I was growing up began to assume their places once again and, in so doing, to help gather that older Woodstock into its perspectives. Suddenly from involuntary memory would appear someone like Sparky, the old man who lived at the jail and took care of Sheriff Moore's sons. In his blue work shirt and his jeans with the high roll in the cuff, he'd walk along the sidewalk on lower Pleasant Street, across from the Wasps' Snack Bar, pushing Buddy, the youngest Moore boy, in the stroller, and his wary, watchful look would announce once again that he was a guardian worthy and mindful of his responsibility. In mid-afternoon, Molly Conners, born in Ireland and proud of it, would emerge from the White Cupboard Inn kitchen in her white uniform, gray stockings, and down-at-the-heel black shoes, and, stooped and muttering and peering over her glasses, begin plodding along the Green on her long walk to her daughter's house on South Street. Mr. and Mrs. Hamilton Daughaday, a very pleasant elderly couple, would be seen once again walking along the sidewalk in front of the Helmers' house on their accustomed route from their home at 24 River Street to the Town Hall Theatre. As always, Mr. Daughaday, who was several inches shorter than his wife and to us children bore a close resemblance to the cartoon character The Nearsighted Mr. Magoo, was a good ten yards in front of Mrs. Daughaday. In the movie theatre they would maintain their relative positions as he sat way down front in the center to see the screen and she sat up back on the right. And I'd once again see Jack Ford, in light colored suit pieces that almost matched, walking somewhat gingerly past the D. A. R. House on his way to town, his porcelain skin patchily shaven and his mood chipper in spite of the brightness of the morning light. Thus, unsolicited, and at the oddest moments, these and so many others of those generations who lived in Woodstock back then would appear and, as it were, pass in review. And all of them in their curiously unaltered condition would seem to be making a quiet appeal against oblivion as though asking us, the survivors who would be crossing out of their time and into the next century, simply to be mindful of the old country, patria, homeland, and, above all, to look back and to remember.

The chapters of this book may be seen as an attempt to answer that appeal. It is offered as a labor of love and gratitude to the people of Woodstock at that time, and dedicated to my mother and father, the two people to whom I am most indebted for the recollections it comprises. For memory, however mysterious its workings and however inexplicable its disclosures and withholdings, can be said to rest ultimately upon a quality of attention to the particulars of life sufficient to give them for years to come a staying power within the mind. And I have come to realize that the love and attention with which my parents introduced me to the world — that is, to Woodstock in the 1940s and 50s — was such as to make my childhood a period of what I can only think of as heightened receptivity. From first to last, their reverence for life illuminated the things of that world and time and gave them such a permanence among changing scenes that, in Nabokov's words, "the long light of those days continues to reach me here." To my mother and father I owe far more than any writing of any sort could ever hope to express.

Pleasant Street and Benson Place

*You must know that there is nothing higher
and stronger and more wholesome and good
for life in the future than some good memory,
especially a memory of childhood, of home.*

DOSTOEVSKY

Whenever I go back to the place that was my childhood home in Woodstock, I instinctively walk softly, almost tiptoeing as though trying not to disturb whatever spirits may be lurking about, and I find myself watching and listening as though, if I am very quiet and alert, maybe, just maybe.... My parents and my twin brother, Howard, and eventually my sister, Jane, and I lived in the small back apartment in the house at 8 Pleasant Street, which belonged to Bessie Thomas and her husband Roy. Our apartment was approached by the lane between 8 Pleasant Street and 6 Pleasant Street, the house belonging to Elba Buckman, a cousin of my mother's, and his wife Gertrude Buckman. Both Mrs. Thomas and Mrs. Buckman were retired principals of Woodstock High School. The Thomases and the Buckmans lived in their respective houses, and each rented two apartments. Although each house sat on no more than two acres, the properties were beautifully landscaped, with terraces of flower gardens and small patches of well kept lawn leveling out behind our apartment into a spacious, enclosed back yard. In my earliest memories this yard was given over to three vegetable gardens, which were spread with manure and plowed and harrowed each spring, and to a small willow-shaded patch of dirt in the corner of our garden, set aside as a play place for my brother

19

and sister and me. Then when the gardens became too much effort for their yield, the land was seeded and turned into a lawn spacious enough to serve us as a football field and baseball field and a prairie for our games of cowboys and a high-jump and pole-vaulting pitch and a fairgrounds for the fair we staged to raise money to buy our first bicycles. In winter the lawn became the place for snow forts and snowball fights and the finish line for the alpine and Nordic events beginning on the top of the huge banks of snow that my father piled up from shoveling the walkway after the seemingly endless snowstorms of those days. These banks, which often rose well above my father's head and approached the second story of the house, were mountains to us children, and we used their slopes as runways for ski jumps built so close to the bottom of the hill that more than a tentative hop meant a bone-jarring landing on the flat packed snow surface of the back lawn. Or they became downhill and slalom courses. In our square-toed boots and cable hitchings, we poled out of our starting gates on our Northland skis and dashed down our thirty yard slope through three gates in imitation of Brooks Dodge, Chiharu Igaya, Othmar Schneider, Tony Speiss, Tom Corcoran, and Egil Stigum, the Olympic skiers we had watched at the Fisk Trophy Races at Suicide Six, and then coasted or schussed to a stop.

The idea, the reality, the memory of summers at 8 Pleasant Street are always associated in my mind with the large screened-in porch at the back of our apartment. In those days it seemed everyone had a porch and made good use of it on summer evenings. You sat out there, sometimes with your neighbors, until it got dark and watched people passing along their accustomed routes at their accustomed times and doing what they always did, and thus you gained the satisfaction of seeing about what you expected to see and of knowing that things were ticking along about as usual. And for some reason peculiar to human nature this was good material for conversation. Occasionally someone new passed by — maybe some "out-of-staters" as we called them — and you remarked on the license plate and wondered who they were and where they were going. Or you exchanged greetings with people who were out for a stroll, and after they had gone by, talked about them and their families and relations and houses; or you saw people you didn't expect to see and speculated on what they were doing out your way. Our porch stood at the level of a second story. It made a good vantage point for the sights and sounds of the neighborhood, and it became in the warm weather an additional room where we often ate our supper and sat to catch the breezes at the end of the day. In between times we would be down on the back lawn playing toss and catch with my father or, my mother included, playing softball with the large ragballs that my father would fashion out of newspaper, pieces of tinfoil, rags, and anything else that could be wadded up and bound within circles and circles of twine. It was an ideal ball for a family game with children in a small yard because its size made it nearly impossible for the batter to miss or the fielder to bobble; its softness meant that we could not hit it far or get hurt by it; and its tendency to become progressively more ragged and misshapen as we swatted it — each ball was good for one evening's play — made the game funnier as it went along. Other evenings after supper on the porch when my father mowed the lawn and ragball field, Howard and I sometimes helped with the raking and threw grass and stuffed it down each other's shirts before picking it up in a big straw basket and dumping it beside the brook. Since just about everybody in those days mowed with a hand-push reel mower, lawns tended to be smaller than they have become since the proliferation of power mowers. Pushing one of those hand mowers around a good sized lawn was a workout. When my father would let Howard and me take a turn, we would each take one side of the handle with both our hands and lean into it and strain and,

21

struggle down a zigzagging strip before giving up. Then we would leave my father to finish the lawn and would join my mother and Jane on the porch to sit and watch the light thicken over the yard and fade from the sky above the Buckmans' roof, and we would catch the sounds that accompanied the end of a summer day back then as they drifted up the damp grass and poppy and peony-freighted air: the murmur of voices from the porches down in Benson Place, the closing of a wooden screen door, and the ticking whirr of lawn mowers telling us that my father and Elba Buckman were finishing up before dark and telling us how they were doing it as well. All of the discontinuous sounds of people cutting grass with those mowers, punctuated as they were by brief silences or by the clacking of clippers, conveyed an image, told us just what the person was doing so that we saw in the mind's eye as well as heard my father mowing a long strip or mowing up close to the flower gardens with quick, repeated bursts or trimming or taking a rest. And then from the different sound the mower made we could tell that he had turned it upside down and was wheeling it to the garage. Then the "pup-pop, pup-pop" of the oil can as he oiled the wheels would be followed by the latching of the garage door, and he would join us on the porch in his white tee shirt and khakis. All of us there together would listen in the gathering dusk to the softer sounds that had been going on all the time but were only now emerging from the stillness — the shrill chorus of the crickets and the continuous rush of the Kedron spilling its waters over the dam, telling its ongoing story.

When darkness came on, we went inside and sat around the radio. We listened to *Amos n' Andy* and *Jack Benny* and *I Love a Mystery* and *Edgar Bergen and Charlie McCarthy*. We heard the broadcasts of Red Sox baseball and, in the winter, from the old Madison Square Garden, of the Knicks' games, which were announced by Marty Glickman, and which always began with Gladys

Gooding's playing of the national anthem on the organ. And once, for a few weeks, my brother and I even had a short wave radio that my father brought from The Woodstock Electric Company, where he worked. It was not conducive to sleep. In bed at night, our faces dimly visible to each other from the small point of light on the radio's dial, we picked up the voice of Radio Free Europe and voices speaking a variety of incomprehensible languages, and, punctuated by strange blips and bleeps and distorted by static, voices coming from trawlers off the Grand Banks, and sometimes a mysterious rushing noise that sounded like the vast, empty spaces of the north, or perhaps like the sea. Eeriest of all was a bleakly industrial, inhuman monotone that someone told us was the sound of the Russians' jamming of the airwaves and which from then on sounded to me like the grating of a huge iron curtain. These transmissions in our darkened room took us on great journeys of the imagination. Many years later I learned that my experience was similar to that of the poet Joseph Brodsky, who was at that time a boy of my age half a world away in Leningrad: he saw the lighted tubes of the short wave radio next to his bed as the great buildings of the cities from all around the globe whose voices were coming to him from out of the night. Then, my travels finished for the night, I'd switch off the radio and, before sinking into sleep, would hear again in succession the old, familiar sound of the Revere bells from the clock towers of two churches ringing the late hour with their different voices. On clear nights when the air was dry, they spoke more distinctly than on stormy winter nights when their tolling came to us intermittently through wind or muffled by curtains of falling snow. First, from just west of us, the Congregational Church announced the correct time with confidence, but evoking as it did so, images of the dark, open belfry rising against the still darker Mt. Tom. And I would sleepily count the strokes until the longer than usual silence said that it was just ten o'clock and no later. Then I would wait, and after a short time, from the other side of us, a little farther away and to the east down Pleasant Street, would come the somewhat deeper, less sonorous answer from the enclosed tower of the derelict Christian Church, carrying with it a picture of the houses from that end of town with their darkened windows and sounding like a sleepy and reluctant confirmation that, yes, it was ten o'clock. In the listening during the silent interval between those clocks' sounding the same hour, there was *no* time. It has long since seemed to me that our location there on Pleasant Street between the two churches somehow belonged to that interval, and that its timelessness was something like the true measure of our lives back in those days.

For those early childhood years, which are the longest of my life, our yard and all that could be seen from it constituted a whole world into which other experiences and other people and places were absorbed. Everything within that world, every detail, was entirely itself and like no other. Each of the stepping stones set in the side lawn and leading from our walkway down to the back lawn had its own shape, its own character, its own way of occupying its clipped space in the grass as I looked down at it and it looked back at me on my way to and from our play place. The same was true of the flowers; I remember my little sister giving the single row of pansies beside our house a wide berth because, as she finally made us understand, she was unnerved by the little lion's face of each pansy regarding her with its own singular expression. Perhaps it is the novelty of everything as it is seen and smelled and heard for the first time that gives to the details of the child's world this special individualized character and its attendant peculiarity of association. I remember, for example, that Howard and I, from a time that must have been during or just after the war in the Pacific, always spoke of the bubbles as we saw or heard them rising in the kerosene tank behind our kitchen range as "darned old Japs." We

were also certain that the high pitched buzzing of the harvest fly
we heard from the front lawn on dry August days was made by the
flying horse on the Mobil sign at Mr. Mooney's service station on
Central Street. Or maybe it is our diminutive size as children, our
being down there close to the ground, that gives us our intimacy
with zinnias and pebbles and grasshoppers and also accounts for
our fascination with things way up in the air so far away from us.
The tops of trees at the very point where they intersect the horizon,
and particularly those trees which appeared as sentinels along the
borders of my small, familiar world, were a continual source of
wonder to me then. The view eastward from our kitchen window
stopped at the top of the pine tree over the Kellys' barn. From my
place at the breakfast table, the sight of its pinnacle reaching into
the morning sky beckoning toward the unknown, suggested long
and distant voyaging. And the top of the pine tree over the Fisks'
barn in the northwest, rising darkly against the glow of sunset, was
like the first glimpse of homeland resting in calm seas and speaking the promise of safe return.

As our world expanded, my brother and I began to experience
Woodstock as the collection of neighborhoods which it was in those
days, each having its own distinct character. Most memorable to
me were my frequent wanderings into the neighborhoods contingent with ours, which I experienced as quite other countries from
the moment I crossed their invisible borders. The nearest such
border was less than two minutes from the front of our house, and
it lay across our main shortcut to the center of the village. We
would cross Pleasant Street, dive down into the small wood behind
Richard Marble's house, and follow its path. This path wound
through the trees along the west bank of the Kedron, skirted the
sun-drenched back lawns and gardens of the Lightbourn house, and
stopped at the wire fence that marked the back of the post office
property. We had simply to climb over this, scoot across the post

office lawn, and leap the barberry bushes in order to land on the sidewalk next to the parking meters on Central Street. In no time at all we had passed from our quiet street through the silence of the woods to the noisy activity of the village streets. But it wasn't this abrupt transition as much as something else that gave to the climbing of that fence and the view across it the feeling of a border crossing. For the last stretch of the path had afforded a view of the back lot of the Mooney house with its derelict cars and its army truck, and the view ahead showed the back of the fire station resting on an iron girder across the Kedron. In making that crossing, I always seemed to be leaving behind the hushed world of elderly ladies with their gardens and bird feeders and entering a province which was predominantly male and had to do with the rituals of manhood and the business of war. It extended from the post office with its four armed services recruitment boards to the Legion House. It took in the fire station and Eddie's Socony Station across the street and the Mooney house, and it was felt to include the Village Tavern and the State Liquor Store. Men congregated and transacted their business in these places. Besides the usual retainers at Eddie's and at the Mooney house, the Legion in these postwar years was a gathering place for veterans; and at the fire station on evenings after softball games and on Friday nights, a crowd of men could be seen standing in the open area in front of the three big doors and sitting on the bottom of the fire escape or perched heroically on the wall overlooking the Kedron. Or, on the first Monday evening of the month, the firemen might be carrying out some practice exercises, and it was worth stopping to watch several of them manning the big hoses and blasting a powerful jet of water back into the brook. Walking or riding a bike through this neighborhood and receiving some of its rough, warm humor felt like a rite of passage or a kind of initiation in which something was expected of me beyond what I needed at home on Pleasant Street, and I hoped to answer their questions or parry their remarks in a satisfactorily offhand manner.

The character and atmosphere of the other neighborhoods we came to know were very much determined by the boys who lived and played in them. Our friendship with Bill Silvernail, an older boy who had once been our neighbor in Benson Place, sometimes took us up to his house on High Street and from there up to the woods and paths of Mt. Peg. With Bill as our guide, we discovered many secret places such as Eagle Rock and Fort Number 4, an impressive stockade made of boards sharpened at the top, and heard with fear and awe stories of his friends and rivals — Eddie McDonald, Eddie and Billy Ricker, Michael Lewis, Donald Cloud, Toppy and Bruce Gould, Fred and Paul Widmer — and of fierce beebee gun battles that were fought there over disputed territory between the boys from High Street and the boys from Highland Avenue. And we sometimes went up there to play on Mt. Peg with the Harlow boys, Bud and Terry, who were schoolmates and distant cousins of ours. Even farther from home, our visits to Vail Field and our occasional dips in the Kedron at the swimming hole on the golf course brought us into touch with the Doubleday boys and their friends from Golf Avenue and Maple Street. These neighborhoods were more rough and tumble than ours, and I was much aware of being among boys who were less cautious than I. Many of them were better swimmers and had graduated to a hard ball from a rubber baseball earlier than I had and had already begun to earn their own money by caddying at the Woodstock Country Club. There was an attractive boldness and recklessness in their play, but crossing into their territory, finding oneself on their turf, felt like entering an atmosphere that was less dense somehow, and I had an odd, indefinable feeling that something was missing. It was, I suppose, although I didn't know it then, an intuitive sense of having entered a world which had hurried its exit from childhood by bartering the imagination for a passel of hard facts.

As I ventured beyond Tribou Park, I came to realize that Pleasant Street became younger as I followed it eastward. Starting from the Congregational Church and cheating a little by going just a ways around King's Corner and a few houses up Creamery Hill and throwing in a couple of tributaries, you could have counted over fifty children within roughly five years of my age who lived on Pleasant Street back in those years: Howard and Bruce Coffin and our sister Jane; Steve Potwin in Benson Place; Bill Kelly, Joan and Zaela Stimets; Lyman and Lyn Amsden (through their back door); Judy, Charlotte, and Susan French; Ronnie and Ann Watts and Mary, Theda, and Charlie Taylor (on Ford Street); Bud and Ann Spaulding; Chuckie Allen and his younger brother (later replaced by Ed and Bill Hackett); Bruce Washburn; Ronnie Hively; Ken Nalibow (from Stanton Street); Bill Leach (in the summertime); and, from Holtermans' Warehouse down, Peter, Jerry, and Lea Hall; Phil, Ralphie, and Dicky Williams — and later, Howard Richmond (over the Station House Restaurant); Peter, Bill, Tom, and Jerry Moore; Connie, Barbara, Nancy, Carol, and Bob Wilson; Art and Jim Donahue and Patty Heath; just around the corner from Richmond's Garage in one side of the two-tenement house, Bernice and Gerald Colby, and in the other, Charlie Dubeau; then on Creamery Hill, Sherry and Brenda Badger; George and Helen Colby; Stanley, Rowena, and Warren Olmstead; and Danny Atwood and Ann Lussier. So if Howard and I hopped on our bikes and rode down Pleasant Street, we were sure of finding plenty to do. We played a peculiar sort of baseball according to a specially concocted set of rules in Tribou Park with the Amsden boys, and we often had some great baseball and football games on the lawns behind the Watts and the Spauldings. Farther east where Pleasant Street ended its long, largely residential stretch and began mixing commerce in among its houses, was another border crossing. One passed the quiet white house of Grace Bowden and suddenly became aware of what seemed like a miniature industrial wasteland in the yards of Holterman's Warehouse which sprawled above Joe Nalibow's junk yard on the banks of the Ottauquechee to merge with the yards of the old Woodstock Railway. This no-man's land had its own fascination, and I often rode my bike along its dusty roadway through rusting machine parts to inspect the circular cement foundation of the old engine roundhouse. I liked to wander among the burdock and brambles surrounding the locked sheds with their peeling paint and their air of desertion and to study from there the barred windows at the back of the jail. It felt as though the railway in its heyday had brought to Woodstock a small corner of White River Junction and dropped it there in the triangle formed by the river and the bend of Pleasant Street on Richmond's Corner. And instead of packing up and departing on the last train in 1933, it took root and stayed and is still there today as a reminder of the old link between the two towns.

Much as I liked to explore this area by myself, I seldom found it deserted. By that curious mutual exchange between people and their neighborhoods, the boys who lived close to these yards and thought of them as their domain seemed to have imbibed some of their atmosphere and to have contributed to it some of their own worldliness. The Hall family had recently moved from White River to Woodstock and settled in the house at 58 Pleasant Street, and their oldest boys, Pete and Jerry, had a certain authority, a kind of savvy and swagger, that seemed to unite them with the Moore boys, who were their neighbors. Peter and Bill Moore, the new sheriff's oldest sons, lived in the apartment on the west side of the jail which was the home of the Windsor County Sheriff in those days. To us, they knew everything about G-men and cops and gangsters, and their games of guns were given a kind of authenticity by their mastery of the language of law enforcement and crime and by the small, seemingly urban jungle behind the jail in the yards of Holterman's and the old railway where they were played. Their home at the jail was also a good place to go on hot summer days. On the lawn beside their porch, they had a big, black, rubber pontoon partially filled with water that looked green and had a kind of inner tube smell and felt pretty tepid. With many of the other children from the neighborhood, we would bounce around on the pontoon and play king of the hill and jump and push each other into the water of the deeper end.

But oftentimes we sought out no neighborhoods at all and simply wandered both sides of the Ottauquechee, skipping stones and looking for driftwood, or fishing for suckers and dace and remembering to stay out of the water because of sewage and polio. Best of all in those days before ecology and environmental awareness, we would find bottles and light bulbs and toss them into the slow moving current and try to sink them with well-aimed stones or throw them against the rocks and watch them burst grenade-style (bottles and jars would crash and shatter, light bulbs would pop – very satisfying). I remember building toy boats out of scrap wood from Frost's Mill and launching them in the race beneath Billings' Bridge. We would jump from rock to rock shouting to each other above the water's roaring, pointing out the small rainbows over the swift, narrow channels, and following the course that the river determined for his particular vessel. One of them might wash up against a rock or a log or become caught in the undertow beneath a tiny falls and stay bobbing in the white water and going nowhere. Some successfully negotiated the rapids only to be becalmed in a slow moving back current, and these we sought to retrieve by throwing large stones out beyond them to make waves that would wash them in to us on shore. But once in a while one of our boats for no apparent reason would pass down the roughest courses upright and somehow find a current that would keep it sailing along through the standing water below the rapids and beating a straight course eastward. Then we would all follow it along the bank, as though under the spell of the force that was guiding it — fate? destiny? — and we would simply let it go...where? Down beyond the Billings Farm fields to Taftsville and over the dam and then to the White River and on to other rivers we had never seen and finally — that small thing that one of us had made with his hands — to the sea, carrying far beyond our last sighting of it, its cargo of our visions and dreams.

Once, in the early spring when the waters of the Ottauquechee were still running fairly high and very cold, Eddie and Billy Hackett and my brother and I tried to give some substance to one of those dreams by building a raft. The Hackett boys, who had attended Camp Abnaki during the summers when they had lived in St. Albans, Vermont, knew something more about outdoor life and about boats and how to make things than did Howard or I, but we were very pleased to be included in the scheme and tried to do whatever we were asked. We constructed the raft on the south bank of the river down behind the Masonic Temple, on what was to be the site of its launching. We built the frame out of materials we found on the spot — that is, out of four logs, two large ones we rolled out of the woods and two somewhat smaller ones we found at the water's edge. As I recall, the idea was simple: just lash the logs together two on two, nail a layer of planks across the upper two logs of the frame, which looked like a giant pound sign, tie a rope to it, push it into the river, and off we'd go to live the life of Huck Finn and Jim. The difficulty, though we didn't know it, was that some of the logs were green and some were waterlogged, and we never thought to test them for buoyancy; not, that is, until the great moment of the launching, which came on a cold, gray afternoon after school. The plan was for Billy, who was the youngest and the lightest and probably the bravest, to hop on board with a pole when the raft

31

was half in the water and then for Eddie and me to push it all the way in and for Howard to hold the rope in case of an emergency. Because of a number of technical difficulties, including the looseness of the lashing, it was getting late by the time we actually succeeded in hauling and shoving the raft to the river's edge at a place where the bank dropped away after a couple of steps into four or five feet of water. And the frustration level was particularly high. Eddie and Billy were, no doubt, feeling as though their self-proclaimed skill as boat builders was being compromised by one unforeseen problem after another, for which they blamed each other and tried to blame Howard and me, who had demonstrated our incompetence in a number of small ways all afternoon. We were all soaked up to the knees and shivering by the time Eddie and I gave one final push and the raft with Billy aboard slipped into the river — "into" the river, indeed, for its logs remained half submerged just long enough to catch their balance and then begin sinking. In considerable panic, Billy, the frigid water rising up his shins, began trying frantically to pole, but to no avail. Seeing that it was no use, he shouted to my brother, "Pull!" But Howard, standing there with the rope absolutely slack in his hands and gazing down the Ottauquechee, was somewhere else entirely — perhaps in some dream of life on the Mississippi, perhaps at home, simply sitting in front of the heater or eating a hot dinner in dry clothes. And Billy's exasperation suddenly reached a sputtering, flailing, crescendo when, in answer to his repeated exhortations to "PULL, DAMN IT, PULL!", Howard asked in mild alarm, "Pull...*IN*?"

Coming home from lower Pleasant Street or from our days by the river always meant coming back into shade and quiet, for ours was certainly the older and more sedate end of Pleasant Street. Indeed, the houses on upper Pleasant Street and Bond Street, largely undisturbed as they were by the traffic carried by Central Street, appeared to have turned their back and to stand aloof from the commerce of the village. By and large, they belonged to people of some taste and refinement. In the brick house at the intersection of Pleasant and Elm Streets lived Luna Converse, an elderly spinster who was the daughter of former governor of Vermont Julius Converse, and her innumerable cats, some of which we thought had grown to look a great deal like her, or vice versa. In the next house, at #4, were Mabel Dana and her charge — an older woman seldom seen and, to us, very mysterious — named Miss Mason, and one vicious dog, a husky named Skylah who chased us and caused us to ride our bikes with our feet up on the handlebars, and one not so vicious, old and mangy looking German shepherd named Gilly. Our next-door neighbors, the Buckmans, rented two back apartments in their house, the one on the first floor to Ada Maynes, and the one on the second floor to a Miss Hall and later to Elizabeth Mitchell, and after that to an elderly couple, Chet and Jane Lawrence. Our landlords, Bessie and Roy Thomas, lived in one of the front apartments of #8 and rented the other front apartment to Roy ("Jack") and Ida Horner and the back apartment to us. Besides our grandparents and cousins and aunts and uncles, these were the people who were most real to my brother and me. Since the living quarters at #6 and #8 were close together and we were the only children, we were reminded by our parents to stay out of the flower gardens and the bird baths and not to go exploring in the garages and cellars and passageways under the neighbors' houses, which we did constantly, and not to snitch the Buckmans' and the Thomases' raspberries, on which we gorged ourselves to repletion for the duration of the berry season every summer. If at times these reminders made it seem to us as though we were under constant surveillance, in actuality our neighbors regarded us with interest and patience and a good deal of real affection, and my earliest memories are inseparable from the sound of their voices and their daily activities. We awoke on summer mornings to the murmur of

Bessie Thomas and Gertrude Buckman remarking on the weather or the news or exchanging gardening tips, and to the sound of gardening tools, and we went to bed to the faint sounds of conversations and radios from the other apartments and their porches. Then there was a cast of minor characters who were interesting because they were less often seen. Since we did not own a car, Mr. Louis Talcott from 15 Pleasant Street rented our garage space for his Oldsmobile. We looked forward to the regular calls of Mr. Bushey, the oil delivery man, and we enjoyed the occasional visits of John Hayes or Robert Walker, men who worked for Stimets, when they came to repair or clean the oil burner. Much less enjoyable, I regret to say, were the house calls — initiated by my mother's picking up the phone and saying the fearful number, "208-W please" — of the kind and venerable Dr. Eastman with his gray Stetson hat and his dreaded black bag, containing penicillin and needle. And sometimes there were surprises, like the Horners' grandson, Peter Lewis, from Aruba, an impish boy with a cowlick who was great fun; and like the time when Mr. Talcott's Oldsmobile started blowing its horn all by itself in our garage. My arm was the only one small enough to reach through the crack at the top of the car window to unlock the door to release the hood so that he could make it stop, and he paid me the extraordinary sum of a dollar for my help. Once in a while would appear a genuine anomaly like Miss Hawkins, a middle-aged lady who strutted forth from the Thomases' one day dressed in jodhpurs; high, leather riding boots; a short, tight riding jacket, and an absurdly small hat such as might have been seen on Buster Keaton's head as he emerged from a haberdashers. She was brandishing a quirt. When Howard and I answered her severe "Good morning" with a cheerful "Hi," she drew herself up in shock and dismay and said, "Oooh, I seem to have made a slight social error!"

Our neighbor Jack Horner was invariably kind and good humored, and the Buckmans and the Thomases were tolerant of my brother's and my trespasses, the ones they knew about, that is, and I suspect they knew about more than they let on. In fact, they seemed to enjoy our company. Roy Thomas took us rat hunting down by the brook one afternoon, much to the disapproval of my mother because he carried a large pistol that until then no one knew that he owned. The fact that we never saw a rat did not in the least diminish the excitement of the hunt for Howard and me. Our landlady, Bessie Thomas, who was known affectionately as Aunt B. to a generation of Woodstock High School students fortunate enough to have had her as math and French teacher and principal, had an apartment furnished with antiques and had, besides the pistol that we knew was hidden somewhere, the wonder of the neighborhood — a bathroom with toilet, tub, and sink made of blue porcelain. I never set foot in the Thomases' apartment without thinking of the blue bathroom and making an excuse to go and see it, even when I was fourteen and sitting at their dining room table, being tutored in algebra and geometry by Aunt B. They also had a television set, one of the first in the neighborhood, and my family and I used to enjoy joining them on Saturday nights in those days just before rock and roll to watch *The Hit Parade.*

Although the Thomases and the Buckmans and the Horners and the generation to which they belonged have largely disappeared, they continue to have a very real existence in my recollections of childhood. When their faces and voices drift back to me, as they often do when I am just on the edge of sleep, they invariably come bearing their benevolence and good will. But the one great presence for my family in those days and for all time was that of Ada Maynes. She lived across from us in the downstairs back apartment in the Buckmans' house, and, although she was no relation to us, we knew her as Aunt Ada. Outside of our family, she was the person whom we most cared for and from whom we received the most constant attention and affection. In many ways, I suppose, she was like many other maiden aunts — neat, fastidious about her appearance, sensitive, always mindful of birthdays and anniversaries, and too generous. Her bureau and her nightstand and the bookcases in her small apartment were crowded with photographs of nieces and nephews and cousins, and on her walls were a number of prints, many of them depicting religious subjects and biblical scenes. A devout member of Our Lady of the Snows, the Roman Catholic Church in Woodstock, she was of Irish descent, as she liked to remind us. In my earliest memories, I recall spending countless hours in her apartment across the way talking and being treated to ginger ale and cookies and looking at movie magazines. In those great days of Hollywood, before television, besides going to the movies (we often went at least twice a week), film enthusiasts liked to read previews and reviews and to keep up with the latest events in the lives of the stars. Out of interest, but also out of loyalty to her sister Peg and her brother-in-law Jim Fountain, who ran the Town Hall Theatre, Ada usually went to more than two movies a week, and she subscribed to more than one movie magazine. As a child I devoured *Photoplay* and *Silver Screen* and knew all about who had starred in what. Ada had her favorites, first and foremost of which was Bing Crosby, for whom she carried a life-long flame, and I had mine. And as I chattered on and she did her household affairs, she usually agreed with me about who the best actors and actresses were, whether she really did or not. As my sister Jane, seven years to the day younger than Howard and I, came along and assumed my place at Ada's, she too caught the movie bug. In fact, she became so fond of Mario Lanza that Mother took her to both the Saturday afternoon and evening performances of the movie *The Great Caruso,* and for quite some time afterwards when we sat down for supper there had to be an extra table setting next to Jane — for Mario himself.

When Howard and I began to spend more time away from Pleasant Street with our friends, Jane had her time with Ada, and what a time it was. To us they seemed inseparable. They were so close that Janie, as we all called her then, even occasionally spent the night at Ada's, something we had never done. Mother would get her into her pajamas and pack her a little bag and make sure she had her special blue blanket and then walk or carry her the fifteen yards or so across the way. Then, at the prearranged bedtime, we would all assemble at our door and they at the window of Ada's den, and we would wave across the darkness between the houses and hallow our goodnights with some flashing on and off of our outside lights. (Janie especially liked to fall asleep in Ada's lap, she told us once when she was very little, because she had "the softest pillows"). In the morning Ada would bring her home with her hair perfectly braided. Sometimes they would sing the songs that Ada had taught her, and even now I can see them perfectly and hear their voices. Together they would sing the opening words to *A Bicycle Built For Two* or *The Sidewalks of New York*, and then Janie would go the rest of the way, perfectly in tune and pronouncing the words as best as she could, Ada all the while waiting to cue her if necessary and trying unsuccessfully to keep her delight and affection in hiding lest she should distract her.

My family's friendship with Ada Maynes began in 1941 before my brother and I were born and ended only with Ada's death in 1979. Although she and my parents had always known each other, they first became friendly when my parents were renting the Woodstock Electric Company apartment that eventually became Dr. Eastman's office, at 5 Central Street over The First National, and Ada and Fern Stockwell owned and operated the Fernada Beauty Shop across the hall. Then, shortly after, we moved into the apartment at 8 Pleasant Street, and Ada moved to the back apartment at #6. In the 1950s and 60s, she and my mother worked as telephone operators at the same time, and we remained as close as ever with Ada after we left the neighborhood and moved to Lincoln Street. She was included in birthday celebrations and was always on hand for homecomings and graduations and departures. I remember her as one of five adults and two suitcases who rode back to Woodstock scrunched together in our Saab 96 from my graduation at UVM. She was usually present at our parties during my college years, especially when she could count on being entertained by a friend of ours who did marvelous Caruso imitations. When Howard finished his tour of duty with the army at Fort Hood, Texas, during the Vietnam War years, the welcome-home party, from which I was sadly absent and about which I am still hearing stories, was held at Ada's apartment. I corresponded with her throughout a year I spent at Trinity College Dublin, and because she was as passionate about peanut butter as I was and was unable to imagine me living without it, in a great gesture of sympathy, she sent all the way to Ireland a large jar of Skippy, thus rectifying that deficiency in the land of her forefathers.

Ada was in on even more than any of us knew in our days together on Pleasant Street. On summer nights when Howard and I were in junior high school and had friends staying overnight, all of us sleeping out on the porch, we would wait until we were sure our parents were asleep and "sneak out", as we called it. We would tiptoe down the porch steps, shoes and socks in hand, and steal off into the night to play car light, to skinny-dip in the swimming pool at the Billings mansion, or to keep nocturnal appointments and carry out liaisons of other sorts. Unbeknownst to us, from her window across the way, Aunt Ada was a silent witness to our secret departures and sometimes also to our auroral returns, as she confessed to us many years later. And all those years she kept it all under her hat, never letting on to anyone that she knew what we were up to.

II

Once in a while an event of some magnitude would actually occur on our quiet end of Pleasant Street, and we would all be drawn into it. One such event took place in the summer of 1950. It was the replacement of the old iron bridge over the Kedron at the top of Benson Place with the bridge that currently stands on that site, and the renovation of the dam just below the bridge. The project was carried out by Miller Construction Company of Windsor, and to Howard and me in particular, who were eight years old at that time, it was all very exciting. Throughout the long summer days we heard the noise of jackhammers and watched the operations of the crane and the steam shovel and saw the course of our brook changed by sandbags. The dump trucks came and went, and through the summer nights the old kerosene lanterns (we called them "smudge pots"), which resembled the bombs of assassins in comic books, burned on the bridge site as a warning to traffic. For a time in the middle of the project when there was no bridge at all, we could look down from the place where the road simply dropped away onto that section of the brook that we had never before seen from above. And Pleasant Street on the other side of the gorge only fifteen yards away was suddenly another continent. The Miller Construction workers took on heroic proportions to us as we watched them operating the big machines and moving girders into place. By asking them questions and offering them lemonade and Kool Aid, we came to know them well enough so that their names still occupy a place in my memory. Bert Kidder was the crane operator; a man named John Bayliss was foreman; a short wiry man called Red was one of our favorites; and we looked with considerable awe at a large man who we were told was a veteran of Iwo Jima. One afternoon at the end of the summer when the major part of the project had been completed and the new bridge was in place and all that remained was the tidying up, we joined Ada in giving a farewell party for these men in her apartment. She nervously spent a great deal of time preparing the food, and my mother helped her. I think she served a variety of small sandwiches cut in triangles and small cocktail franks and punch and cake for dessert. I remember those muscular, tanned men looked different with their hair combed and their shirts buttoned up as they crowded somewhat self-consciously into Ada's cramped living room, watching where they put their feet and being careful not to upset the knick-knacks. Mingled with our excitement on that occasion was a sense of sadness in all of us that the job, and with it the summer, was almost over, and that autumn and school were just around the corner. Their departure left us with a new bridge but also with a great silence, and life seemed pretty dull for a while.

Actually, as it turned out, the excitement was not quite over. The bridge they built has performed its service well, but the dam project was less successful. It had involved tearing out the rotted and sagging remains of the old wooden dam and replacing the dam with a riprap, a packing in of huge, flat boulders sloping down to connect the upper and lower levels of the brook where the dam had been. They did not long remain in place. Each year, depending on the severity of the winter and the length of the spring thaw, when winter finally did relinquish its grip on the Kedron and the ice broke up and let go, the spectacle could be quite dramatic. I remember as a child waking in the middle of the night to a tremendous thundering sound and being carried downstairs by my father and peering out the kitchen windows and finally going out onto the porch and looking out into the roaring darkness toward the brook. Out there at a height to which the Kedron had never risen, we could see huge slabs and blocks of ice rising and heaving up against each other and grating against the retaining walls in their cramped passage as they were swept downstream on the suddenly released currents. In the most spectacular of these early spring events, those newly placed, huge blocks of stone were simply torn out of their setting by the departing ice and scattered like pebbles down the course of the Kedron.

Except for such unusual events of construction and destruction, little occurred to break the somnolence and the long hush of our days at the quiet end of Pleasant Street. But, whether many people knew it or not, it was also the enchanted end because of two places which offered to my brother and me endless possibilities and inexhaustible material for the imagination: the Little Path and Frost's Mill. "The Little Path" was the name we gave to the acre of woods extending from the Marble house on Elm Street to the Kedron Brook. Since this wood was right across the street from our house, we often used its path through the trees as a shortcut for running errands upstreet, but more importantly, it and other paths we made served as roads into uncharted wilderness which we explored and settled as pioneers, or into the darkest jungle or, best of all, into Sherwood Forest. In the shade of its trees and tangled vines and in the coolness of its ferns, we established outposts, camps, forts, hideouts, but at night it was notoriously unsafe and was to be avoided as the dwelling place of fabled beasts, most notably the red fox. Where the rumor of that creature originated, whether Mr. Marble had mentioned to someone in the neighborhood a sighting of a fox or whether we just conjured it out of our active imaginations, I don't know. But while we were under its spell, the Little Path, even in daylight, was beyond the pale as a shortcut or a place to play. I remember one summer evening at the height of the scare, sitting on our steps with my mother and Howard and Bill Silvernail. Bill, a boy two years older than we, towered over us, and his belt would have gone around both of us with some left over. A little like the character Pud from the Double Bubble Gum comic strip of those days, he was massively overweight, but he was also such a combination of placid and mild mannered, on the one hand, and physically strong, on the other, that nobody ever picked on him about his size. On this particular evening as we sat there speculating on the probable location of the red fox's den and on the range of his nocturnal wanderings (my mother listening good-humoredly), the darkness deepened, and Bill, who was at first a little skeptical, became pretty quiet. When it was our bedtime, we said goodnight to him and went inside. Quite some time afterward when Mother went to switch off the outside light, she saw Bill again sitting there on the steps. She went out to him, and he reluctantly confessed that "this red fox business" had made him "a little nervous." Evidently, after saying goodnight, he had made two attempts to reach his grandparents' house in Benson Place. On the first of these, he went behind our house and encountered darkness; on the second, he walked around to the front of our house and found himself looking directly into the Little Path across the road. So he ended up back where he started and might have sat there indefinitely, too frightened to make it home and too embarrassed to admit it, had my mother not spotted him and sympathetically walked him home. She swore us to secrecy, and we never let on to Bill that we knew a thing about it. And after a while the legend of the red fox lost enough of its potency so that we could once again play in the Little Path with nothing more than a little uneasiness now and then.

The other great place of enchantment was Frost's Mill, which occupied the roughly triangular two-acre piece of property in Benson Place extending back to the point where the Kedron runs into the Ottauquechee. Except for its one remaining house, Benson Place today is just a parking lot. Anyone seeing it now for the first time might have trouble imagining it as the busy little neighborhood it was back then. In those days as you turned off Pleasant Street at the bridge and followed the arrow of the black and silver sign reading "C. C. Frost Lumber Building Materials," you went down the dirt road toward the Benson house on the right. Built straight up from the spillway of the Kedron dam, with a glassed-in gallery overlooking the brook, this beige colored house with brown trim had two apartments separated in the front by a lattice-divided, built in porch. At the back, a small side porch extended toward the roadway and looked over onto the house across the way, which is the only house still standing in Benson Place, and which in those days was the same color as the Benson house and had four apartments. The Benson house took its name from Mrs. Bertha Benson, who lived in the apartment on the brook side. She rented the other apartment to Alfred and Nannie Robinson, an African-American couple who had come from St. Louis to work for Mrs. Bryson in the big house at 39 Elm Street. Mr. Robinson, who drove a rubbish truck, at one time had raised chickens and had a number of chicken coops at the back corner of the Bryson property behind the mill. Later, in our last years on Pleasant Street after Mrs. Benson and the Robinsons had died and the ownership of the house had passed to Ed McCann, this apartment was occupied by Robert and Peg Hendricks and their son Bob and daughter Faith, good friends of ours, and I got to see the interior of the place for the first time. The house across the way belonged to Sumner and Maud Wardwell, who lived in one of the apartments and rented the other three — one to John and Bessie Potwin and their daughter Ruth, one to Fred and Laura Ransehousen, and one to Sonny and Jerry Potwin and their son Steve and their black cocker spaniel, Chichi. From Benson Place our access to the brook was a narrow strip of lawn sloping to the water's edge between the Benson house and a long, low building housing a number of garages, one of which Elba Buckman rented for his Ford. A narrow passage separated the farthest garage from a curious building belonging to the mill. It was painted brown like the mill and, with its lean-to roof and its attached exterior wooden stairway going up the mill side, it looked to us as though it had come from a western frontier town. The main floor of this building was used to store lumber and bags of gypsum and cement, and the doors were always secured with large padlocks. It was of considerable interest to us because the second floor had once served as the living quarters for one of the mill workers, a man named Ernest Rennie. We knew little about Mr. Rennic except that he had died before we were born, that he was missing a number of fingers, and that during his time at the mill he was often to be seen in the evening sitting on the bench in front of the Benson house, smoking his pipe and regarding the weeping willow across the brook. After his death, his rooms had simply been closed up more or less as they were so that from the top of the wooden staircase we could peer through the dusty glass of the door into the dark interior and see an old dishpan and part of a bed frame. On the other side of the mill yard, the space between the Wardwell house and the southwest arm of the mill was used as a parking place and an access, through a gate in a wooden fence that still stands, to the Bryson property. The rest of Benson Place was occupied by the buildings and the yards of Frost's Mill.

From our back porch and from the windows along the eastern side of our apartment, we became accustomed to the regular sights and sounds of Benson Place — to Phil Tierney and Ed Maynes easing the delivery trucks loaded with cement bags and lumber and building supplies up the dirt road and to the rattling sideboards of the emptied trucks when they returned; to the comings and goings of customers in their pickup trucks; to the maroon LaSalle and later the green Packard that Mr. Frost drove to work; to Mr. Frost's bookkeeper, June Whitcomb, walking to and from work in her dark blue coat, and Sumner Wardwell laboring up the road with his crutch on his way upstreet; to the arrival at the end of the day of Oliver Ferguson and Ruth Keck, who took their evening meal at the

Wardwells. But it was Frost's Mill itself that commanded our attention. Under its seeming acres of gradually sloping, tarred roofs crowned by its great cupola, it sprawled across Benson Place in a bewildering variety of angles, lines, and surfaces and suggested to us infinite possibilities. From my earliest memories of walking there with my father and later of riding my first bike in the mill's backyard after supper, I was fascinated by its tiers and its rooms and hiding places. I remember its cupola and weathervane in the daytime as a fixed point for gauging the motion and direction of slowly moving clouds, and in the evening as a home for bats, a rallying point for flights of swallows, and as a place belonging more to the sky and its remaining light than to the mill yards filling up with darkness. On rainy nights, behind the fog that had come in from the brook and the river to shroud Benson Place and wander around its lone streetlight, the mill would appear and disappear like a ghost among tall cliffs of shadow.

All through those years of childhood, we spent as much time playing around Frost's Mill as we did witnessing its activities. It was our castle, our fortress, our frontier town, our stadium. Approaching it as we did from the enclosure of Benson Place, we saw it as looming up in front of us, the great culmination of the buildings leading up to it on both sides. I imagined hitting towering homeruns into its upper decks and onto its roofs to thunderous applause from sellout crowds in the tiers surrounding me, and I imagined jousting in medieval tournaments before royalty seated along the rail of its elevated porch, and stealing through its passages to overcome the infidel and fly the flag of Christendom from its battlements, of defeating by stealth and sabotage its occupying Nazi forces, and, as I faced single-handed the outlaws just arrived on the morning train, of spotting just in time the rooftop ambush and toppling him from his perch with a single shot from my six-gun. When we were not running up and down the mill's endless stairways or hiding among the lumber piles, we were sneaking around, trying to keep from being seen by Mr. Frost and the men who worked there, and spying on them. Our presence in and around the mill was largely overlooked, and if we ever were questioned, we had our excuse. We were on our way to the scrap room, and more often than not we really were. We would crawl under or climb over the sloping gate in the passageway between the two main buildings and duck through the first door on the left — hitting the light switch on the way — into the small room with the bin where scrap lumber was kept. This room was situated just under the shop on the main floor that housed all of the saws and planes and joiners. As the scraps fell from the machines, they were tossed or swept down through a square opening in the shop floor. From the large pile beneath this opening, we picked up pieces we needed and took them home and nailed them together or carved and whittled them to make machine guns for our games of war, or swords for our games of Robin Hood, or small boats to sail on the Kedron and the Ottauquechee. If the scrap lumber pile was high enough, and it usually was, and we heard the whining of the machinery above us, we would climb up the pile and poke our heads up through the opening in the ceiling and spy on Jack Horner as he cut and fashioned wood to fit the mill's orders. Sometimes we would ask and receive permission to watch him at his work, but it was, of course, against regulations for safety reasons. Other times if we heard no sounds at all from the shop, that meant that it was lunch time and that the coast was clear, and we would boost ourselves up through the hole and tiptoe around, looking at things. Such prowling was unnerving because we might be noticed by anyone, even Mr. Frost himself, from the main office, situated just one glass paneled door away. We were more relaxed but also spooked when, at the end of a day with the rest of the mill locked and the men gone home, we found the door to the scrap room unlocked and we stole up through

46

the hole into the strangely silent room with all of its quiet machines and its cobwebbed corners. Dusty shafts of slanting sunlight lit up patches of sawdust and wood on the old wide boards of the floor, and beneath the screened off interior of the cupola rising from the raftered ceiling, the air was heavy with the fragrance of wood chips and shavings.

Our other favorite place in the mill was the enclosed walkway, like a bridge of sighs, that served to connect the two main buildings. It was situated over the gateway into the storage buildings and yards. Since it was up on a level of its own slightly above the second story, we ascended to it and descended from it by a small staircase at each end leading, on the one end, to the main shop, and on the other, to one of the many lumber storage rooms. But while we were up in this narrow gallery with its floor to ceiling windows on both sides, we were in neither place, in suspension. Even time seemed to stand still there as we looked down into the yard on both sides, dazzled by the sunlight and the close air and heat, the enclosed stillness broken only by the buzzing of a trapped fly beating against a windowpane.

Since we seldom entered the main office of the mill, which was reached by the long stairs leading up to the front porch and the front door, we were rarely in the presence of C.C. Frost himself. Mr. Frost wore dark suits and appeared to us as tall and gaunt and somewhat scary. One detail in his office did require periodic inspection and was worth thinking up an excuse to go and see. That was the single, rectangular picture frame containing five portrait photos in a row of his five daughters, who were several years older than we and of whom Ada had often spoken fondly. Arranged oldest to youngest, they were fascinating as so many variations on a theme, and Mr. Frost once named them for us in order.

This was Frost's Mill as I recall it. After the death of C. C. Frost, the mill was sold by his daughters to two enterprising businessmen, Ranulf Ueland and William D. Wood, who turned around and sold it to Laurance Rockefeller on the very same day they bought it, 11 September 1968. Rockefeller razed the buildings but retained ownership of the land, which he leased to the village of Woodstock as a parking lot. As far as I know, there are no pictures of the mill as it was in the 1940s and 50s. It can be glimpsed as a blurry presence in certain snapshots of my brother and me taken in Benson Place. Ivan Albright's abstract rendering gives a good idea of the cupola and, studied carefully, suggests other familiar features, but it is too non-representational to give anyone a clear idea of the mill's real appearance. A watercolor in the Mertens House catches the west side and back yard in winter from an unusual perspective, but the result is simply an unidentifiable huddle of sheds half buried in snow. The Woodstock Historical Society's only photograph of the mill, taken just before it was torn down, shows it stripped of its signs and denuded of its front porch, and thus barely recognizable to anyone who knew it in its heyday. All that is left of it now is the weathervane from the cupola and the mill sign that stood at the top of Benson Place next to the bridge. They are in the possession of Esther Frost at the Frost family home on Pleasant Street.

We left 8 Pleasant Street in the fall of 1958 and moved to what had been my grandfather and grandmother Coffin's house on Lincoln Street. Although our apartment had scarcely been large enough for a family with one child, let alone three, and the house was big enough so that we could each have our own room, I didn't want to go. In fact, I was so reluctant to make the move, to leave behind that small, entire world of first memories, of meaning and association, that I stayed two extra nights in the nearly empty apartment after the rest of the family had gone. For a while after we moved, we looked in on our old neighbors periodically, but eventually the Thomases and then the Buckmans passed away, Ada moved to an apartment on River Street, and the two houses were sold to strangers. Years later at the invitation of a friend, Janet Houghton, who happened to be renting the apartment we had lived in, I went back to have a look and found the interior so completely renovated that I wouldn't have known where I was, had it not been for the view from the east windows. The screened-in porch in the back, however, had been left just as it was in our day, and it was good to stand there for a while and remember.

Over the years I have often returned to the old neighborhood. I've explored again the Little Path, and have gone back to Benson Place with its one remaining house and poked around the parking lot where the mill used to be. And I have walked the banks of the brook and the river, looking for some scrap, some trace of all that was there, but I have not found a thing. At such times I've usually ended up at the very back of what was the lumber yards on the bench that someone has placed on that narrowing point of land where the Kedron meets the Ottauquechee. Sitting there empty-handed, I am always reminded of how little help is ever offered from artifacts in any task of reconstruction, of how much it all finally depends upon that something in us that makes us return again and again to the places we used to know. And in that one place in Woodstock where the brook and the river can be heard simultaneously, I often give in to an impulse to recreate it all just as it once was, bringing back the buildings and summoning the people to reoccupy them. The sound of the water on both sides helps, and as that world and time begin to reappear before the mind's eye, I sometimes imagine I am hearing the different voices of the Kedron and the Ottauquechee. The Kedron in its course through the village runs close to the backs of houses, and its chatter is overlaid with snatches of conversation from back lawns and porches all along its way; with the imprecations of generations of golfers glaring into its waters; with the shouts of children who swam at the first bridge on the golf course and in the dammed up place behind the

Doubledays' house on Maple Street; with the splash of home run balls and the faint honking of car horns from Sunday afternoon town team baseball games on Vail Field; with the clopping of horses on the Cross Street bridge by Costello's Garage, returning to Ferguson's Stables at the end of the day's Trail Ride; with the words of the village crew drifting out the back windows of the sheds on Mechanic Street; with the furtive whispers of boys hidden in the willows under the footbridge trying their first cigarettes; with the tall stories of hunters weighing their deer at the old fire station; with the echo of the fire whistle signaling from the middle of the village its countless, faded noons; with the wading of fishermen into the water by the Pleasant Street bridge; with the blowing of sawdust out of the pipe and onto the sawdust pile at the side of Frost's Mill. The Ottauquechee's voice is deeper, its perspective longer. Negotiating its rapids, then barely moving through its standing pools, then picking up again, it passes beneath the span of higher, wider bridges, skirts spacious lawns sloping to its banks from older and more grand and distant houses, and wanders under wider skies through broad expanses of pasture and field. The affairs of the village are none of its concern, for it is more reflective, more self-regarding, and all down its long reaches it is intent on something outside our moment, something far beyond us altogether. The Kedron chronicles, and its voice is narrative; the Ottauquechee meditates, and its voice, which is itself a kind of listening, is oracular. Standing by the water's edge, I have often tried to spot the exact point of their confluence. The Kedron broadens at its mouth and unravels as if in anticipation, rippling around and skipping over stones as though expecting its arrival to be a gathering and culmination of events. But its currents suddenly just disappear into the deeper course of the Ottauquechee in its running east, then north, then finally east again, like years passing into memory, time into eternity.

Upstreet

*In the theatre of the past that is constituted
by memory, the stage setting maintains
the characters in their dominant roles.*

GASTON BACHELARD

W hen my mother worked in Gillingham's Store, she had a
kind of standing joke going with Clara Richardson, the slight, bespectacled, seemingly ageless lady who worked there as bookkeeper
for so many years. I think they may have even played it a few
times. To a customer inquiring about an item which the store did
not have — for example, an adaptor for an electrical socket — they
would say, "Oh, no, we don't carry it any more because we couldn't
keep it in stock." The reaction of the customer, reported or imagined, was an acquiescent "O.K., thank you," followed, as he turned
to go, by a sudden expression of momentary perplexity and confusion. That joke has stayed with me for years, perhaps because it
subtly honors a vanishing sense of time, both as an essential factor
in a longstanding tradition of dry, Yankee humor and as a function
of retail as it was carried out before the age of the consumer. It
conjures up an unhurried world, part real, part mythical, of small
shops where items had been placed on the shelves to stay put for a
while, at least, and where too much business was considered as
bad as too little. It was a world that offered enough time for personality to enter into business transactions and for character to
emerge. Perhaps for that reason, my early memories of the stores
and businesses in Woodstock are inseparable from my memories

of the people who ran them and the clerks who worked for them. In those days Woodstock offered the spectacle of a wide variety of distinctive characters that was irresistible to any young person with a developing curiosity about the world. So I never needed to be asked twice to run an errand, and I seldom did so, either on foot or on my bike, without making an additional stop or two in the stores.

The center of Woodstock is located at the intersection of Route 12, which runs north and south, and Route 4, the main east-west artery across central Vermont. Within the village, these routes become Elm Street and Central Street respectively, and most of the stores and shops are situated in the blocks of two and three storied nineteenth century buildings laid out on both sides of these streets. The most impressive approach to Woodstock was and still is from the north on Route 12. One passes the Billings Farm and then the hedges and lawns of the Marsh-Billings-Rockefeller mansion on the top of the hill to cross the bridge over the Ottauquechee River and look straight up Elm Street to the center of the village. We called the business district "upstreet" in those days. Since people from Golf Avenue or Maple Street, for example, said "downstreet", and all of us got there without ascending or descending, and since Mrs. Wolstoncroft, the grandmother of a friend from Mountain Avenue, said "overstreet", I will accept the theory of a friend of mine that it might be a matter of whether one walked with or against or perpendicular to the flow of the Kedron. My route to the village was so often the same — up Pleasant Street to the Congregational Church and then along under the great elms of Elm Street — that in memory and imagination it is the way I always go when I take a walk through the streets as they were then, revisiting the stores and reacquainting myself with their proprietors, their clerks and, in some cases, their clientele. Just beyond the Dana Historical House, I come first to the Elm Tree Press and then to the large white clapboard building of the Tracy Block with its three entrances, the first for Stimets' Electrical Service with its showroom window; the middle one, an open foyer with photographs by Joe Stone behind glass on its walls and an open staircase leading up to his photography studio and to Jerry and Ruth's Beauty Salon, Jerry Potwin and Ruth Needham, proprietors; and the third for a shoe repair store that was operated by Roger Chamberlin. Between the Tracy Block and the Gillingham Block was an alley for deliveries to F. H. Gillingham and Sons in its current location, and beyond that, in the Gilman Block, was Winslow's Clover Gift Shop and the New England Telephone Company, with Persis Gilbert and Mary Howes' Yarn Shop above it. At the end of that block, a driveway lined with lilac bushes on both sides led back behind the stores to the old White Cupboard Inn barn. Then on the west corner of Elm and Central Streets stood the White Cupboard itself without its deck and with its kitchen situated in a cramped, narrow room along the west side of the building.

Crossing over Central Street and turning left by the side of the Vermont Savings Bank to walk eastward along Edson's Row, I come first to the Budget Shop (Katherine Mosher, proprietor), which was always painted white. Just beyond it was the First National, which was red, and then the Woodstock Electric Company; then W. H. Mitchell (Elmer A. Emery, proprietor); then Tony's Barbershop; then the Woodstock Pharmacy (W. D. Clough and later Joe Nalibow proprietors); then The Great Atlantic and Pacific Tea Company, known simply as the A&P; then W. H. Shurtleff; and at the end of the block, Carter Insurance Company, with The Green Beauty Shop at the back, and down the steps in the basement Eric and Jane Maynes' store, The Yankee Bookshop. On the other side of the alley where Mechanic Street began was the Economy Store (Reno Casellini, proprietor), and then the Village Inn, better known as the Tavern, which was owned and operated by Rose Bergante. Across the Kedron the stone building stood in ruins from a fire in 1938 that had gutted its interior, leaving only its exterior walls intact. In the attached building was the state liquor store at 49 Central Street, and, set back from the sidewalk, at the bottom of High Street, was Eddie's Socony Station (Ed Leonard, proprietor), with the service area in the middle and the office on the end, where some years later Bernie Mayo had his barbershop. The only business I can recall in the corner between the service station and the liquor store was a music store run by Hap Ellis.

Across the street next to the Mooney house, where Francis Mooney would some years later install gas pumps, stood the fire station, painted gray. It fronted the street with its three large doors for the fire trucks, and its fire escape leading up to the second floor looked directly down onto Kedron Brook, in those days a lively little stream filled with good-sized trout. Walking over the bridge and heading west on the north side of Central Street, I pass the red brick, 1930s post office on its present site. On the end of the block beginning on the other side of the post office driveway was R. E. Morgan, Plumbing, Heating, Kitchen Ware; then The Town and Country Shop (Frank Lewis, proprietor), which had formerly been Livingston's and which we still referred to as such; then the Central Market (R. B. Houghton, proprietor); then Earle M. Slack, Grocer; then up the steps to Maynes and Wards Groceries and Hardware, a store painted gray, which I also remember as Remington's. Between this store and the next, a wide staircase led up to apartments on the second floor, one of which was later renovated and occupied by Elmer Atwood as a barbershop. Next to the steps at the bottom of this staircase were the steps to the back entry of The Woodstock Fruit Company, better known as the Fruit Store (Ed McCann, proprietor), and on the corner were the steps leading up to the front entrance.

Around the corner, starting down the east side of Elm Street, I come first to W. D. Cabot, Home Furnishings; then to Joe DeRosie's

54

barbershop just before the bend in Elm Street. The next store space was also occupied by Cabot's, but no doorway from the street opened to it. Then the wide stairway led up to Sterling's Sporting Goods, which was managed by Douglas Hunter. Under that was Sterling's Pharmacy; then The Woodstock Market (Paul Kenefick, proprietor); then up the steps to Peg Godsill's Women's Shop, which later became The Men's Shop under Larry Angwin. At the end of the block was the Woodstock National Bank. On the other side of the drive in the white clapboard block was the English Sports Shop, Aubrey Lightbourn, proprietor. Next to that was The Vermont Standard, where Benton Dryden was editor; and finally the last door led up the stairs to the rooms used by W. D. Cabot in his capacity as funeral director.

Of all the stores, perhaps Gillingham's has changed the least over the years. My first memories of it go back to the time when my grandfather, Clarence Coffin, was completing the last of his more than fifty years with that establishment. The days when he hitched up the horses at the Gillingham barn on lower Lincoln Street and drove the delivery route, taking orders in the morning and then going to the store and filling them and delivering them in the afternoon, had passed, and he spent his days working in the store. From the moment my brother and I entered Gillinghams with our parents and sometimes our grandmother, we would be looking for Grampy Coffin among the clerks, who wore identical tan work coats. These clerks included the poker-faced, timid, but very kind Elizabeth Rose; Richard Marble, a Harvard man and former principal of Woodstock High School, whom people recognized and depended on as an ornithological expert; the ever serious and ageless Bill Chandler; and a short, wide bulldog of a woman named Alice Mae Snyder, who looked as though she had missed her true calling as the matron of a women's reformatory and who went on to run the state liquor store on Central Street as though she were an undercover agent for the W.C.T.U., refusing to allow a bottle of spirits to cross the sales counter until she had scrutinized innumerable proofs of age from anyone bearing the slightest trace of youth. Joining this company in my memory is the redoubtable Bob Walker, a man of roughly my grandfather's vintage who came along after my first recollections and worked in Gillingham's into his nineties. A slight, bespectacled sparrow of a man, he took up various positions in the store and stood there immobile with arms folded like some stone idol. He preferred speaking to being spoken to, as a customer discovered one day when he approached Bob with a packet of seeds that he was intending to purchase and asked him if they would grow. Came the only answer to such a question in a sonorous, stentorian voice, "They will if you plant them." The idol had spoken.

Grampy Coffin was usually to be found stocking shelves or waiting on a customer in the way that they did in those days before shoppers helped themselves to the things they needed. As he went around, he wrote down each item and the price with a thick blue pencil on a pad with carbon paper that he kept in the vest pocket of his coat. He was a gentle man with carefully parted straight gray hair combed close to his head, his most extreme gesture being the delight he expressed on seeing us. I always hoped that we would find him in the back of the store near the freight elevator. Once in a while he would take us for a ride on it, and we would watch the motion of the great wheel and ropes as we rose into some quiet and distant storage rooms that seemed like quite another world. Downstairs we would walk back past the offices with their roll top desks and ledgers and look there for Clara Richardson, the bookkeeper, who, though she seemed elderly to us then, was destined to live another forty years. And we loved to explore the hardware section and to walk among the barrels of produce. Sometimes we would catch a glimpse of Rolfe or Warren Gillingham themselves, who seemed to personify the Coolidge idea that the business of America is business. In the grocery section of the store, which back then carried the same aroma of coffee beans as it does today, the prices of the items on the shelves were displayed in plastic numbers that fit in between two metal tracks running the length of the shelf edge. Having no idea what these numbers were for, I used to play with the ones I could reach, moving them along the shelf and causing who knows how much havoc until my mother saw me and, with some alarm, explained why I was not to touch them. I recall feeling pretty guilty and hoping that I had not made Grampy Coffin's job hard for him and that he would not hear what I had done.

Various places in Gillingham's had their fascination for me at different times. Each year at Christmas time a Santa Claus would miraculously appear in one of the niches of the display windows, as though through a secret door at his back, and that particular rectangular space set in the wall had and still has an aura of magic about it that has always attracted my notice. In the winter my attention was mostly fixed on the back left hand side of the store with its rack of Northland skis. Then, as spring came around and the woods beckoned, I would go back to the same part of the store to gaze into the display case of jackknives and hunting knives. In the fall around Halloween, we would go to the back rooms to have one of the clerks scoop whole or split peas into bags for us for our peashooters.

Gillingham's, in spite of its expansion and its alterations, has retained much of its particular look and atmosphere and has preserved its unique character. And my association with that store has been oddly continuous: as in my childhood, I have often been able to visit someone in my family who was working there — first my grandfather, then my father who, after working in the store briefly after high school, helped them take inventory on New Years Day for several years; then my mother, who worked there as a bookkeeper from 1962-1969; and finally my daughter, who worked there summers and vacations during her school years.

The same sort of connection gave me some familiarity with the inside of the place of business that was probably least well known to the people of Woodstock — the Woodstock Office of the New England Telephone Company. My first visits to the telephone office were made with my mother when she would stop in with my brother and me to see Aunt Ada Maynes, who worked as an operator there. I remember standing behind the fenced-in area just inside the door and seeing the tyrannical Bessie Gobie, chief operator, seated at her desk on the right. She was a short, squat woman whose flushed face was framed by rope colored hair done up in a permanent, and whose mouth, compressed by puffed red cheeks, did its best to turn its fixed expression of disapproval into a smile whenever anyone besides her employees entered the office. Opposite her at the switchboard, sitting on their high rotating chairs were four corseted, substantial women, busily pulling up plugs on the ends of cords, reaching them across a huge tangle of other cords and pushing them into the holes of what looked like a huge, standing parcheesi board as they spoke into the little microphones of their headsets.

The telephone system then was more public and more human than the one that has replaced it. You couldn't pick up the phone to make a call without talking to someone, even if the party you were calling was not at home. Instead of the innocuous dial tone and the various sound signals of today's automated systems, you were engaged by the voice of a live operator saying "number please" and "thank you" or "that line is busy", and you knew those voices — Ada's clipped, professional tone, Lucille Paige's husky tenor, Elizabeth Rose's adenoidal drawl — and could put a face and a personality to them. Sometimes you asked the operator if she would call you when the line was no longer busy or if she knew where the fire was. For the telephone operators knew *everything*. They knew who was calling whom and when, who was distressed and trying to reach the police, who was sick and trying to reach the doctor. In those days before beepers, the doctors kept in close touch with the telephone office. When one of them was going out on call, he would phone in to tell the operators, and they would put a clip on Dr. Eastman's or Dr. Thomas' office numbers, with a note on them where they could be reached.

Nosiness is a well-known small town condition and one that those of us who were on party lines were able to satisfy better than those who had the luxury of a private line. Though it certainly could be a great inconvenience, the party line provided easy access to the lives of other people. As children, we listened in on others' telephone conversations and discovered that even though they were so sure someone was eavesdropping as to ask us to hang up, if we stayed quiet, they'd lose their suspicions and would carry on, confident that they had the line to themselves. Thanks to the party line, we were that much more able to keep up with each other's business.

My mother worked as a telephone operator from 1956 to 1962, when the dial system came to Woodstock and the office closed. In the last years of the telephone office, when I was in high school, I actually got behind the fence and had a closer look at it all. She worked the night shift from 11 PM to 7 AM, and I used to stop in to see her on weekends and talk with her as she did the four hours or so of work — checking and putting into order the tickets for the out-of-town calls and handling the occasional late night call — before she could put on the late night buzzer and go to sleep on the cot in the comfortable sitting room in the back.

Recently I discovered in the Vermont Historical Society in Montpelier a switchboard, considerably smaller but otherwise very much like the one that had been in the old Woodstock office of the

New England Telephone Company. Standing there picturing the way it used to be, I was struck by how few telephone operators were left from those days. To my knowledge only Bernice Atwood of the older generation and the last three operators to have been trained in that office are still living: Winifred Allard, a shy, dark girl from South Pomfret who trained for the job at the same time as my mother; Sylvia Strong Doten and Zaela Stimets Strong, who grew up in Woodstock and have made it their home; and Bernice Colby, valedictorian of Woodstock High School's class of 1958, who went on from her job at the phone company to become budget director for Radio Free Europe in Washington. It seemed strange to me that someone of my generation should be among the very last to speak from actual experience of working the old system there in the office on Elm Street. And the old switchboard that was now an artifact reminded me of the curious and ironic fact that of all the calls to have come through Woodstock over the years, probably the most important one was handled by my father in his brief stint as a night operator when he was in high school. On the night of August 3, 1923, he put through a call from Washington, D.C. to Secret Service men in Bridgewater, Vermont, informing them to carry the news of President Harding's death to Vice-President Coolidge at his home in Plymouth, where he would be sworn in that night by his father.

My father worked at the Woodstock Electric Company at 11 Central Street for forty years from 1929 to 1969, a period which included the first thirteen years of its incorporation into the Central Vermont Public Service Corporation. The Electric Company supplied electricity and maintained electrical services for the town of Woodstock and employed quite a number of people in a variety of jobs: there was a line crew, whose job it was to keep the power lines in good working order; an office staff of accountants and book-keepers; and a number of salesmen for the electrical appliances displayed in the front of the store. My father worked as a repairman and a salesman. My mother also worked there from 1935 until November 1941, just two months before my brother and I were born. Although the Woodstock Electric Company is long since gone and the CVPS gave up the old store to a jewelry business and moved its offices, I often find myself drifting back there. In one of my earliest recollections of the store, my brother and I are riding our tricycles all over the first floor, and my parents are watching us. We had gone there on a Sunday so that my father could put together our trikes at his workbench, and he let us try them out before taking them up to ride around the sidewalks of the library and the courthouse. He propped open the back door of the store so that we could zoom down the ramp and race up and down the showroom, pretending that the aisles were streets and the refrigerators and ranges we passed were the buildings of the village. And in my memory I still stop in, as I used to on my way home from grade school, to see my father. The water cooler next to his workbench was just the thing whether I was thirsty or not because it was fun to work and because I knew just which cupboard to look in to find the long box of paper cups made from overlapping folds of paper like tiny Venetian blinds. And then I could push the button to turn on the water and wait for the bubbles to blub-blub to the top of the tank.

Any stop at the Electric Company might include a few dramatic moments with the company's treasurer, Rob Woods. Wherever I met him, whether inside the store or on the front step or strolling in the village, Mr. Woods, as we were taught to call him, would stop, and that was the signal for me to do the same. He was a short, portly, balding man who always wore a hat, a three-piece suit, complete with a vest pocket watch chain, and a diamond ring, and he smoked cigars. A diehard Republican, he refused to take Roosevelt dimes in change. Pretending to be serious, he would study me with a skeptical and seemingly dissatisfied manner and say, in his crackly voice, something like, "Now where do you think you're going?" or "What do you think you're doing?" No matter what I answered, he would pretend that it had further confused him, and he would tip his hat back and put his thumbs in his vest coat pockets and wrinkle his brow. Often he would end these episodes by poking me in the ribs and making a funny noise with his mouth and giving me a dime. Though he could be difficult and demanding, as anyone knew who worked with him, at his best, Mr. Woods kept up a spirit of impish good humor in the Electric Company office. He was "full of the devil," as we used to say. When he fell asleep leaning back in his chair at his desk with his Stetson on, my mother and bookkeeper Louise Fraser would take hold of its brim and jam it down around his ears and regale themselves watching him struggle and swear in trying to get it back up so that he could see. Not to be outdone, he could be depended on to even the score. To bother her, he tended to call my mother "Oileen" instead of Arlene. Somehow he got word that she had agreed to take a singing part at a meeting of the Teago Grange in the small, nearby farming community of South Pomfret, which was her home. One day when she was working at the Electric Company office window, Mrs. Chapman, a blue-haired, socially prominent lady from Elm Street, came in to pay her bill. As my mother was politely waiting on her, Mr. Woods sidled up and said, "Are you going up to the Grange tomorrow night, Mrs Chapman, to hear Oileen sing her song?" My mother always remembered her embarrassment and clearly recalled that at the Grange hall performance Mr. Woods was in the audience, making it difficult for her to keep her composure.

When my father was not to be found talking to a customer in the Electric Company's large front showroom, I would look for him at his workbench at the east window. Usually if he was not there, Bill Woodbury at the sales counter on the right, with its great roll of wrapping paper, would tell me where he was and when he would most likely return. Sometimes I would stop in to use the bathroom upstairs or at least use this as an excuse to wander around on the second floor for a short while. Up there at the top of the long, banistered staircase, one black-ribbed rubber mat extended diagonally across the wide floor of the mostly empty room to the narrow shop where Dick Leonard and Carl Hively repaired radios, and another mat extended all the way back to the bathroom at the back of the building. I'd walk quietly to the north end of the room to look out the windows down into the square and watch the activities of the village from this unique vantage point. It was always worthwhile being upstairs just on the chance that the door to Mr. Woods' room, situated directly over the office downstairs, was open and I could catch even a momentary glimpse of the antiques and memorabilia which that large room contained: jars of old coins, including Indian head pennies; music boxes and musical clocks; the bell of a railway engine from the Woodstock Railway; old photographs and posters and stamp collections. The fact that this room was so often locked greatly increased my curiosity and speculation about the treasures that it housed. At the end of the hall in the bathroom was a sign which my father said Mr. Woods had put over the toilet, and I was puzzled by it for some time: to the bottom half of a war bonds poster showing a red and yellow Uncle Sam leaning out of a black background, pointing at me and saying "You too can help," Mr. Woods had attached a hand-lettered notice printed in ink on white poster board: "Stand close or sit down."

Another advantage to being upstairs was that in descending I could see over the partitions and down into the main office where the accounts of the Woodstock Electric Company and the Woodstock Aqueduct Company were kept. Since I was not tall enough to see from the first floor what went on in there, the staircase gave me a chance to see, beneath the great glass lamps suspended from the ceiling, the desks and tables and combination safes of the sort that were always being cracked in western movies. In what seemed a privileged glimpse of important business being transacted and a vision of warm lamplight on varnished wood, I could stand with my hand on the banister and see Irene Burke, a lovely and soft spoken woman, in her high office chair at the window where people came to pay their bills; and, seated at her desk, accountant Anna McManama, whose Irish sparkle and humor always made it a pleasure to see her; and sometimes Mr. Woods with his hat on seated in his swivel chair at the long table at the back of the office, snoozing.

The back of the store and its outbuildings always seemed to me to offer an intriguing maze of variously lit coves and warrens. The back entrance led down past the office and my father's workbench to the end of the corridor where an office was set behind a partition with large windows. This office, which was occupied by Carroll Bennett, the good-natured company superintendent, whom we knew simply as Ben, had been Wilfred Smith's when he was the company manager. Mr. Smith was a great favorite of my mother and father, but I knew him only from a photograph on the desk in the office. Next to this office a door that never latched opened to a built-in ramp leading to the back storage area and a long, narrow office. Beyond that, the double doors opened onto a loading platform with steps down the side next to the space behind Elmer Emery's store where he always parked his dark blue jeep. Behind the Woodstock Electric Company in the area that is now a metered parking lot, the company shop was situated. This two-storied building, which had few windows and was always in need of paint, was encircled by a dirt driveway. The shop was the headquarters of the line crew and the place where Olin Fullerton, who had shared an apartment with my father when they had attended trade school in Boston in the 1920s, repaired ranges and refrigerators. In its dark and cool interior among workbenches covered with tools stood

64

dollies and large coils of cables and wire. On afternoons during World Series time, a radio was always kept on in the shop, and people working in the stores on Edson's Row would come out to check on the score of what always seems to have been a classic Yankee-Dodger showdown. I remember sitting on my bike and leaning against the shop's concrete loading platform and hearing the voice of Mel Allen in the early autumn air and seeing the weathered faces of the line crew — Kit Sawyer, Bill Lantz, Bicky Bates, Max Spaulding, Maurice Rogers, Ronnie Colby, and others — as they gathered around the radio in their low-slung, heavy leather belts and tool holsters, or stopped in for a moment to listen. A black and white group photograph of the personnel of The Woodstock Electric Company taken on the occasion of the opening of the new power plant in Taftsville in June of 1943 captures them all. They are assembled before the great open doors of the brick building in the bright midday sunshine. The women from the office wear light-colored dresses gathered at the waist. Almost all of the men, including some of the line crew, wear white shirts and ties, and the older men, the stockholders, wear dark suits, though some have shed their jackets. There is a small boy near the front with his father, both of them unidentified. Hair tonic is much in evidence, as are wire-rimmed or rimless glasses. The camera click catches some people looking down or slightly askance, but most of them, kneeling as they are in the front row or standing in the three rows behind, are looking straight ahead, and there is good humor in their faces and also some sense of the occasion, of the moment. My eye is drawn time and again to the center of the photo because my father is there and, not far from him, my Aunt Julia, my mother's sister who replaced her in the office when my brother and I were born. But my attention keeps wandering to so many of the others, looking at me, just as I remember them from my childhood, across exactly sixty years and meeting my gaze here, in what seems the instant of my life. I can almost hear their voices. The last of these forty men and four women, Lucy Houghton, died in July of 2004.

II

In those days the stores in the village had about anything that anyone might need. Even without a car we were not disadvantaged. Although we did sometimes order things from the Sears and Roebuck and Montgomery Wards catalogs, the shops in Woodstock could be relied on to supply most of our requirements. All of our shoes came from Shurtleff's, and we always liked going there. For one thing, it often meant a new pair of sneakers, the black or brown Ball Band or Keds high-tops which all the boys wore. For another, it gave us a chance to look at the squirrels and the pheasant and the other stuffed and mounted animals which were to be seen at various places along the walls and on the top of the high shelves. This collection of taxidermy was not to be compared with the one in the back room of Alan Potter's Teago Garage in South Pomfret, which had a bobcat, but it was still interesting. So were the guns which were also sold there, particularly the pistols in one of the windows and in the display case just inside the door. Sometimes Mr. Shurtleff himself, in his three-piece suit and his one built-up shoe, would emerge from his town clerk's office in the back and quietly wait on us, sitting before us on one of the low stools with the sloped place for a foot on the front, and then disappearing into the basement or behind one of the floor-to-ceiling cases of shoe boxes. Until his return, we would hear only the ticking of the old pendulum clock and try to meet the glassy stare of the great horned owl from the top of a display case. In our visits to Shurtleff's, we always hoped to be attended to by Ruth Harvey, in my mind one of the most delightful people ever to work in a store in Woodstock. She always pretended to be put out with us, always knew we were up to no good and approved of that, always tickled us in the ribs, and, according to her, we always put out the wrong foot when she was helping us try on shoes.

The rest of my clothes for school or for summer came from the same places every year. Upstairs in the Town and Country (Livingston's), Alice Leonard, full of kindness and gravelly laughter, helped my mother and me find just the right swimming trunks for the Red Cross swimming lessons sponsored by Camp Kitchigamink at Silver Lake. Jeans, or "dungarees" as we called them then, were pretty much all we wore year-round, and we bought those in W. H. Mitchell's, which everyone knew simply as Elmer's. Elmer Emery was a tall, good-looking man with wavy hair who wore bow ties, chewed a toothpick, and kept a tape measure around his neck. His stock of Lee Riders was kept stacked in the large drawers under the long wooden display and sales counter. He would measure my waist, and I would go down into the cluttered basement to try on a pair and come back up and stand in front of the mirror on the other side of the store and tell him and my father whether or not they felt right. The length didn't make any difference since we always rolled up the legs. Sometimes we might buy a tee shirt or two or a striped jersey as well. These fittings usually took place after my father had closed the Electric Company on Saturday (later Friday) night and stopped into Elmer's next door to shoot the breeze for a short while before walking home.

Later, in the mid 1950s, as I entered junior high school and became more clothes conscious, I was able to find at Larry's Men's Shop at 17 Elm Street the button-down plaid shirts and pink dress shirts and chinos with the belt in the back and the green and white campus coats that were the fad back then. I always liked to go up the steps into that curiously elevated attractive store, redolent with cigar smoke, simply to look at the shirts and trousers on display.

We could just as easily shop for groceries without leaving the center of the village. Although there was nothing resembling a supermarket in Woodstock until Raymond Houghton opened Houghton's Red and White at 12 Central Street in 1954, there were many grocery stores very near to each other. We had the choice of Gillingham's or the First National or the A&P or Maynes and Wards or Slack's store. My recollections of Maynes and Ward's, which also sold hardware, are sketchy and incomplete, probably because it was not until the store was purchased by John Remington, from Long Island, in 1954, that I had my own reasons for going there. However, I do recall going up the steps into a store with old shelves reaching to a high ceiling and, at the front on the right at a narrow counter with a light bulb suspended over it, being waited on by Margaret Ward, a gray-haired lady who always seemed more busi-ness-like than friendly. She was wearing one of the gray coats worn by the clerks in those days. And I remember Joe Ward and a man with a hat on, who, I was told, was Jim Maynes, reaching up for items on the top shelves with a long pole with pincers on the top end which could be worked by a metal device on the other end. Since the Railway Express had its office in the back of Maynes and Wards, Newhall ("String") Jones, who drove the Railway Express truck, was often to be seen there. At 6'5" tall, String was one of the largest men in Woodstock. A quiet, mild-mannered bachelor with a sharp wit and a dry sense of humor, he was a sort of adopted member of my father's high school class, the class of 1925, and often attended their annual Alumni Day reunion, although he had graduated in 1916. If this was his way of staying young, it worked, for he outlived most of the members of both classes, dying at the age of ninety-four in 1992. Perhaps String's strangest cargo in his years as railway express driver was a human one. When Dick Ster-ling was suffering from a bad back, he and String made an arrange-ment whereby at the end of the day String would back the big, green express truck from its parking place behind Maynes and

Wards over to the back entry of Sterling's Drug Store so that Dick could, without having to negotiate steps at all or to assume the sitting position, walk straight into back of the truck to be transported (balancing himself in some fashion) and delivered to his home on the other side of town. Upon arriving there, String undoubtedly maneuvered the truck so as to permit Dick an equally painless exit.

When Maynes and Ward's became Remington's, I stopped there to buy Root Beer Barrels, Tootsie Pops, and the kind of penny candy that we had always bought from Slackie until his store closed in 1953. But most important were the Topps baseball cards, which came wrapped with a flat stick of bubble gum and cost a nickel a pack. In our eagerness to see whether we had finally landed a Mantle or a Mays, we sometimes opened the packs right in the store after we had bought them, only to find just another Bubba Church or George Zuverink or Eddie Pellegrini. These we either stored away for trades or tossed into the Kedron next to the fire station. One day John Remington surprised Ronnie Hively and Dave Harrington and Howard and me as we went to pay for our usual purchases. Placing our small piles of candy and baseball cards on the counter, we said "just these," as we always did, to which John answered, "plus what you've got in your pockets." We chuckled and didn't quite know what to say until we got outside the store and down the street, and then we stopped and laughed ourselves silly. Our pockets were, in fact, empty, but we felt that we had just been given a great idea.

Among all the merchants in the village in those days, Earle Slack — "Slackie" — was my favorite. Perhaps more than any other place, his store, Earle M. Slack, Grocer, represents for me a Woodstock that has long since entirely vanished. Any time we could put together a few pennies, which we usually did by collecting returnable bottles and then hauling them upstreet in our red wagon, we headed to Slackie's to exchange bottles for candy. Twelve-ounce soda pop bottles and beer bottles were worth two cents apiece, and quart bottles were worth a nickel. For a reason that is now easier for me to understand than it was then, my father advised us to transport the empty beer bottles, especially if there were quite a few of them, in bags. We pulled our loaded wagon along Bond Street and Central Street to the front of Slackie's and left it there under the awning and carried the bags and bottles in, checking the glass case on the right to make sure that it was well stocked with candy. Slackie waited on us at the counter on the left, where the cash register was located. He was a large, broad-shouldered but somewhat stooped man who dressed in charcoal gray suit pants — quite often without the coat in summertime, suspenders, and striped dress shirts with elastic arm bands to shorten the sleeves. He wore steel rimmed glasses and had bushy eyebrows. Above his large ears were tufts of reddish gray hair. The hat he wore in and out of the store — I remember a straw one — was pushed back far enough to show that he was balding on top. Over his ear was a pencil which he used to tally up purchases on a brown paper bag before putting the groceries in it. Although we must have tried his patience with our petty transactions, no matter how many stops we made during the day, he was patient with us and always seemed glad to see us. Walking with a stooped swing of the shoulders, he carried our bags of bottles to the back of the store and then came out from behind the cash register to open the sliding door at the back of the candy counter. To keep from bending way over and trying to peer into the small cupboard, the contents of which were more visible to us through the glass front and side, he would ask us to direct his reach, and I can still see his large hand with its thick fingers moving about behind the glass among the open boxes of Kits and Double Bubble in response to our requests and directions.

Mr. Slack's store, which he had inherited from his father, was largely untroubled by the spirit of commercial enterprise. Its ceiling was lower than that of some of the other stores, and its dusty shelves did not reach as high or contain as much. Some of their contents, cans of beans and corn and soup and boxes of starch and baking soda, looked as though they had sat there for years. At the back of the store near an old stove among empty cartons and boxes and bags, Slackie carried on a laundry business. This area was a meeting place for old men. His regular customers included senior citizens such as Ed Kenefick, John Dunbar, Perley Wheeler, Mino Harris, William Soule, and others who used to pass the time on and around the steps at the bottom of the stairs leading to the upper floors of the French Block. Since they were permanent fixtures there on good days, we assumed that they had always been there and that they had always been old. An ever ready source of history, they had the good fortune to spend their last days in the sunshine with each other and to have, just a few steps down the street in Slack's Store, both a ready source of news and tobacco and a place to shelter from a sudden summer shower. On the wall at the back of the store where the old men congregated, Slackie kept a list of his plug tobacco customers and their preferred brands. When one of them died, he simply drew a line through the name and the brand. During gatherings around the stove, if Slackie heard a customer stray into the front of the store, he was known to instruct his cronies to "keep quiet and maybe they'll go away." In response to someone's asking him how much a can of Campbell's soup cost, he replied, "whatever you paid for it last time." He was an authority on aging cheeses, and he sold good fruit and always told us which of the grapefruits and oranges sitting in crates with tissue paper were ripe and which were not. On a late summer afternoon he could be seen cranking up his awning after another day's business.

In those days in the early 1950s, there were three meat markets in Woodstock. Two of them, the Central Market and the Woodstock Market, were in the center of the village. The other, Wheeler's

Market, was located at 47 Pleasant Street in the long, low building that has been occupied by a number of businesses since then and is presently a laundromat. As a child I thought it strange that the Central Market, which we called Houghton's Market because Ray Houghton was the proprietor, did not have a front step as did Slack's next door; rather it had a sloped cement walk that led into the store so that the front door was at sidewalk level. It always seemed to me that it should have been the other way around so that we could have pulled our wagons full of bottles right into Slack's to unload. I remember walking into Houghton's with my father and going to the counter on the right past the display case for meats and buying ground round. Ray Houghton ground the beef for us and caught it in a white container as it came out of the small holes in the grinder. Sometimes we were waited on by Irving Whitcomb or John Staples, and we could see those men busy in their white aprons in the space at the back of the store between the counter and the meat locker. A relative of ours from Barnard, Naoma Hull, also worked there and I used to look at her with some curiosity and a good deal of sympathy because her having been born on February 29 meant that she would have enjoyed so few birthdays. Among the details of the store itself, I seem to recall that a cone of string was situated up above the counter so that when the clerks wound the string around the packages of chops or ribs or ground beef wrapped in tan or white paper, I could see the cone bobbing up and down as it spun around.

Paul Kenefick's Woodstock Market was located at 15 Elm Street. When I first went there to shop with my mother or father or to run an errand for Ada Maynes, customers on entering the store picked a small, white, circular card with a number on it from a hook at the end of the shelves near the door. They then presented that number to Annie Kenefick, seated at a slightly elevated desk at the end of the aisle near the meat case. In that busy and efficient store, customers were waited on in the order of these numbers by Paul himself or his white-aproned clerks. Paul leased as a kind of storage building the small gray house behind a gray rail fence just south of Ferguson's Stables at the intersection of Court Street and Cross Street. Known as "the castle" to Paul and Annie and their help, it housed a cheese cave and a big walk-in cooler, and Paul's truck could often be seen parked there or making the trip between there and the store.

The Woodstock Market was also one of the unofficial residences of Fluffy, a black male cat who for many years was to be seen in and around the store and roaming around the village. Friendly by nature and the object of much affection in the community, Fluffy nevertheless had his turf. After being shooed out of the way in the store by a somewhat imperious elderly lady of those days, Fluffy waited until she bent over to pick something off one of the lower shelves and then demonstrated the territorial imperative by testing and penetrating the thickness of her corsets with his claws. Fluffy's other domicile was the offices of *The Vermont Standard* under the direction of Benton Dryden. Though it offered up-to-date coverage of the town's most important events and informed editorials, the essence of the *Standard* was its "personals," which kept readers informed of such news in Woodstock and its surrounding towns as the following:

Ric Davis has been confined to his house by injuries received when he was kicked by a cow.

Several gardens have been plowed here over the weekend.

Mrs. Angie Abbot has been quite ill the past week with Dr. Eastman in attendance.

Wilmer Peoples went trout fishing in South
Woodstock with his grandfather Rhodes.

We can't set a date for our Community Club
meeting for we are to have movies and don't
know where we can get a machine.

Having a good rain this morning. Too bad the
rivers are too high for fishing and it rains too
hard to work outside. Why find fault, we can't
change it. Just what we need.

Benton Dryden was a likable, red-faced, serious country editor who
paid my brother a dollar for every account he wrote of a Woodstock High School sports event. His mood had a way of brighten-
ing on Wednesday afternoons when long-time employees Vince
Maynes and Larry Godsill started the aging presses rolling. It was
in part through Benton's efforts that Fluffy came to enjoy something of a reputation for feline immortality. Having disappeared
for a time sufficiently long to encourage Benton to write and pub-
lish an obituary, Fluffy later turned up ten miles away in South
Woodstock at the Kedron Valley Inn, whose owner reported that he
was, contrary to all reports, alive and well.

The smallest and the least centrally located of Woodstock's three
markets was Wheeler's Market. Until the Wasps' Snack Bar made
its first appearance as a frozen custard stand in 1950, Wheeler's
market sat more or less by itself across from the entrance to
Holterman's Warehouse. Its proprietor Reu Wheeler had operated
in the Tracy Block a legendary tavern and bakery that my father
and his brothers never tired of recalling. Even without the benefit
of those stories, I would have found Reu Wheeler very funny. He
was a short, friendly-looking man with thin hair and mischievous

eyes. I liked to hear him talk because he spoke with a sort of drawl in a voice that sounded as though it were coming from the side of his mouth, and he had an infectious laugh. Reu and his wife were twice blessed with twins, the second being born some dozen years after the first. Shortly after their birth a lady who had come into the market to do her shopping simply couldn't contain her astonishment over the glad event: "Twins again, Mr. Wheeler! How do you do it?" To which Reu replied, "Well, you go home and take a nice bath and put on some powder, and I'll show you."

Although my parents did not often shop at Wheeler's because of its distance from where we lived on the other end of Pleasant Street, I sometimes went there for a bottle of coke when I was playing with friends from that end of town — Ronnie Watts or Jerry Hall or Ronnie Hively or Gerald Colby, whose mother, Gladys Colby, worked in the market. The other employees I remember were Leonard Cone, a large, broad-shouldered, gray-haired, energetic man who bustled around in his white apron; and Gardiner Maccarty, a quiet, dignified looking gentleman with glasses and snowy white hair and a prominent and neatly trimmed white mustache.

Just as we had some choice of markets, we also had some choice of barbers. My first recollection of a visit to the barber is not a happy one. For no apparent reason my brother and I hated having a haircut. I remember my mother dragging the two of us, much against our will, up the long staircase between Carter Insurance and Shurtleff's to Arthur Godsill's barbershop, where each of us in turn sat on a board placed across the arms of the chair and sniffled and fidgeted and not very stoically endured whatever it was that made us so reluctant to be shorn. In my grade school years I would go to either Tony's Barber Shop or Joe's Barber Shop. Having a haircut at Tony's at 15 Central Street meant being pretty much on display. The only thing that obscured the view of people passing by on the sidewalk was the large potted plant, in the barbershop window. This plant was identified by a small sign next to it: "MISS B. GONIA. Slipped in Woodstock July 4, 1923. GROWING OLD GRACEFULLY. A. Sabatino." The sign stands today beside a comparatively small descendant of the original plant in the home of Tony's grandson Edmund Paige. Tony was a short, balding man who spoke English with an Italian accent. A quiet and mild mannered gentleman, he took an interest in my activities, asking me questions about midget league baseball and basketball, and in my family, for he knew my father and his brothers well. When Tony was busy, I sat on the round, metal-backed chairs along the west wall, breathing in the fragrance of hair tonics, looking at *True Magazine* or *Life* or *Field and Stream* or watching pedestrians passing by the large plate glass window with its faded lettering until it was my turn. I always wondered about the white metal spittoon on the floor at the end of the row of chairs and about the days when it served its true purpose.

I usually went to Joe Derosie's small barbershop at 3 Elm Street for my summer crew cut. I got my first and only flattop from him, and he sold me a stick of butch wax to make it stand up. Unlike Tony's, where I could always see how busy he was from the sidewalk, Joe's barber shop had curtains across the lower half of the windows, and people were always sticking their heads through the door to see how long the wait would be. Joe was a dark, swarthy, preoccupied sort of man with black, curly hair and dark eyes. From time to time Joe would disappear behind the curtain that hung across the entrance to a small, closet-sized room at the back of his shop and then reappear. On the large mirror on the north wall of the shop were a number of photographs of three men from town having their heads completely shaved by Joe. Having nothing else to look at when I was in the chair and faced in that direction, I always looked at them and wondered why anyone would go to a barber for the purpose of becoming bald. Later when Elmer Atwood opened his barbershop in the large front room over Remington's, I went there for haircuts. His unique vantage point from his second floor windows gave him a privileged view of Central Street, and he often punctuated his tonsorial activities with prolonged glances over his glasses at the events below.

III

The businesses in Woodstock that exerted the most irresistible attraction on me were the corner Fruit Store and the two drug stores. So much so that they have come to represent to me something fundamental about the life of the village as it was back then. My recollections of the Woodstock Pharmacy as Clough's Drug Store merge with and are somewhat obscured by later memories of the same store after it was bought and managed by Joe Nalibow. Sterling's Pharmacy was always just Sterling's. In my earliest memories both drug stores along with their soda fountains had a small area in the middle of the store with two round, marble-topped tables and wrought iron chairs. A customer who wanted to enjoy a soda or a dish of ice cream in more privacy than what was offered at the counter could be waited on at those tables. Of the two drug stores, Clough's offered the better perspective on the activities of the village since its L-shaped counter and soda fountain and stools were situated by one of the large front windows that looked out on the square. At Sterling's the view from the straight line of stools onto the less active Elm Street was partially obstructed by the partition which separated the window from the counter. Business at the soda fountains was best around lunchtime when people from the various stores stopped in and made their selection from the cold sandwiches displayed behind the counter on small glass shelves. These sandwiches had their crusts cut off and were wrapped in wax paper and labeled "tuna" and "egg salad" and "cream cheese and olive." But it was the large jar of doughnuts as much as anything else that caused a pretty steady flow of customers on coffee break throughout the day. They were made by Laura Perry. She was an old friend of my Grandmother Jillson from the days when they both lived in South Pomfret, and for years after my grandmother's death in 1958, she paid homage to that friendship by calling my mother on my grandmother's birthday. Just about any day Mrs. Perry could be seen with her neat print apron on in the kitchen of her home at 25 Linden Hill, making her famous doughnuts according to a recipe which her grandson Peter Wells claimed she had not divulged by the time of her one-hundredth birthday and which she ultimately took to the grave with her. They were hands down the best dough- nuts I have ever tasted.

Each soda fountain had its more or less faithful clientele, often drawn from the neighboring businesses. Employees of Cabot's such as Fred Maynes, Aunt Ada's brother, and Alice Messer used to go to Sterling's, as did Elizabeth Rose and Clara Richardson from Gillinghams and Larry Godsill from the Standard Office and Peg Godsill from The Woman's Shop and Ray Messer from the post office and Mimi Bergstrom from lawyer Paul Bourdon's office. Carl Bergstrom, caretaker for the French and later the Rockefeller man- sion, stopped there regularly as did sometime newspaper correspon- dent and girl scout leader Rhoda Teagle. In the summertime a boy two years older than I, David Lamb, who has since become well known as a journalist and author, was a fixture there at the counter in his baseball cap and with his copy of the *Sporting News* sticking out of the back pocket of his Levis. Frank Stillwell always took a coffee break there from his custodial duties at the Congregational Church. As his assistant for two years, I came to know Frank well through our work and our great conversations when we raked leaves together or when we ascended the stairs into the church belfry at the end of the day to wind the clock and striker. Frank wore his hat indoors and out and spoke of someone he liked as "a good scout." I've never worked for a better person. Seated next to him there at Sterling's soda fountain were often to be seen the boys from the Elm Tree Press, Chester Dix, Wayne Walker, and William Robison, with their ink-stained hands, though they patronized both drug stores. Regulars at Clough's included Cecile Hively, a war bride with a heavy French accent and mother of my friend Ron; Bernard Laramie; and June Whitcomb, all from the Green Beauty Shop; Theresa Mosher from the Budget Shop; Allan Brownell, who introduced the Saab to Woodstock at A&B Motors; and local characters such as one-eyed, hard-swearing Bill Lussier, who looked like a pirate; and Fred Woods, a sometime photographer who worked for Gene Roy in his oil business and was famous for his store of jokes and baffling turns of phrase and for greeting his friends in even the most public places by flashing them what he called the "E. E. Roy salute" — a simple, emphatic extension of the solitary middle finger.

Which drug store I patronized depended on a number of factors. The prices were the same. A small soda, i.e. a glass of Coke, root beer, cherry, vanilla, or lemon and lime, cost a nickel; so did a Nab or a doughnut or a pack of gum or a candy bar or a single scoop of ice cream. A large soda, which was served in a paper cone wedged into an hourglass-shaped metal holder, cost a dime. A root beer or coke float — a scoop of ice cream in a ten cent soda — cost fifteen cents, and it required a long handled spoon and a straw selected from one of those dispensers that you had to be careful not to lift too high or they would blossom and spread their straws centrifugally all over the counter. Milk shakes and frappes and ice cream sodas were around twenty cents or a quarter. We chose our drug store largely on the basis of the soda jerk and the quality of his or her sodas, which in those days were made from thick syrup pumped into a glass and topped with seltzer water. Some finesse was required to get them just right: too much syrup was as objectionable as too little; not enough stirring would leave the ingredients unmixed; too much stirring would take away some of the fizz. In The Woodstock Pharmacy Charlie Clough mixed a mean Coke, and Stewart Hill wasn't bad either. Later on, Mary Ostrander was good at it, and we had lots of fun with the diminutive Laurie Desautels, who had to stretch to reach the counter top at the soda fountain. But Sterling's had some interesting stock both in the store and upstairs in Sterling's Sporting Goods — baseball gloves and beebee guns and hunting knives — that made it a hard place to walk by without stopping. Besides, their Nab selection was better and more reliable. Among the boxes of Nabs on the shelf at the window end of the soda fountain, I was pretty sure to find the malted milk peanut butter crackers, packaged as they were back then in a stack of five and labeled on the end. Also Sterling's selection of candy bars was better. Their candy counter remains imprinted on my memory because of an extraordinary event that took place there one afternoon. I was standing with David Doubleday, who had just completed his afternoon paper route. He had his *Valley News* bag slung over his shoulder and was trying to select a chocolate bar. I had chosen my usual wintergreen patty and suggested that he try one. He did just that. He reached up, took one down, looked furtively around, unwrapped it, took a large bite, moved it judiciously around in his mouth, made a sour face, swallowed with some effort, and then carefully wrapped the rest of it until it looked as though it had never been opened and put it back on the shelf, settling instead for a Milky Way.

At Sterling's, besides John Resner, who, in a good natured way, was willing to take a stand on any issue that might be discussed, and Harry Tarleton, with his endless supply of off-color jokes that he was anxious not to have us overhear, Natalie Barrup herself was worth the stop. Although probably a less up-to-date source of the latest news than her fellow employee Louise Birmingham, she was certainly more tolerant of our nonsense. In fact, she could adapt to our zany sense of humor, and she did unexpected things like actually serving us a pine tree float (a toothpick in a glass of water) before we could ask her for it. I often looked forward to a stop at one of the drug stores on my way home from school, and on long summer days their clean, awning-shaded interiors, cooled by the slow-turning ceiling fans, beckoned like oases.

Across the square from the White Cupboard Inn, on the east corner of Elm Street, was located the establishment that seems to have been open throughout all the days and nights of the years when I was growing up in Woodstock. It was called the Woodstock Fruit Company, but we knew it simply as the Fruit Store. Its name was misleading, for the fruit that it sold, or attempted to sell, attracted more flies than buyers. It was displayed in crates in the steep pitched, narrow space in the lower part of its large windows and was therefore more visible from outside than from inside the store. The Fruit Store consisted of one large room that was part soda fountain and lunch counter and part beer joint. It also advertised and sold good ice cream, and magazines and newspapers could be bought there. One entered by going up the steps on the corner and in through the narrow swinging doors or by going in through the side entry, of which there is now no trace, on Central Street. This entry stood at the top of wide steps, the bottom half of which were open and the top half of which were enclosed within the facade of the building. The corner and main entrance to the Fruit Store opened to the section that had the counter with its soda fountain and long row of stools and a number of booths of light stained wood, the seats of which, like the stools, were covered in red leather. This section of the store catered to people who came in for a sandwich from the grill or a soda or some ice cream. Beer was served only to the booths in the back nearer the kitchen. At the middle of the store and easily accessible to all its customers was one of Woodstock's few jukeboxes.

I made my first stops in the Fruit Store with my father to get an ice cream cone or one of those round, white quart containers of ice cream that the waitress would fill and pack down with a broad, flat spoon or an ice cream scoop and then seal up for us to carry home. The Fruit Store's proprietor and short order cook was a man named Ed McCann. He was a somewhat flaccid man who was almost always to be seen there behind his thick glasses and in his begrimed white apron, perspiring and hurrying back and forth in the narrow aisle that ran the length of the store from the kitchen to the west window. His wife Melba also worked there, and their daughter Pam, who was a year younger than I, could usually be seen in the store or by herself on the sidewalk on Central Street under the store's awning, playing hopscotch or skipping rope and looking forbiddingly streetwise, near the old scales that stood there and, if they had worked, would have told your weight and fortune for a penny.

The Fruit Store served the biggest ice cream cones in town to anyone who knew what he was doing. When I used to stop there for a Coke, I didn't have to be selective about who served me — Ed or Melba, Dot Cloud, Peg Olmstead, Viola Wardwell — it was all the same. But with ice cream it was different: Lois Longe was the only one, and if she was working, it was worth employing delay tactics until she was free to wait on me. For a nickel I received from her a scoop of coffee or black raspberry ice cream that extended out beyond the top of the cone all the way around and had an extra dab or two on the top.

In contrast to the drug stores, the Fruit Store was considered not particularly clean and somewhat disreputable. Although my father advised me not to hang around in there, at times the place was irresistible. Most of the stores in Woodstock used to be closed on Thursday afternoons and open until 9 PM on Saturday nights until the merchants, in August of 1952, voted for Friday nights instead. On the night when the stores stayed open and people from the village and its outlying farms and communities came to town to do their weekly shopping, the Fruit Store would be busiest. Once the shopping was done and the supplies were loaded, people sometimes stopped there for a beer or two and a bit of news and left their children outside to amuse themselves. This was a great time to gather about the bike stand on the corner and to chase around the sidewalks and dart into the darkening alleyways with schoolmates, some of whom did not often come to town, and sometimes to eye suspiciously — or to become friends with — boys we didn't know, until it was time for them to climb into the back of the pickup for the long trip home.

An encounter with one such boy has left me with a very clear memory of the corner steps leading up to the swinging doors of the Fruit Store's front entrance. He was a stranger to me until he introduced himself as Douglas Rampona and made it clear that he was a summer boy from an affluent family in Princeton, New Jersey. When he was not out at the Woodstock Country Club, he was sometimes to be seen hanging out in the Fruit Store or the drug stores attempting to win some friends among us townies by impressing us with stories of what he owned and where he had been. Cocky and self-assertive, he boasted, among other things, of his "collection of ivy league shirts," as button down collar shirts were first called back then. Since I had one such shirt, a red and black plaid one I had bought in Larry's Men's Shop after weeks of stopping by the store to look at it, I had no way of understanding why anyone would collect shirts. Did he simply purchase them to have them on show in drawers or in display cases in his house? Did he ever take them out of pins and put them on? One early Friday evening I was going up the corner steps into the Fruit Store just as he was coming out, and he blocked my entrance and would not let me by. He was a good deal heavier than I and much more muscular, and we got into a pretty unfriendly pushing and shoving match until I lost my temper and took a swing at him. I caught him on the side of the jaw, and, because he was slightly off balance, knocked him down the last two steps onto the sidewalk. My first concern was that he was hurt; my second concern was that he was not, and that we might be just getting started. But, evidently mistaking me for a seasoned fighter, he showed no wish to continue, and I shakily went on into the Fruit Store, leaving him to dust himself off. Years later, one summer during my college years, I dated a girl from Princeton. When I found out where she was from, I told her that I had met only one other person from there and named him. To my amazement, it turned out that he was her neighbor on Nassau Street and that they had grown up together. Since he was no favorite of hers, the story of our little scuffle made me just a little heroic in her eyes, and that summer I offered silent, belated thanks to Dougie, as he called himself, for being a sucker for an old right hook.

It is a hot afternoon in late July in the early 50s. The parking places including, for the moment, police chief Wes Krupinsky's on the White Cupboard corner, are empty, giving the streets a deserted look. The businesses except for the Fruit Store and the telephone office are closed, and their storefronts with their awnings rolled up seem to dozing in the bright sunlight reflecting off the windows. The square is so quiet that even the occasional car passing through and going up or down either side of the park looks bewildered and causes only a ripple in the stillness. My bike is the only one parked in the bike stand. Inside the Fruit Store it is hot and sticky. The lazy, black ceiling fans rather than cooling things off just circulate the smells of the grill from last night's hamburgers and the scent of overripe bananas from the windows. Since the town team is play-

ing baseball in Springfield, there's not much to do. I'm sitting at the counter, making a large coke with ice last as long as possible and trying to decide whether to ride around on my bike or to go up to the park and watch cars and maybe carve my initials in the bench I'll sit on propped against a tree. Ed McCann is sitting on the ice cream cooler, reading the Sunday funnies. Three stools down from me on the end of the row sits Larry Goodell in his faded blue, sleeveless work-shirt, rolled up workman's dungarees and black, high-top sneakers. The village handyman, he keeps the sidewalks cleared of snow in the winter and is always there for any job of lifting or trimming or fixing that needs to be done in any season. Just now his hands are stained with dirt from the flowerbeds that he tends beneath the large war memorial on the lawn between the library and the courthouse. He is squinting through the smoke of the short cigarette dangling from the corner of his mouth at a matchbook resting in his left hand and trying to recall whether he already has it in his famous matchbook collection. With his right hand he stirs and stirs his coffee. From the jukebox the voice of Jo Stafford languidly crosses the air, telling us to "see the pyramids along the Nile, watch the sunrise on a tropic isle." I have a dreamy sense of those places being very far away, but the time is passing so very slowly on this hot summer afternoon in Woodstock that I know I'll have forever to follow her advice.

Besides the Fruit Store there were three places in the village where you could get a drink in those days: there was the White Cupboard Inn's cramped, drafty bar which, with its peculiar murals of underwater scenes — seahorses, mermaids, seaweed — was rather like a fish tank; the Pine Room of the Woodstock Inn; and the Village Inn, known locally as the Tavern. Occupying the eastern two-thirds of the block in which the Economy Store was situated, the Village Inn at 39 Central Street was accessible by two

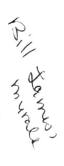

entrances. The west and more formal entrance opened into a hotel lobby with double, glass-paneled doors on the far side leading to the restaurant. The lobby was of light varnished natural wood, and its most prominent feature was its short staircase stopping at a landing from which other stairs angled to the right and led up to the second and third floors. In the old days, when this building had housed the Commercial Hotel, the rooms on these floors had been let to traveling salesmen who arrived and departed on the Woodstock Railway. The large, faded, vertical "Hotel" sign that was bolted to these upper stories and still looked up and down Central Street, announced that the Village Inn still rented rooms. Over the east entrance was a small neon "bar and grille" sign. This entrance opened into a long, dimly lit room with booths covered in dark blue leather along the walls and tables in the middle and a small bar at the far end. Next to the bar was a jukebox.

As a bar, the Tavern catered to a somewhat more respectable, though perhaps less colorful, clientele than the Fruit Store. The slightly urban, distinctly night-clubby ambiance was undoubtedly the creation, or perhaps simply the extension, of its astonishing proprietress, Rose Bergante, who lived in the rooms above. Even in The Tavern, in her own atmosphere, as she directed operations or sat behind the bar as cashier or sometimes served drinks herself and chatted with her customers, Rose attracted attention. You noticed her, and, once having done so, whether you intended to or not, you continued to look. And nothing in all your years in and around Woodstock, except perhaps some moments in the darkened Town Hall Theatre with Marlene Dietrich and Mae West, had quite prepared you for what you saw. Walking up the sidewalk on Central Street in broad daylight, she sounded an alert to the senses. You heard the quick tapping of spiked heels on the pavement, saw a tall bleached blonde with her hair arranged in a high and complicated configuration on top of her head. She had long, painted nails and a great deal of expertly applied makeup, including what at least one male observer referred to as "the traveling mole", a curious itinerant beauty mark, and you were dizzied by the scent of perfume that announced her approach and arrival and lingered after her on the smitten air. Her perennial knit sheath dresses brought to the spectacle a certain sense of poetry in motion and emphasized the fact that, in Chaucer's words, "hardily she was not undergrowe."

Not in any sense a dumb blonde, Rose was a touch of class. It was obvious to anyone who saw her that she had presence and that she had experience and that she had dignity. She was a good businesswoman and, according to those who knew her, an intelligent and understanding person. She was described as "the soul of kindness" by one of her waitresses who was having family problems which made it look as though she would have to stop working to take care of her children. Rose instructed her to bring the children to work with her and she herself would look after them so that the waitress could continue to earn her much needed wages. She was good to work for, and she supported her employees. When Barbara Fleming came to work at the Tavern from Bridgewater, "not knowing a Manhattan from a martini," Rose was patient and encouraging in teaching her how to tend bar. A much more sympathetic person than her brother Marty, who assumed some role in running the place, Rose instantly rehired Mary Audsley after Marty had fired her for shutting off his friends when they had a drop too many taken. For years Rose looked after the Tavern's handyman, Stanley Pease, and his mother; and she was always pleasant to such people as retired teacher Sarah Maxham, who rented a room there by the month, and to regulars in the restaurant such as florist Rob Eaton, who walked up from his greenhouse on Pleasant Street to take his meals there, and to locals Bill Woodbury and Maggie Ward, who sometimes went there for dinner. Rose also loved flowers, and she was often to be seen in her jewel-neck white sweaters outside at her window boxes. With a spray bottle in her hand, she would be water-ing her petunias and geraniums and picking off the spent blossoms.

I remember being in the Tavern once or twice with my father on his way home from work on Friday night, and thinking that Rosie was very pleasant in her quiet and soft-spoken way. On another occasion when I was in junior high school, a friend of mine, Ronnie Hively, and I stopped in the Tavern one evening on our way home from the movies to play *Hernando's Hideaway* on the jukebox and to have a Coke while we listened. Being pretty young for such an unchaperoned stop, we attracted a certain amount of attention in the form of bemused and suspicious looks from the clientele, and we began to feel pretty self-conscious and uneasy when we saw one of the waitresses, Rita Edwards, looking our way and having a word with Rosie. But we were served, and we left as soon as our Coke was gone and our song was over, feeling a little more worldly and certainly no worse for our experience.

Actually it is to Rose Bergante that I owe my most indelible impression of the old First National Store at 9 Central Street. I was in grade school at the time. I had just gotten my summer crew cut at Joe's Barber Shop, and I was with my mother, who was grocery shopping. We were standing at the counter at the back of the store, being waited on by Francis Hathorn, when Rosie entered. She took her place behind us, and then she ran her fingernails lightly over my scalp, and when I turned around, she said in her low and breathy voice, "Hi, Butch." The old First National, just as it looked at that moment, has stayed with me ever since.

IV

Around Christmas time certain shops in Woodstock took on a sort of aura that never quite disappeared throughout the rest of the year. During the Christmas season most of the stores stayed open in the evening until nine o'clock. That gave us plenty of time to shop but also to make repeated stops in the Economy and Cabot's to gaze at some of the things that we hoped would be waiting for us under the tree on Christmas morning. Even today when I walk into a very different Economy Store, my feet automatically direct me to the back along the left hand side where the toys were on display. Although I spent much more time than I did money looking at the metal cars and trucks and cap pistols there, Reno and Sylvia Casellini never seemed to mind. At Cabot's, Willard Cabot, Aubrey Curtis (known as "cowboy" Curtis to at least some of his neighbors because of the way he drove his black and white Nash up and down Linden Hill), and the other employees were just as patient with my brother's and my Christmas browsing. Every year in early December much of the back room where paint and wallpaper and other such merchandise were kept would be given over to toys of all sorts displayed on shelves reaching up to the high ceiling, with narrow corridors running between them. In those days before we had seen anything resembling a department store, coming around the corner from the main room of the store with its furniture displays and confronting a world of toys was always a breathtaking experience.

Mrs. Winslow's Clover Gift Shop, which had its own cloistered, evergreen smell, gave me the feeling of Christmas all the year round. Mrs. Winslow was a gracious and kind and delicate looking little woman with rimless spectacles. She always seemed happy to see us, and I remember that we tiptoed around in her shop and spoke quietly. Across the top of the partition separating the front part of the shop from the space at the far end ran a little sort of picket fence. I seem to remember dolls' houses up there and stuffed animals looking down, but I may have only imagined them in that strange land magically suspended between the floor and the ceiling. Many of Mrs. Winslow's gift items were made of glass, and each one reflected light in its own way. Among them was the first snow globe I had ever seen. It was a heavy glass paperweight filled with liquid with a miniature village inside. By turning the globe upside down and then right side up again, I could make the snow descend slowly onto the backs of the little deer and into the small, safe world of the white house and the white church.

Woodstock itself was one such small, safe, snow-filled world at Christmas time back then. During every Christmas season, the little white church that has made an occasional appearance in recent years was set up outside one of the second floor windows of the Woodstock Electric Company. Through speakers in the interior of this church, carols that were played on a turntable in the radio shop could be heard coming out over the streets of the village. On the evenings when my father worked in the store, it fell to him to go upstairs and change the stock of records, a task which he did not relish and which he gladly allowed my brother and me and, some years later, our sister Jane, to perform. It gave us a feeling of importance to select the 78 rpm records for the whole village to hear. We would put on the old Capitol or R.C.A. Victor or Decca or Columbia recordings of Gene Autry's *Rudolph the Red-Nosed Reindeer* and Bing Crosby's *Adeste Fidelis* or *White Christmas* and others (Rob Woods had forbidden the playing of *Silent Night* until Christmas Eve), and start them playing and then peer into the interior of the little church, complete with its own stained glass windows. And while the records played, we looked out of the second story windows of the Electric Company and hoped to be noticed. The snowy streets were decorated with strings of many colored Christmas lights radiating outwards from the dummy and stretching across Elm Street and Central Street above the traffic. And way up on top of Mt. Tom in those days before the star, the cross would be lit up, illuminating the edges of the trees nearest it and the snow at its base. Gazing into this spectacle of lights and snow, we would watch shoppers bundled up against the cold, moving about on the sidewalks, which were separated from the streets by high banks of shoveled snow reflecting light from the store windows. Hearing our music, some people would look up in our direction, and since we both wondered how we appeared to them, Howard and I took turns at going out and looking up at each other in the window next to the church. But what we saw was something that still required the imagination by being just one person short.

This Woodstock is far more real to me than the one which has replaced it. I have no recollection of how or when the change took place. Without my being aware of it, time passed, and the place and the people of my childhood passed with it. Tony Sabatino's obituary in September, 1968, refers to him as "the last of the old-timers in the business square in Woodstock." He may have been. At any rate, by the time of his death, one by one the old merchants that I had known had closed their doors and disappeared from the streets of the village. And some flavor of life, something sage and seasoned, had departed with them. Yet because the actual configuration of the blocks has remained the same and because memory has its own strange laws, a native who has been away and approaches upstreet from any direction finds himself peculiarly astonished not to discover in the shops themselves some dusty corner left completely unaltered, some counter still tended by an old, familiar face. All that remains is some of the store entrances and, oddly enough, some of the front doors. In March and April between the winter and summer inundations of tourists, when the streets are quiet and Woodstock almost returns to itself, there is time to indulge in a kind of reverie. Going into the stores, I sometimes pause for a moment with my hand on the same old door in a grip that feels like a handshake, and I close my eyes for a second to listen for the sound of the latch or the sweep of the door slowly opening before I cross the threshold into a largely unfamiliar and unresonant interior. And for one bewildering moment touch and hearing conspire to suspend me between a present which is simply there, and a past which is rich and real and strangely still open.

I recently realized that for many years now, on passing through any town, I have been in the habit of looking up away from the storefronts and letting my gaze travel to the stories above and farther upward to the various configurations of the rooflines. What, exactly, I am looking for I'm not sure, but I know that my eye always rests on any painted or carved date. And I feel gratified by the vacant look of unwashed, high windows, their old curtains or their flashes of sunlight or reflections of cloud and sky suggesting that time has not yet risen from its activities in the retail space and the streets below to penetrate those rooms above and encroach on a sort of permanence reigning there. Perhaps it all began once when I was young and I sneaked up the second floor and then the third floor stairs of the French Block. The door at the top was unlatched, and I opened it and found myself looking into a long, large room. Without knowing it, I had stumbled upon the G. A. R. Room, the old meeting hall of the Grand Army of the Republic. As I was to learn many years later, my father as a boy had once stolen up those same stairs to peek in upon a meeting of the local Union Army veterans of the Civil War, one of whom was quite likely my great grandfather, Elba Jillson, who fought at Fair Oaks in Virginia. I only saw that room that one time, but I have carried an impression of it ever since. It was spacious, with faded wallpaper and pictures on the walls. At the west end was a slightly elevated area, a low stage for speeches and presentations. It had an evocative, musty smell as though its air had long been sealed, and the sun shining through its eleven long windows filled the entire room with light. No business, as far as I know, has ever occupied it, and no one has ever lived there. So, in its association with the past centuries and in its position high above the center of the commercial life of the village, that room has always seemed to me to be simply a repository of years, a timeless backwater regarding through its undecorated windows the tides of fashion and change that have swept Woodstock and judging them as unworthy of both the wisdom of old men and the wonder of young boys.

Bikes

*The new thing in me
has always included the old.*
ROBERT FROST

W hen I think of Woodstock as it was in the late 1940s and
early 1950s, I always think of bicycles. The bicycles which we
rode in those days were nearly all balloon tire bikes of the sort you
rarely see nowadays unless you come across one on display as an
antique. Some years ago I was in a bike shop with my children,
standing among rows of the latest models that they knew all about
— delicate looking, sophisticated, high-tech, 10-speed and 12-speed
and 18-speed and even 21-speed racing bikes and touring bikes
and mountain bikes, feather weight aluminum bikes so light they
hung from the ceiling, seeming to belong more to air than to earth,
with shifts and cords and wires running every which way and with
sprockets on sprockets like epicycles. I wandered around, disoriented, vulnerable in my ignorance as my son and daughter confi-
dently transacted their business with the specialists who operated
the place. Suddenly there it was, by itself, confronting me as a
solid fact — a white-sidewalled, balloon tire, green and white Columbia RX-5, completely restored, with pedal brakes and the horn
in the tank and the carrier on the back and the light on the front
fender. After the shock of recognition came a rush of memory and
an impulse to walk this fellow anachronism out of the shop and to
get on it and let it take me back onto those elm-shaded sidewalks

and quiet streets I used to know.

In those days there were more children living in the village of Woodstock, and most of them had balloon tire bicycles with pedal brakes. Nearly all of these bikes were two-toned, as were many of the cars of that day; the second color, usually white, was used for the pinstriping and the scrollwork on the fenders and the frame. A good representative selection of the bikes of that time could have been seen each year on Memorial Day at the end of the parade. Boys and girls wove concentric circles of red, white, and blue crepe paper through the spokes of their wheels, flew small flags from their handlebars, and followed along at the end of the procession of veterans and marching bands as it passed along the parade route. And most of the bikes of the village — J. C. Higgins, Schwinns, Hawthornes, Columbias, Western Flyers, Firestones, Huffys, and Roadmasters in the standard 18- and 24- and 26-inch sizes — were parked in and around the bicycle stands in front of the elementary school on South Street on spring and fall weekdays and on the lawn at the front of the Town Hall Theatre on Saturday afternoons. We converged on the theatre, paid 14 cents apiece, read comic books with Eugene Blake, argued over who was sitting next to whom until the show started, then sat on the edge of our seats in the dark, misbehaving as much as we dared under the watchful eyes of Jim Fountain, the man in charge of the theatre, until the end of the movie, and then spilled out the front doors and exits under the spell of the World War II or the cops and robbers thriller or the western we had just seen. There we feigned fistfights and gunfights and enacted scenes of violent capture and resistance and then grabbed our bikes, now transformed into horses or motorcycles or jeeps or police cars or getaway cars, and chased each other, whooping and shouting, off into the village.

I suppose every boy remembers his first bicycle and the proud feelings of ownership and independence which it gave him. In the early summer of our eighth year, after what seemed years of saving our money and gazing at the picture in the catalogue, my twin brother Howard and I got our first bikes. They were identical, red-and-white 24-inch Hawthornes, which was the brand name of the bicycle made and sold by Montgomery Wards. We brought them home in my grandparents' Plymouth from the Wards store in Claremont in big boxes, and my father assembled them in the shop of the Woodstock Electric Company where he worked. Once they were put together, I do not remember how we told them apart, but it did not take long for them to look very different. I had a head start on Howard since I had learned to ride a little on my friend Sandy Morse's 18-inch bike on the sidewalk between his house at 15 Linden Hill and the Lantz house next door. My father, in order to give me practice and to teach my brother to ride, took us in the evenings down back of Frost's Mill to the lumber yard. After I had demonstrated some proficiency in handling my bike, he gave me permission to ride up and down Pleasant Street from the Congregational Church to Tribou Park and to ride on Bond Street, but forbade me to go upstreet. Thinking I was ready for anything, I risked a ride on Central Street on a Saturday night when the stores were open and there was plenty of traffic. I was doing fine until I rode into Eddie's Socony Station at 55 Central Street and, finding that I could not step back on the brake with the pedals at twelve o'clock and six o' clock, plowed onto the back of a car that was parked there. I pitched off sideways, scraping my elbow and knee, and, worst of all, bending the fork of my bike so that the front fender scraped on the frame. Ed Leonard and the driver of the car, Larry West, were worried that I was hurt and helped me up and looked me over for bruises. I had a sorry trip home over Bond Street, limping and pushing my damaged bike and feeling a great deal of guilt and humiliation and some fear of what my father would say. However, the spectacle of misery which I must have presented apparently softened his exasperation. Seeing that I had learned a lesson, he fixed my bike as best he could so that I could ride it, though the bent fork gave it a slightly snub-nosed look. After that mishap, I was a more cautious rider for a time.

So difficult is it to think about one season at the middle of another that at the height of summer I couldn't imagine putting up my bike for the long winter months. But when the time came, it didn't seem such a hard thing to do. For bike riding in the late autumn had its drawbacks: with mittens or gloves, my hands tended to slip around on the handlebar grips; without them, they would begin to freeze. Then too, the cold made the bike slower as though it were tired and inclined to begin its annual hibernation, and heavy clothes made pedaling laborious. Sometimes, I went out on a sort of nostalgic last ride around the village and wondered what sorts of things would have happened in school and during the basketball season by the time I rode around those streets again. Other years, in the excitement following an early snow, I would realize that when I put my bike away for the night just yesterday, I had in fact ridden it for the last time until spring. Then for the next five months or so I would see it in the garage parked next to my brother's when I went there to get my skis or one of our sleds, and wonder whether there really had been and would again be a time for racing around town on it without my shirt on.

Sometime in April, with the dregs of winter still hanging around in spite of some warm weather, the waiting would seem unbearable. When my father and I finally went down to the garage and turned my bike upside down to lubricate the brakes and chain, the long days of summer were already there in the smell of the oil. Then I'd wheel my bike out into the bright, cool sunlight under the bare butternut tree and get on, a little awkwardly, and ride it up out of Benson Place and into the world. That first ride would be the most conscious of all, reminiscent of my first times on a bike. Every year it always took a few minutes to get the feel of it again and to recall the peculiarities of *this* bicycle — the sound of the chain, the one slightly crooked pedal I had forgotten about — and to realize that I had grown since I had ridden it last. There would be puddles glistening in the sun and best negotiated by putting the feet up on the handlebars, and there were places where the ground was still too soft to ride, like Vail Field and the paths in the park. And I'd have to be careful riding along the sides of the streets not to slip in the dry, sun-warmed sand and gravel — the leftovers of what had been spread by the sanding trucks. A cool wind like the one I had felt on my last ride before winter would be blowing, but from a different direction and bringing with it the promise of baseball and swimming instead of skiing and snowball fights. Riding up Elm Street toward the center of the village and catching once again the familiar rhythm and sound of a bike were like coming back into possession of a country I had lost, and every turn of the pedal seemed to be taking me closer to the long days of summer.

From the time I first owned a bicycle, I was nearly as attentive to other people's bikes, especially those of the older boys, as I was to my own. I was fascinated by Schwinns, and since the Schwinn seemed to confer a special status on its owner, I secretly and quietly admired anyone whom I saw riding one. Whenever anyone went by on a Schwinn, I gazed after him, and whenever I saw one parked, I had to stop and reverently note all of its features. The best place for such bike gazing was the Vail Field during Junior League baseball practice when the bikes of the players, Woodstock boys four and five years older than I, would be leaning on their kickstands behind the home team bench or in the area between the bandstand and the grandstand. I spent as much time studying the bikes of these boys as I did admiring their baseball gloves and their feats on the diamond.

The Schwinn in those days was the Cadillac of balloon tire bicycles, and I never tired of comparing the Schwinn Phantom and the Schwinn Panther with their differently shaped tanks. My favorite was the Schwinn Phantom with its cantilever frame, its chrome fenders, its metallic colors, and its chrome, rather than white, trim. I knew which Schwinn belonged to which boy and where in town, besides Vail Field, these bikes were most likely to be seen. Outside the drug stores and the corner Fruit Store stood the old green, wooden bicycle stands that were a common sight in those days. We bumped our bikes up into them and left them parked between the vertical slats. I could count on seeing Bill Leach's green and white Schwinn parked outside Clough's Drug Store, usually next to Bud Spaulding's red and white Schwinn, which was interesting because Bud had customized it by replacing the standard seat with a small motorcycle seat. I often admired Bill Boardman's green and chrome Schwinn and also Dave Corkum's and Bob and Muffy French's maroon and chrome Schwinns outside Sterling's Drug Store and Donald Cloud's maroon and white Schwinn outside the Fruit Store. In studied imitation of these bikes, I did my best, without much success, to make my 24-inch Hawthorne into a Schwinn look-alike by replacing the small seat with a larger one and getting rid of my small handlebars for some large, angular longhorns with colored, finger-grooved grips.

Just as people did not travel as much in those days, so we did not go much of any place on our balloon tire bikes. Once in a while a few adventurous youngsters in need of a change of scene and a swim would pedal the ten miles or so up to Silver Lake in Barnard and then enjoy a primarily downhill ride on the stage road or the gulf road on the way home, but such excursions were infrequent. Hills were the enemies of those bikes. Whenever we came to a long, formidable hill such as Church Hill or Creamery Hill, we ended up walking and pushing them. I remember competing to see who could ride the farthest up Church Hill and in the process standing up and pumping and weaving back and forth across the road to decrease the angle of ascent and pulling up on the handlebars for leverage and going more and more slowly until I simply could not bring that upper pedal down from the top one more time. Then it was time to hop off and push. The farthest we usually rode was the relatively level mile up to Willow Vale to spend afternoons swimming in the brook behind the Eatons' house. The village was the place for us and our bikes. Perhaps we were content to stay within its confines because it was a more human, more accommodating place back then than it is now. For one thing, there were fewer people in town in the summer than there are now and therefore fewer strangers. We never worried about theft and rarely saw bicycles with locks on them. We simply left our bikes in one place, for example at the River Street Cemetery or on Mountain Avenue, in the morning, and when we came down off the mountain after a day of playing guns or exploring, there they were right where we had left them. Since there was far less traffic in those days, there was far more room for bikes. To anyone accustomed to the tourist mecca which Woodstock has become, any photo of the village in the early 1950s looks as though it must have been taken on a holiday when all the stores were closed. Remarkably few cars are to be seen either parked or passing through the streets. Parking spaces stand vacant everywhere. But then as you look more closely, you notice that among the pedestrians some are clearly going into and coming out of stores, some are carrying parcels, and you realize that this photo captures a moment in the ordinary weekday life and commerce of Woodstock as it was back then. Boys on bikes had more room. Although the sidewalks in front of the stores were narrower, we could leave our bikes leaning on their kickstands outside places that did not have bike stands without inconveniencing pedestrians or annoying store-owners. Even the dummy, the traffic divider at the main intersection of Central and Elm Streets, seemed to have been designed with bicycles in mind. It had two levels like steps all the way around it so that when we pulled our bikes up to it, we could lean a leg over onto whichever step suited our size and could rest and survey the activities of a summer day from dead center in Woodstock. Or we could use the dummy as a convenient place to switch riders.

You seldom see two people on a bike nowadays. Today's bikes are not built for passengers. But back then we often gave short distance lifts to friends whose bikes had been laid up with a flat tire or impounded for their coming home late to supper. The balloon tire bike had four places for a passenger, each with its advantages and disadvantages. The most common place was the crossbar, seated sidesaddle. This was probably the safest and most stable place since the balance was natural and both rider and passenger could hang onto the handlebars. The bad news for the passenger was the way his backside began to feel after only a very short distance, and for the rider, was the discomfort of pedaling bow-legged. You could also carry someone on the back fender, which was bad for the fender, or, better still, on the back carrier if the bike had one, but this way always presented a balance problem and made pedaling difficult by weighing down the rear wheel. The way girls often doubled up, since their bikes had no crossbar, was by the passenger sitting on the seat and the rider standing up and pedaling. For us this way was considered kind of sissy because girls did it and because the passenger had to hang onto the rider's waist. The most macho way was for the passenger to sit on the handlebars facing forward: advantage — stability and balance; disadvantage for the rider — lack of visibility and difficulty in turning; for the passenger — trying to balance by grasping what he was sitting on and trying to get on and off without injury. Whichever way we doubled up, there we were — two pals with summer crew cuts and grimy tee shirts, black hightop sneakers and dungarees — headed home on one bike with two baseball gloves swinging from the handlebars.

Although we traversed the same streets day after summer day, we saw to it that bike riding never became boring. En route to one place or another we had our regular stops at the nickel, and eventually the dime, Coke machines at Eddie's Socony Station and Costello's Garage and A&B Motors, and we often stopped at Tracy's Esso for ice cream on a stick and popsicles. We rarely crossed the Middle Bridge without pausing next to the back porch of Henry Cushing's house long enough to encourage his parrot, Don Pedro, to begin cursing, which was usually not very long. And in our riding, of course, we improvised. We rode with no hands, competing to see who could go the farthest, pedaling away along straight stretches and around corners with our arms folded across our chests. It seems we were always racing. Howard and I had a sort of tacit understanding that on the way home at 9 PM from the first show of the movies we would race from the top of Pleasant Street at the Congregational Church to the door of our house. Riding down Elm Street, we began making sure we were nearly abreast as we talked casually, trying to catch each other off guard and thus to gain a few feet of head start. Then, as we turned the corner of the Marbles' house and the last streetlight shot the huge shadows of us and our bikes out ahead of us onto Pleasant Street, we both stood up on the pedals and took off. We gained plenty of inspiration from the dark wood on the our right and went neck and neck even through the narrow alley that led to our door, then skidded to a stop and bolted up the steps and leapt for the door handle that was our finish line. Many of us often struggled up Rose Hill and Lincoln Street and Highland Avenue (no one that I can remember ever dared Stanton Street) and came careening down. But the best place to race was on Mt. Tom. My brother and I and Dave Harrington and Ed and Bill Hackett and Ronnie Hively and others used to push our bikes all the way to the top and then race down the mountain road from the cross to the Billings Farm, passing each other and shouting and yelling and putting out a foot for balance as we leaned and went tearing around corners. A couple of us went so far as to strip down some 24-inch bikes and race down the winding Faulkner Paths, even taking some of the vertical shortcuts in the process.

Considering how we raced around and dared each other and attempted stunts, I am surprised that we had no serious bicycle accidents. My closest call came one day when I was not being reckless but simply inattentive. I pushed off from the dummy to cross Central Street, heading east into oncoming traffic without seeing George Howe returning to his job at Richmond's Garage in his blue 1951 Ford until I heard the squeal of brakes just to my right and saw his car swerve and skid to a stop in the middle of the street. It was a close call, and he was pretty alarmed and upset, as was my father, who, unfortunately for me, had witnessed the event front and center from the window of the Woodstock Electric Company. He told me in no uncertain terms that it was my fault and that if I were not more careful I could forget about my bike for quite some time to come.

One of the most common causes of minor bike injuries or at least of considerable momentary pain was actually an operational fault of the old balloon tire bike and not the judgment of the rider. Occasionally a bike would skip; that is, an inner part in the rear hub would not engage properly and the pedal would simply drop from the top of its cycle to the bottom and send the rider, if he happened to be standing up on the pedals, crashing down onto the crossbar and often losing control of the bike in the process. The only way to ride a bike that had that tendency was to pedal from the sitting position. The worst skippers were bikes with Bendix brakes, for once the horseshoe clip in those brakes broke, as they sometimes had a tendency to do, the pedals would skip about as often as they would engage. The worst skipping bike that I ever saw was an old brown-and-white thing that a friend of mine, Bing Watson, rode one summer when I was in junior high school. It skipped so badly that he did not stand up on the pedals at all. One morning as we were crossing the park on our way to Vail Field, the bike began to skip so as not to engage the hub at all. Fortunately, since we liked to race across the park, Bing had up some pretty good speed. As the bike began to lose momentum, he pedaled faster, driving the pedals around in cycle after skipping cycle, his legs pumping faster and faster in a ridiculous spectacle of increasingly furious motion's producing steadily declining speed. For us who had slowed down to wait for him, it was funnier than Buster Keaton or Charlie Chaplin or The Three Stooges, and better yet, the futility of his increasingly strenuous activity was accompanied by a string of increasingly impressive curse words until the bicycle's slowing forward motion ceased and he got a leg down just in time to keep from falling. He got off, kicked the tires, swore at us, picked up the bike and threw it onto the ground. For purposes of our amusement, we urged him to get on and give the bike another try, and we challenged him to a race, and then we rode off and simply left him there.

Those old balloon tire bikes were heavy and ruggedly built, made to withstand a certain amount of punishment, and it was a challenge to get them airborne. One place where it was possible to jump them was along the sidewalks on Elm Street where the asphalt humped up over the roots of the elm trees. On our way home to 8 Pleasant Street, Howard and I would stand up and pedal for all we were worth and cross from the road to the sidewalk between the Elm Tree Press and the Historical Society and hit the best of these bumps outside Margaret Johnson's house with enough speed to get both wheels off the ground momentarily. Becoming proficient at bike riding also involved mastering a number of ways of getting on and getting off our bikes. The most admirable way of mounting a bike was not tamely to swing a leg over the crossbar onto the top pedal and push from the ground with the other leg for a start; only learners did it that way. Neither was it to step onto the bottom pedal with the outside leg and then to put the bike in motion by pushing from the ground with the inside leg before swinging it up around the seat and over onto the other pedal, though this method was more acceptable since it meant getting onto a moving bike. No, the real hard rider would grasp the handlebars, casually jog a couple of steps alongside the bike, and then simply vault into the seat. It was just as important to demonstrate some inventiveness in dismounting. We quickly learned to get up speed and then to jam on the brake and skid around in a half circle to a stop. That way soon became passé and was replaced by a semicircular, 90- to 180-degree skid to a stop without applying the brakes at all. On a suitable dirt surface such as that of the drive leading onto Vail Field, or at the angles where the walks crossing the park intersect the central walkway running stem to stern, we pedaled up some speed and then put a leg out on the twelve o'clock pedal side and, without braking, simply laid it down; that is, leaned until the tires and bike went out from under all but our anchor leg in a fast, flat skid. The few of us who could do this were much applauded and envied by the ungifted multitudes who, for want of nerve or balance or both, could not. Another dismounting stunt, and this one had more entertainment value, was to get off the bike while still moving and "let it go," as we called it. A boy would come steaming down onto Vail Field, pedaling like mad, and be greeted by a chorus of "let it go" from the boys already assembled there. To comply, he would simply step off the bike as though he had forgotten all about it in the interest of seeing his friends, who would be standing and gazing in gleeful expectation after the riderless bike as it rocketed in a straight line past home plate and across the third base foul line. It

106

would continue onward as though with a will of its own and a destination in mind and then, depending on the unevenness of the terrain and the precarious balance produced by the decreasing speed, would go into a series of lunatic wobbles and spastic handlebar and front wheel lurches that brought it to an uproariously slapstick collapse on the grass. The comedy of this spectacle was heightened by the infrequency of the performance, for most of us respected our bikes enough to know that such treatment would eventually damage them.

Although we needed little encouragement toward antics and stunts, sometimes we would witness something truly inspiring, something like Joey Chitwood's Hell Drivers as they performed at the Hartland Fair. Those of us who watched those daredevils go through their high-speed, seemingly death-defying weaves and two-wheeled turns and soaring jumps from ramp to ramp came home full of ideas which we wasted no time in spreading. We built some ramps and set them up at Gil Emery's house at 6 Mountain Avenue in the long driveway, and Gil and Howard and I and Tom Brownell were doing our best to emulate Joey Chitwood until Tom pitched over the handlebars of his bike and Gil's father put a stop to our performances. Similarly inspired, Don Eaton and Allan and Richard Atwood worked out some skillfully executed weaves and jumps in Don's yard without any accidents or injuries. The most consistently fearless and innovative bike rider that I can remember was one that needed no inspiration beyond his own reckless daring. His name was Richard Cushman. He was a tow-headed boy with thick glasses who was two years older than I and lived in Woodstock for only a short time when I first began to ride a bike. He had a small brown and white bike with one of its fenders missing, and it was plastered with Hires Root Beer decals of the sort that were popular back then. I can still see him tearing down the driveway that used to slant down from Slayton Terrace to Lincoln Street between his house at #25 and the house next door at #23, and I seem to recall that he rode some of the steepest streets without brakes.

Another way of diverting ourselves and varying the pattern of our bike rides around the village was to go off the beaten track in a number of ways. Private property was tempting, especially if it offered some interesting paths and obstacles and we did not have to come out the way we went in so that the owner had no second chance to catch us. Keeping an eye out for the Lightbourns' care-taker, Alva Hazard, we sometimes dared each other to slip through the gate behind the Vermont Standard Office at 25 Elm Street and go racing down across the Lightbourns' back lawn, along the paths between the flower beds, down onto the path through the Marbles' woods by the Kedron, and up onto Pleasant Street opposite our house at #8. The beautifully raked and edged, winding paths cut into the side lawn of Margaret Johnson's house at 30 Elm Street always tempted us. Beginning between two cedar trees at the side-walk and snaking back between some decorative slabs of petrified wood onto the back lawn, these paths seemed to beckon to bike riders. But because of their extreme narrowness and their tight curves, it was impossible to ride them with any speed and thus to avoid the watchful eye of the caretaker, Elbridge Brown. When we rode our bikes on Mountain Avenue, we usually darted off the road and behind the hedge at Lucy Daniels' to follow the curve of the semicircular driveway past the front of that brick house, which is no longer there, and back out onto the road. We also took some shortcuts and never tired of riding on what we called bike trails. One such shortcut bypassed the park and connected South Street and Court Street and eventually Central Street. To ride it once again in one's imagination is to recall sights and sounds that have long since disappeared from all but memory. Riding home from Vail Field on the east side of South Street, we passed the elemen-tary school and the high school, with its long, Y-shaped walkway and tall evergreen tree, and rode by the Powers' house and Ethel Nutting's house, with its long, narrow front porch, and then came to the large, brown-shingled building which was the Woodstock Inn annex. Seasonal help who worked for the inn lived there and were always to be seen between meals or on days off sitting in chairs or on the steps of the two front stoops. At the north end of the annex, we turned east and rode out along the wide, dirt driveway between the inn and the annex, passing on one side the small garage where Dave Beach, the inn manager, or Dicky Page, the desk clerk, parked his car and the old inn kitchen with its raised back porch and the boiler room; and on the other side, the annex parking lot and the circular wooden fences enclosing the riding rings behind Ferguson's Stable. I remember the texture of that roadway with its patches of ash and crushed coal, and I can hear the occasional snorting of a horse being exercised by Ruth Keck, the pock...pock of tennis balls, and the quiet sighing of the great pine trees along the grass at the south end of the inn tennis courts. Then we rode across Court Street and out Mechanic Street past George Sharon's welding shop and the village sheds and the garages of the Woodstock Electric Company; past Nelson Lee's garage, where Rodney Hatch, the blind man, was to be seen in the shadows caning chairs; and past the footbridge and the fence at the back of the Moon house and past the small back porch of the Tavern, where Stanley Pease was often to be seen taking a break from his kitchen duties, and out the alley and onto Central Street.

The bike trails crossed both public and private land, and no one complained about our riding them. Although every boy growing up in Woodstock must have known them, we thought of them as secret and concealed routes, and we showed them only to our best friends. We would be pedaling along the north side of the park, and suddenly, to the surprise of an unsuspecting companion, we would turn and dart out the driveway between Mrs. Norman

Williams' house at 7 The Green and the White Cupboard annex at 9 The Green and speed across the back lawn past a small greenhouse and a fence to the dark, pine needle-strewn lane along the north side of the old White Cupboard barn and out into the yard behind the Gillingham block and the White Cupboard. Then we would ride along the driveway between rows of dusty lilac bushes and come out at the Town Crier. There we would stop to receive the expressions of surprise from the rider whose initiation into the secret of the bike trail had just been completed.

Another bike trail connected School Street with Prospect Street and wound past some buildings that are no longer to be seen. We would turn off School Street behind the Catholic Church and ride out the dirt driveway that veered off from the church parsonage driveway and sloped down to Ara Thompson's Fix-It Shop and to his house. If we kept on going along a path between that house and the shop, we would come out in the shady back yard of the old, derelict Methodist Church. We would ride past the dilapidated church sheds and alongside the church itself with its small wilderness of burdock and ragweed and come out onto Prospect Street between the church and 22 Prospect, the house that then functioned as a dormitory for the Woodstock Country School when it was on Church Hill. Riding on this trail always meant stopping at the Fix-It Shop, which was one of the great places of my childhood. On almost any day in those summers when the proprietor, Ara Thompson, was not working in his shop, he was to be seen in the shop's front yard, sitting under the big maple tree in a wooden chair padded with cushions, or coming out the back door of his house and across the porch to receive his customers. If his shop was closed, that usually meant that he had run out of cigars and had gone down to Slackies to replenish his supply. I can still see him as I used to meet him sometimes on that trip, loping along in front of the library in his thick glasses and his gray work shirt and denim overalls, his gray hair swept back from his forehead. In those days when my bike needed servicing or repairs that were beyond my father's and my capacities, my father would advise me to "take it to Thompy," something that I grew accustomed to doing whether anything was wrong with my bike or not.

In those days Ara Thompson was a man in his mid-sixties who made his living repairing lawn mowers, baby carriages, and, primarily, balloon tire bicycles, which he fixed up and sold. His four children, the oldest of which was my age, were usually to be seen riding bicycles or tricycles in the yard; and his wife, Hazel, rode a blue and white bike around the village on her errands, which included selling Christmas cards. The dark, cigar-fragrant interior of Thompy's Fix-It Shop would capture the attention of any boy interested in bicycles. As you crossed the threshold and your eyes adjusted to the dim light, the first thing to be seen, on the corner of a workbench, was a bubble gum machine — one jaw-breaker for a penny. Beyond that lay a world of bike frames without wheels, wheels without tires, tires without tubes, tubes without air, bicycle handlebars, reflectors, fenders, seats, chains, chainguards, forks and spring forks and Gene Autry handlebar grips; lawn mower wheels and blades, baby carriage parts and parts of children's red wagons. The next room with the large window was always in the process of becoming a showroom for bicycles ready for sale. In the shop and its yard, with Thompy's help, we could make the sorts of minor adjustments we were always needing — raising our seats, lowering our handlebars, putting our handlebars in bottom side up. And we filled hours with bicycle talk about why J. C. Higgins bikes were junk, about whether the pieces of cardboard that we clothespinned to our forks so that they flapped against the spokes and made a motorcycle sound really did loosen our spokes, about whether bicycle sirens were or were not against the law, about how much better New Departure brakes were than Bendix brakes.

111

The second and last bike I owned came from the Fix-It Shop. When I finally outgrew my 24-inch Hawthorne, I was able to trade it with Thompy for a good 26-inch bike, which I think was a Western Flyer. Since the bike was a secondhand one, it was mine to fix up, and it seems that I was always painting and customizing it in one way or another. Those balloon tire bikes with their wide fenders offered limitless possibilities for painting and striping and decoration. The bike was red when I got it, but I soon painted it pink and trimmed it with black. Whatever I did, I always rode out for Thompy's approval, and he always gave it. Of the last and most ambitious of these customizing jobs, I have a peculiarly vivid recollection. I carried out the work in the basement of our next door neighbors, Elba and Gertrude Buckman, at 6 Pleasant Street. It involved sanding down the frame and painting it blue, replacing the pink and black fenders with a new chrome set, which I purchased from a catalogue and outfitted with white mudflaps and matching handlebar grips. I remember my mother and father coming down through the bulkhead on those cool, early spring evenings to offer a hand and to admire my efforts, and I remember, as one always does remember the last of things, how seriously and intently I worked to bolt in the fenders tightly, to center the mudflaps exactly, to brush out the brushstrokes until they were nearly invisible.

I suppose I half knew that I was working against time, that my interest in bikes had begun to be replaced by other more complicated and confusing things. In laboring as I did in the dim light of the Buckmans' basement, I may have been trying to hang onto the innocence and simplicity of those earlier days, trying to preserve undimmed, in the life of the different person I was becoming, something of the sense of wonder and excitement that attended my first solo bike rides through the village and something of that vision of Woodstock as mine which those rides had given me. Whatever, I know that when I finally carried my newly renovated chrome and blue and white bike up into the spring sunshine and rode it upstreet, something seemed to be missing, something had gone.

The balloon tire bike probably continued to enjoy popularity and sales after I had passed along to high school and to cars and dates, but I think I was in on its heyday. In our bicycle talks among ourselves and with Ara Thompson, English bikes were sometimes mentioned. They were then certainly not as anomalous as either Gerald Colby's buggy-sized antique tricycle that I recall seeing him turning around in the widened sidewalk space outside the Station House Restaurant at 60 Pleasant Street, or as the large-wheeled unicycle occasionally ridden in the village by a student at the Country School on Church Hill. But they were curiosities to most of us, and they were visible enough so that we had begun to refer to our balloon tire bikes as "American bikes." There were a number of Raleighs around: David Sa'adah had one, as I recall, and so did Blythe Weatherby up on Linden Hill. Jim Brownell rode a top-of-the-line, dark green one, and his brother Tom had a hybrid English and American model, and I am sure there were a good many more. E. K. Parker, who may have been a Raleigh dealer of some kind, always had one or two of them in the large, somewhat empty looking offices of Woodbury Label Company on the second floor of the Whitcomb Block at 14 Central Street, but the number of English bikes did not appear to be growing. Although all of us were fascinated by the idea of a bike with gears, a bike you could actually shift, we all pretty much agreed with Thompy about the instability of their narrow tires and the danger of their hand brakes. But then when Sandy Morse outgrew his first bikes, he replaced them with an English bike, and then Don Eaton did the same.

We did not know it, but as we sat in the shade of the maple tree in Ara Thompson's yard and carried on our ongoing bicycle conversations, the days of the Fix-It Shop were numbered, and so were the days of the balloon tire bicycle's greatest popularity. Its virtual disappearance in all but the mini bike and dirt bike models was something I failed to notice in the interest of continuing my education and traveling and pursuing my vocation. In fact, I might not have thought much about bicycles at all had it not been for my children. The discovery that I could not fix their ten-speed bikes because I could not understand them — and that I could not safely ride them because whenever I needed to stop I kept pushing the pedals backward onto thin air — left me looking around for one of my old balloon tire companions. I finally found one such bike, an old girl's Columbia belonging to a friend, and borrowed it to go riding on summer evenings in Woodstock with my children, who were not used to riding in town. My first impression on once again viewing Woodstock from the seat of a bicycle was that something was missing. In some cases it was buildings, and in others it was the people that some part of me must have expected to see still sitting out on their porches. Then too, the village seemed to have shrunk since the time of my boyhood. I was amazed and a little disappointed at how quickly we could go once around the streets, and I kept thinking, "Is this all there was to it back in those days?" To my children, however, who were riding along with me, Woodstock as they were coming to know it and as I had once known it, was as large as the future, its streets extending outward and branching off into realms of endless possibility. They were traversing ways along which they had walked with their parents just as I had with mine before being old enough to ride a bike. Watching them, I could see that they were experiencing something of the transforming power of the bicycle, of the way in which it allows us to explore by ourselves and to possess the details of even the most familiar houses and streets and lawns and trees in such a way as to add them to the furnishings of our inner lives. And so, pedaling an old balloon tire bike similar to the ones I used to ride, sometimes leading, sometimes following my son and daughter on the bikes of their day along Elm Street and River Street and finally along all the streets of Woodstock, I felt myself sharing something of the excitement of their discoveries. And sensing some of my own exhilaration from thirty years before, I began to experience that peculiar feeling of both loss and recovery in seeing so much in the village that was unchanged and in recollecting so many of the old buildings and the old bicycles and the old faces, that seemed suddenly to have simply vanished into the summer air.

Vail Field

*The memories I value most,
I don't see them ever fading.*

Kazuo Ishiguro

In the days of my childhood and youth, all of Woodstock's out-door athletic events took place on Vail Field. Those events re-flected the town's and the nation's priorities at the time. Vail Field was deeded to the village by Henry Vail in 1895 for the purpose of recreation and athletics. Since it was developed around the turn of the century when baseball was rapidly growing into the national pastime, this six-acre tract of land was laid out primarily as a base-ball field. Its grandstand and bandstand were designed and situ-ated so as to afford fans the best possible views of the action on the diamond and in the outfield. When I was first becoming aware of sports in the early 1950s, baseball at all levels, all the way from midget and junior leagues to junior legion and high school up to the American Legion semi-pro league, was played there. But those six acres were also made to accommodate a football field for the nearby Woodstock High School, although it was a squeeze. The goal posts of that field which ran parallel to South Street were set so that a forward pass to the end zone, if overthrown, could end up in the brush at the base of the massive pines bordering the country club, and at the other end a point-after-touchdown kick might land in the bandstand. This makeshift gridiron's having to appropriate nearly the whole first base half of the baseball diamond in order to fill out its northeast corner gave it even more the appearance of an afterthought.

For me and for many of my schoolmates and friends, these were fields of glory which gave us our first visions of athletic prowess, real and imaginary. We spent the better part of our free time in organized league play and in pickup games in the days of summer and autumn, striving to emulate the feats of our local heroes on the very ground where we had seen them performed. We took our cues from the baseball and football practices as well as games we watched on Vail Field. On school-day afternoons in the fall, if we didn't follow the high school football team as they jogged out to practice, their cleats rapping a tattoo on the sidewalk along the west side of South Street, it was because we were already out at the field waiting for them. In our improvised after-school and Saturday morning games of tackle football, we didn't bother much with passing, our delight being in running the ball. Any time I could gain yardage by breaking through the line and shedding a tackler or two before being pulled down, I delighted in the thought that I was on my way to becoming a fullback like Jim Paul. A long run off a quarterback fake and reverse had me thinking I was the next Albert Bassett, baffling yet another defense with the famous end-around play that Bob Dailey brought to Woodstock and used so effectively in his first years as football coach. And with any long touchdown jaunts, I could imagine I was Charlie Soule giving the crowd another breathtaking display of broken field running.

So completely were sports associated in our minds with Vail Field that not even our first major league game at Fenway Park in 1953 could dissolve the spell. When we saw Ted Williams homer against the Washington Senators, my brother and I were both astonished not to hear the fans respond with the customary Vail Field practice of honking their car horns while he rounded the bases. In fact, the very words "home run" to this day summon an image of a baseball rising in slow motion, against a backdrop of Kedron willows, up into the summer sky to lift over the high chicken wire fence and clear the brook. The memory and the talk of Vail Field homers so often features references to Kedron Brook and its fence because the short left field line of approximately 290 feet made Vail Field a paradise for right-handed pull hitters. However, homers were also hit over the outfielder's head to straightaway center and to right field. I remember legion team catcher Bob Harrison, a blocky, short-legged man who worked for the Billings Farm, hitting a shot that cleared right field, bounced on the pavement on South Street, and landed on the other side of the road. And outfielder Dick Maynard hit one of the longest home runs of the 1949 season when he clouted one that cleared South Street in the air and ended up in the grass on the bank beneath South Street extension. Right field in those days was a bit different from what it is now. The bank sloping up to the sidewalk was steeper, its grass was left uncut, and in damp weather the shallow ditch along its bottom was wet and muddy. Outfielders sometimes backed into it in tracking fly balls, and a referee in a high school football game was shouldered into it by Woodstock lineman Bruce Washburn when he got in the way of a tackle. Sometimes a ball hit in that direction that shouldn't have been a home run turned out to be one simply because the right fielder, in his frantic pawing through the long grass, could not come up with the ball before the hitter had made the full circuit.

There was great baseball to be seen on Vail Field back then, baseball of a caliber to make the men of my grandfather's generation recall the days just before and after World War I when more than a thousand fans used to be on hand to watch the Woodstock team battle such rivals as Bridgewater and Windsor and teams from as far away as Keene, New Hampshire, and Holyoke, Massachusetts. Once in a while out of those recollections passed on to us by my father, a name would emerge and attach itself to a person known to us. And then the sad-eyed, gray-haired man keeping the dilapidated store that sagged over the bank and seemed ready to slide down into the Ottauquechee River in Bridgewater would turn out to be Bump Davis, the legendary first baseman who had played semi-pro ball in the Boston area and who had hit some of the longest balls ever seen on Vail Field when he played for Woodstock. Then we would regard him with new interest, and the faded baseball posters and pictures on the back wall of his store would make sense, and we would recognize as the real thing the card he carried in his wallet identifying him as a scout for the Cleveland Indians.

But of course we had our own contemporary baseball heroes. They were drawn from the great American Legion teams, including the one that won the state semi-pro championship in 1952 and especially the team of 1950 that won that championship and won the regional championship by beating the Massachusetts state champions from Athol in two straight games and went on to compete in the national tournament in Wichita, Kansas. The story of that summer has been told and retold and deserves to be passed on down through the decades to come. I was eight years old at the time, too young to realize the full significance of their achievement but old enough to experience the baseball fever that spread through Woodstock and to idolize the players who just kept on winning until they got to Wichita. By itself the fact of their two straight defeats which eliminated them from further play in the national tournament is somewhat misleading. Even their first round loss of 8 to 5 to the Plymouth Oilers of Sinton, Texas, was nothing to be ashamed of. After a shaky start which left the Woodstock team down 4 to 0 at the end of the first inning of that game, pitcher Pinky Johnson settled down, the offense got going, and they gave Texas all they could handle. At the beginning of the eighth inning, Woodstock was out in front 5 to 4 when a Texas player hit a long fly ball with men on base, and it got away from right fielder Lars Beckman. Catcher Tom Flower can still recall watching that ball dance around in "that Wichita wind" and thinking that a major league outfielder would be lucky to get under it. Then extra runs scored on a wild throw to third, and the Oilers came out on top. In the words of a sportswriter from Wichita, "Until the eighth it looked like it might be one of the most amazing upsets in the tourney's history. The young Vermont team did not field a single ex-pro while the Texans had almost an entire squad of ex-minor and a few major leaguers." According to Flower, all but two members of that team, the second baseman and the shortstop, had played double A ball or higher, and their roster included Babe Dahlgren, who had replaced Lou Gehrig on the Yankees, and Tom McBride, MVP of the Texas League, who had played outfield with Ted Williams and Dom DiMaggio on the Boston Red Sox team that had won the 1946 pennant. The Oilers went on in their next game to demolish 13 to 1 in only five innings a North Carolina team that had the young Dick Groat of Pittsburgh Pirate fame playing for them. The second game against the Arkansas Lions of Eldorado, Arkansas, could have gone either way, and Woodstock's loss of 3-2 speaks for itself.

The tremendous excitement that inspired the people of Woodstock to raise in only two weeks' time the three thousand dollars necessary to send the team to the national tournament brought several hundred fans into the center of the village at night to listen to those games as they were being played. Speakers were set up on the dummy, and Wendell Cameron, serving as announcer, recreated the games from the play-by-play reports as they came in over Teletype at the Western Union Office at Sterling's Drugstore. On the night of the team's homecoming, the square was once again the scene for a large gathering of their loyal fans. That night was a memorable occasion for me because I was allowed to be there with my father for what turned out to be a long wait. Since the trains from Wichita to Albany were delayed, the team did not arrive until two hours later than expected, thus affording me a chance to stay up late and to enjoy the entertainment provided during the long interval. A platform had been erected in front of the Woodstock Electric Company at 11 Central Street, and Charlie Clough, who had spearheaded the fundraising drive for the team, acted as master of ceremonies. A pickup band was assembled, three members of Woodstock's comic Snozzlefrew's Band made their contribution, recorded music was played over the speaker system, and the twelve-year-old boys Bill Leach and Bud Spaulding tap-danced on the platform. The improvisational nature of the entire evening is still conveyed to me in the curiously indelible image of Squee Leach, Bill's mother, standing on tiptoe and reaching up to the platform to hand him his shiny black tap-dancing shoes which she had just fetched from their summer home on Pleasant Street. Finally around 11 PM the cars that had gone to meet the train in Albany began to pull into the square, and the players made their appearance: Howard Richardson, Morgan Vail, Jim Fleming, Lars Beckman, Ed McGee, George Goodrow, Pinky Johnson, Don Perkins, Tom Flower, Ray Langhans, Dick Maynard, Bernie Carr, Stan Rice, Ed Fleming, Stan West, and Stubby Spafford. They had not lost any of their stature. In fact, in my eyes they had even gained some by having taken on the country's best in a place so very far from home.

Indeed, the legion teams of those days might very well have invited comparison among Woodstock's older fans with the great teams of the past. Rightfielder Lars Beckmans' occasional tremendous home run shots to deep left field, one of which I remember clearing the fence and the brook to bounce off the top of Fred Bates' barn on Maple Street, may have challenged the longest balls hit by such former greats as Bump Davis and Emmett Racy. Perhaps unequaled in Woodstock baseball history was infielder Morgan Vail's great power hitting, especially with men on base, that carried the 1950 team all the way to the midwest. In fact, the play of some of Woodstock's best was good enough to attract the notice of the big leagues. Vail received a letter from the Red Sox in 1941, but World War II prevented his being able to accept the call. In the state tournament in 1946, his play for the Rutland Royals attracted the notice of the Brooklyn Dodgers. In the late 30s and early 40s Tink Reed's fastball had landed him in Binghamton, New York, where he played some minor league ball with the Dodger franchise, and in the 1950s catcher Bernie Carr was given a tryout in the St. Louis Browns' farm system.

Nor was the lighter side, which has its own place in legend, missing from the games of those days. Before one of the exhibition games played under the lights at Hartford in the summer of 1950 to raise money to send the team to Wichita, one of the Woodstock players was suffering from a nervous stomach. Since the ballpark was without facilities, he had to settle for the privacy of the trees beyond center field and to make use of what nature supplied, which, unfortunately turned out to be poison ivy. As a result, although he was able to make the trip west with the team, he was unable to play in either of the tournament games. In a less gruesome anecdote which afforded my father many laughs over the years, catcher Stubby Rice went out to the mound to talk with southpaw Tink Reed, who was getting shelled. When Stubby told him to give up on his curve ball because it wasn't breaking, Tink, with a cautionary gesture that took in the batter and the man on deck and the rest of the opposing team on the bench, answered, "Shh, they don't know that!"

It might be said that the great legion team of 1950 had a decided advantage because the Vermont semi-pro tournament was held that year in Woodstock, as was the regional championship. But in playing on Vail Field, opposing teams were perhaps not as disadvantaged as they might have been in playing on the road in other parks. For Vail Field was a beautiful baseball field. Its all-dirt diamond was spoken of as "the pride of southern Vermont" and celebrated for its "billiard-like smoothness." It was tenderly cared for by the people who did the groundskeeping. In their time Bob Dailey, John Wells, Ed Brehaut and others kept the grass cut short, the puddles dried, and the edges of the infield weeded. Before games the diamond was dragged by a heavy metal screen behind a small tractor, and all the stones down to the smallest pebbles were carted away. Then, as part of the manicuring, it was raked in the necessary places and rolled before the baselines and the batter's boxes were laid down and the bases and the rubber on the mound were pounded in. All of the equipment for grooming the field was kept in a locked storage area under the bandstand.

Vail Field was as great a place for the spectators as it was for the players. Many fans drove onto the field and parked facing the diamond on both ends of the grandstand and bandstand and watched from inside or outside their cars and tried to protect their roofs and hoods from foul balls. The grandstand, which had been erected in 1897 to accommodate three hundred spectators, was situated a suitable distance behind home plate, and it offered a shady place to watch a game on a hot Sunday afternoon. The bandstand was positioned on the first base side several yards behind the home team bench, and it afforded a fine view of the action. Avid fans had their established spots. Rob Wells, a small, elderly, gray-haired man with rimless spectacles, had his place two or three rows up to the right of center in the grandstand. My father preferred the bandstand, where he occasionally sat on the steps, but usually stood, sometimes leaning against the wooden rail. It seems now as though he may have had some tacit agreement to watch at least part of each game there with Rob White, a bushy-browed, gruff, gravelly-voiced, diehard old fan of Woodstock sports. When Rob disagreed with umpires and refs, he was, in my father's words, "apt to get off a good one," as he did when he loudly informed a football referee who had just called back a Woodstock touchdown for illegal motion that the stripes on his jersey ought to be running the other way. As they talked or exchanged the occasional remark, they kept their eyes on the game except when Rob, who chewed tobacco, walked across the bandstand to spit off the backside.

The loyal spectators who gathered there sometimes included Mr. Vernon S. Gray, who strolled, or drove his Oldsmobile, out to Vail Field from his home at 79 Central Street opposite Tribou Park. Colonel Gray, as he was sometimes called, was a tall and portly southern gentleman with an appreciation for good cigars and good bourbon. On summer days he dressed in a straw hat and light colored, three-piece linen or light cotton suits, the trousers of which were rumored to have been specially tailored at Campions in Hanover so as to allow him to hitch them, without inconvenience, above his ample stomachs. He wore glasses and had a classic schnozz that invited comparison with Jimmy Durante's. My father was fond of Vernon and much amused by him, and was always pleased to see him leave his customary position of standing behind the Woodstock bench to come up into the bandstand to deliver in his rumbly Tennessee bass his perceptive and often humorous observations on the progress of the game. One of my friends and I mischievously delighted in speaking to him in passing in the village, for no matter how abbreviated or informal our salutation, whether it was "hello, Colonel Gray" or simply "hello" or even just "hi," we were answered with a somewhat preoccupied tip of the hat and the invariable "fine and dandy, how are you today, suh?" In 1949 Vernon Gray had served as Vermont State Baseball Commissioner, and in that capacity it had been his pleasure to throw out the first ball of the state tournament, which was played that year at Vail Field.

The bandstand was the gathering point for some of the older and more serious baseball fans. Children and youths were welcome if they were quiet and they behaved. Those who tried chasing each other up and down the steps or went there to dare each other to jump off the sides were tolerated just so long and then were told by my father and others to go elsewhere, and they did. More often than not, they went to the grandstand. The grandstand's location some thirty yards or so behind home plate and bordering the dirt drive made it a kind of unofficial boundary between the baseball field and the playground, which occupied the north end of Vail Field. As such, it separated the two purposes specified by Henry Vail in his original deed — recreation and athletics — and, in a way, unified them. The back of the grandstand included a storage area for playground equipment. During summer morning playground, which was supervised by coach Bob Dailey and assisted by high school athletes such as Nancy Wilson and Valerie Ward, youngsters participated in organized games and activities including arts and crafts as well as sports. They also had free time to use the swings or the teeter boards or sandbox or to shoot baskets at the old hoops and wooden backboards attached to telephone poles in the open area where the hockey rink is now located. When a sudden summer shower sent everyone scurrying up the metal stairs into the grandstand, the youngsters seldom minded, for the grandstand, whether during playground hours or baseball games, was irresistible to children.

For a time in the late 40s and early 50s the back west end of the grandstand housed a food concession which operated during legion baseball games. It sold chocolate bars for a nickel and hotdogs for twenty cents and small bags of Wise Potato Chips for a dime. Most importantly, also for a dime, it sold soda pop — Coca-Cola, Hires Root Beer, Fanta Orange, Fruit Bowl, Grape Ade — all in the tall bottles of thick glass and served with a paper straw. I remember running over to the bandstand and asking my father for ten cents for a Coke and running back to wait for the concession to raise and hook the wooden slat that boarded its window. Then I'd step up onto the low platform and reach my dime up to the narrow counter covered in oilcloth and be handed, fresh from the water filled cooler with the bottle cap opener on the side, a wet, cold bottle of Coke. After the few blissful nose-and-throat-stinging moments it took me to guzzle the 6 and 1/2 ounces, my first thought was for the empty bottle, for empties were returnable, and the competition for them was fierce. Five of them brought back to the concession meant another dime or a dime's worth of goods. But also, soda bottles were needed for water fights. We could fill our bottles from the grandstand's restrooms at the east end or from the water fountain conveniently located at the base of its iron fire escape stairs and platform and chase each other around the playground area or rush up into the highest row of seats and soak our opponents from above. Or we could peer out of the open space between the back of the top row and the roof until we spotted unsuspecting victims and then drench them and be turned around and innocently watching the game from another seat by the time they came up looking for us. From time to time some aspect of the game really would capture our attention, as when the honking of horns would signify a great catch or a long ball, and we would look up to see runs crossing the plate; or when a foul ball would send its booming sound rippling down the length of protective chicken wire stretched across the grandstand's front or announce itself by a thump on the grandstand roof. Then we would go jumping down the seats and racing down the stairs to try to find where it had landed and be the one to carry it back to the team bench. Or the crunching of base-ball spikes on the crushed stone at the base of the water fountain would signify that one of the players had come over for a drink, and we would break off our foolishness and look down respectfully at the tilted cap and the uniform number on the bent back as he drank, and wonder in horror what he would do to anyone bold enough to baptize him from above even with as little as a single drop.

Inside and out, the grandstand had a well-used look. The wood along the half-dozen or so wide levels which functioned as both steps and seats had been worn down by the feet and the backsides of generations of fans until its grain was ridged and shiny. Layers of jackknifed initials, some of the letters of which were rubbed shallow and barely legible or were superimposed with fresh carvings, recorded youthful affairs of the heart down through the years and testified to the grandstand's appeal and use as a place of romance. Occasional knotholes invited peeps down into the enclosed and darkened area below. This curious place probably proved irresistible at least once to every boy in Woodstock. Either by yourself or, more likely, behind a more experienced comrade on afternoons when Vail Field was quiet, you found the indented place in the border of tall grass under the iron stairs and slithered in under the building on your stomach. As you stood and your nose became accustomed to the smell and your eyes adjusted to the darkness, you saw a cavernous space extending from one end of the grandstand to the other and punctuated by a line of huge support beams running front to back at intervals of five feet or so and situated some three feet above the hard-packed dirt floor. And whether it was the fetid air or the litter of paper and cigarette ends and matches and broken glass, you recognized this hideaway as a place of the forbidden. I remember sitting on one of those beams just long enough to share with a friend a corn silk cigarette before my claustrophobia began to get the better of me and I wriggled back under the edge and out into the dazzling sunlight and the welcome summer breezes.

If at times our attention to the baseball games in progress was at best minimal, the atmosphere of Vail Field during legion team games prevented our ever being very much unaware of baseball for very long. In fact, we always had our gloves with us, and someone usually had a ball and bat, and we improvised games on the old tennis court in the northeast corner of the field. As baseball diamonds go, it was eccentric, though less so than the one we fashioned in a sloping meadow above Lincoln Street on the side of Mt. Peg, where it was a hike from third base to home plate and where a batter could see only the top half of anyone playing deep left field. Having become accustomed up there to bushwhacking for anything that was hit into right field, to watching grounders slow to a stop, and to losing sight of the bases in the high grass, we found the weed-strewn remains of the old Vail Field tennis court to be perfectly level and comparatively well groomed. For first base we used one of the iron posts that had once held the net. Since home plate was located on one service line and second base somewhere near the other, this was a diamond without an outfield, and any fly ball either hit the tall, rusty fence that still enclosed both ends and the Kedron side of the old court or cleared that fence to land in the brook or out on the grass near the path that ran behind the opposing team's bench and led to the footbridge and Maple Street.

As my schoolmates and I reached the age for organized baseball, we began to realize that the legion team, though unquestionably the best, was not the only show in town in those days. The boys on the junior league and the junior legion teams coached by such long-time baseball specialists as Chick Wells and Ken Miner were then developing the skills and the chemistry that would bring them, under Coach Bob Dailey's direction, the high school Class B baseball championship in 1956. During their practices and games, I spent countless hours on Vail Field behind their bench. As it seems to me now, I admired everything about them — their baseball skills, their remarks, their antics, even the curve in the visors of their caps and, of course, their gloves, which I studied carefully. Back then before baseball gloves were preformed, five-fingered models designed so that from the moment they left the store they could scoop or snag even the hardest hit balls, you had to work to break in a glove. Whatever the price and the model, whether three-fingered, four-fingered, or five-fingered, the glove required exercise and shaping before it would serve you well. The job was to make a good pocket for your catches, and in order to do so, you worked with the glove incessantly, playing toss and catch or, when by yourself, putting it on and slamming a baseball into it over and over again or socking it with your fist, oiling it, folding it around a baseball or two and tying it up or even sleeping with it under your pillow. The kind of pocket I had in mind was usually determined by which of those junior league players' gloves I admired the most.

Even more intriguing to me than the native Woodstock boys who played at this level — for example, John Wells, Bud Spaulding, and Tom Barnard — were a few summer boys who joined them and strengthened the junior league team's play. These new players - first baseman and outfielder Bill Boardman from Texas, fastball pitcher Charley Murphy from Massachusetts, the Lockman boys (Aime Bourdon's grandsons) from Virginia, and shortstop Al Rocco from New York City — brought with them to Vail Field different manners of speaking and also the fascination of distant and unknown places. Rocco especially captured my attention. Dark skinned, good-looking, and somewhat solitary, he spent a number of summers as a fresh air boy with highway commissioner Gerald (Pete) Perkins and his wife at their home on Rose Hill, and he played baseball with considerable style. The fluid way in which he fielded even the most sharply hit grounders by scooping in the ball and drawing back the glove to the low sidearm throwing position and then released it, seemingly all in one motion, had no doubt been picked up at Ebbets Field or Yankee Stadium or The Polo Grounds.

Under the spell of his defensive play, I strove hard to emulate all aspects of his game, even going so far as a studied imitation of his batting stance, although I don't recall his being a particularly good hitter. Like Rocco, some of the boys who went to Wendell Cameron's Camp Kitchigamink in Barnard were city boys who showed a different style of play; and the midget and junior league showdowns against Camp K were played with great intensity because a number of Woodstock boys who were campers there were in uniform against their schoolmates and friends.

It was always worthwhile to be out at Vail Field to watch the emerging young star of that day, left-hander John Wells. Along with a strong supporting cast, which included pitcher and outfielder Bob Fleming from Bridgewater, shortstop Tom Barnard from Woodstock, outfielder Roger Jaycox, catcher Reggie Barron, and third baseman Chick Chase, all from South Pomfret, Wells led a nucleus of his former junior league teammates to the high school title in 1956. The same summer he and Tom Barnard went on to play for the Hartford junior legion team that won the state title, Barnard collecting key hits and RBI's in the clutch and Wells showing his prowess as both a hitter and fielder at first base, right field, and center field when he was not leading the way to victory on the mound. A pitcher with a number of weapons in his arsenal and great control, John pitched for Springfield College and Lyndon State College before being drafted by the Milwaukee Brewers and playing for a time in their farm system in Boise, Idaho. As a high school pitcher he was awesome even in defeat, as he showed against Springfield High on Vail Field in May of 1956 when he pitched the entire fourteen innings of what was thought to have been the longest game in the history of Woodstock High School baseball, allowing only a sprinkling of hits before finally losing 3–2.

John also coached junior league baseball during the years when I was beginning to realize that I was not and never would be a baseball player. At the end of the arduous and instructive practices that he conducted, he would sometimes agree with us that it was time for a little comic relief. If team managers Don Eaton and Charlie Racicot had been shirking their duties to carry out their self-designated task of insuring that our various young female fans were maintaining an interest in the game, John would send them, against their ardent protests, into the outfield by themselves to demonstrate their inability to judge a fly ball. But John himself, though a dedicated and able coach, was not completely incapable of a similar sort of neglect. His girlfriend usually accompanied him to games and acted as our scorekeeper. However, on one Saturday afternoon she was evidently unable to go along with us for our game against the team from Enfield, New Hampshire. Enfield's pitcher that day was a big righthanded fastballer without a great deal of control. My brother, who batted leadoff, had a good eye and drew a lot of walks, and in his first time at bat, he started things off by taking a couple of balls. Suddenly, John called timeout. "Look," he said to my brother, "I don't want you standing up here waiting him out all afternoon. I've got a date. Swing away." Realizing that, given the speed of the pitches, he had little chance of connecting with one, Howard followed orders and went down swinging four times in what I can only hope proved to be a suitably short contest for our impatient coach.

Some of our most memorable times in practices with John came when we could persuade him to show us some of his best stuff. Then, one by one, we would step up to the plate and, trusting his control, dig in against him. Most of us were hilariously fanned in a few pitches. The trouble was that no two of his pitches were the same, or, just when you discovered that they weren't going to be, they were. It was simply no good trying to second-guess him. A sucker for a curve ball, I was helpless against John's breaking pitches, which could go both ways. His fastball was less easy to see than it was to hear when it exploded into the catcher's mitt behind me. My only hope was in getting hold of a change-up, but John's off-speed pitches tended to float in when I was set for the fastball so that it seemed as though I had already corkscrewed around on a tremendous swing just as the ball was reaching the plate. That much wiser, I was caught with my bat on my shoulder for the next pitch, which was a scorcher. And like most good pitchers, John seldom delivered a good strike. About the only one of us who could hit him was a classmate of mine, Ed Brehaut. A power hitter with a tendency to go to the opposite field in his early days, Ed began getting the bat around on John when he learned from Eddie Potwin and Morgan Vail that hitting is, as my father used to say, "all in the wrists." In the legacy of Woodstock baseball, Ed credits those Vail Field veterans with introducing him to the secret that enabled him to go on to hit .400 for Lyndon State College in 1963, the second highest average in college baseball in that season.

Most of my best baseball experiences on Vail Field came in practices and not in games. Since I was a weak hitter, I preferred fielding and throwing to standing in at the plate, and I loved infield and outfield practice. During our junior league workouts, I often got to fill in for first-string shortstop Bing Watson, whose part-time job in the kitchen of the White Cupboard Inn prevented him from getting to practice on time. One day in particular when John was hitting us grounders and I had just taken the flip from the second baseman on my way across the bag and thrown to first, I remember John shouting, "Bruce, you look like a million dollars." But in games it was always different. From the corner of my eye, the sight of the runner heading for first would distract me so that I bobbled the ball or booted the grounder or hurried the throw, and I had trouble shaking off an error. No, for me baseball when least formal was most enjoyable. The greatest times were when a number of us would be playing the usual sort of undermanned pickup game and Ken Miner would turn up with a fungo bat and a few balls. Ken was a well-known photographer and sportswriter who lived with his wife Ellie and their (then) three children across from Vail Field in the house that was attached to, and later became part of, A&B Motors. A great baseball enthusiast, Ken had played third base for Middlebury College, and his active involvement in Woodstock baseball included coaching the junior legion team which fielded players from a number of towns of the upper valley including Woodstock, Lebanon, and Hartford. Summer afternoons would often find us on Ken's front porch talking sports, and it was never difficult to persuade him to come over and work with us. I remember the first time that a half-dozen or so of us gladly gave up our attempt at a game and spread ourselves across the green expanse of the outfield to shag the flies that Ken hit to us. The first ones that came off the end of that fungo had us all confused. They lifted and continued to lift until we thought they were either going to carry over the pines and onto the golf course or to become lost in the blue depths of the sky over Vail Field. We hadn't the faintest idea how to get under them, but as we kept trying, Ken talked to us. With his son Jimmy catching for him in front of the old backstop of metal and rope, he kept up a battery of comment, encouraging us, advising us to save our arms by setting up a cut-off man, telling us to watch which way the ball was coming off the bat. Then we started to catch on. And he would cheer us as we began to judge even some of the deepest flies, and when one of us would snag one on the run, he'd shout his approval.

Those afternoons of shagging flies were the best times I ever had with a baseball, better than any actual games I ever played except for one summer in something called the In-Town League under coach Tony Pratt. The In-Town League, which I think may have been the creation of the Rec Center, and ran for only one summer, was made up of boys from Woodstock and a few from Bridgewater. In that summer enough boys signed up to put together four teams which held practices and played games on Vail Field. Tony Pratt may very well have been its organizer as well as its coach. Whatever he was, he was a new face in town; none of us had ever seen him until we showed up for the first day of practice. We assembled in a line in the grandstand to step up to where he sat and to tell him our names and the position we wanted to play so that he could write them down on his clipboard. The line was moving slowly, and, seeing some of my pals who had gone through ahead of me and were beginning to play pepper on the diamond, I leaned forward to one of the smaller boys and asked him to sign me up for pitcher. Not knowing that Tony had overheard me, I turned to go and was stopped dead by a booming "Sign up yourself, you lazy bum!" Humiliated, I quietly resumed my place in line and decided that whoever this stranger was, he wasn't going to be any push-over. Tony was a good-looking young Yale student in his early twenties. He happened to be in the area for the summer, staying with his father, Lowell Pratt, at their summer home, "Sunningwood," at the top of that section of North Bridgewater known locally as the Gold Coast because of the number of wealthy families that owned homes there. Tony was some five feet nine inches tall, somewhat slope-shouldered but solidly built, and he carried himself like the athlete that he obviously was. He had played baseball at Andover and Yale, where he also played trombone in his own Dixieland jazz band. His most arresting features were his light blond curly hair and light blue eyes and his all-knowing smile, which let you know right away that he had your number but that he liked you nevertheless. He commanded our respect, and we all took to him immediately. Somehow, throughout that summer he managed to organize our teams; create a smooth running schedule of practices and games, which he supervised and umpired; coach all four teams; and, in the process, teach us a good deal about baseball. Still, although — or perhaps because — we looked up to him from the start and wanted to earn his recognition, some of us felt it necessary to test him by horsing around and doing things our way rather than his. One afternoon during practice at the beginning of our season, we were fielding flies in the outfield and making the sort of high, lazy throws that were slow enough to allow any runner to beat them and probably even advance a base by the time the ball landed somewhere near where it was supposed to go. Tired of telling us to keep the throws low and to send them in on one hop, Tony put down the bat, called us in from the outfield, told the infield to stay put, picked up a glove, and headed for shallow right field. This was our chance, and so as not to miss it, we hastily elected Bing Watson to hit them out to Tony. Bing could really get under them sometimes, and the first one he hit went just where we wanted it to go: into deep right center. Seeing it was beyond even his best efforts as a fielder, Tony loped after it until he got out to where it had rolled to a stop, picked it up, wheeled, and without winding up at all seemed to let the ball go from the shoulder, half throw, half shot-put from where he stood. And we saw something then that we had never seen on Vail Field in seasons of high school and even legion team baseball — an arm like a rifle, a genuine major league throwing arm. Like a pitch, the ball seemed to carry in a downward trajectory all the way from where it was released to where it touched ground on the bounce and slammed into the astonished third baseman's glove. By the time Tony came in fifteen minutes or so later to take the bat from Bing, he had shown us, in fielding as well as throwing, how to play the outfield, and from that moment we all tried to do it just as we had seen him do it. We loved playing for him, and we were usually out there early for our practices and games, waiting for him. When he appeared in his old, dark blue Ford pickup with the Bridgewater boys in the back, and drove down onto Vail Field, we wasted no time in hopping on the running boards and crowding around him.

Besides baseball, the main event on Vail Field back then was softball, which was usually played in the evening two or three times a week. It caught on, I think, after the war, around 1946 or '47, and in some cases represented a continuation of the recreational softball played at the military bases to keep the men busy. Though my Vail Field memories don't go back that far, I have seen some of the old team photos and heard about the long ball hitting of Ed Lord, the speed of Buster Johnson, the base running of Don Eaton, Sr., and of the infield play of Art Paul at second and Chick Wells at third. Among the best teams were the Fire Department teams, and for a number of years at the time of the state firemen's convention, some team would challenge a team from Woodstock, usually to go down in defeat. The game was fast pitch softball then, and I remember seeing, in something like their twilight years, the invincible battery of the Potwin brothers, Sonny on the mound and Eddie behind the plate, and being amazed at the motion and the speed of Sonny's windmill release. When legion baseball faded and finally died sometime in the mid 50s, softball became Vail Field's main sporting event. Then Woodstock fielded a number of teams, including Paul's Painters, a fire department team, and Paul's Motors (Paul Ellis and Paul West), and Bridgewater and Pomfret brought teams into what became a good-sized league, big enough to have two games going on at the same time, one on the main diamond and one out on the grass diamond in the far southwest corner of Vail Field. I would often ride my bike out there on summer evenings and drift back and forth between games. I remember that I had an eye for three players in particular and would tend to favor the field on which one or all of them happened to be playing. I looked for Jack Stillson at third base because of his arm. There would be the sharply hit grounder down the line, the scoop, and then, as though Jack was challenging both himself and the runner, the slight hesitation before the explosive release that astonished me by smashing into the first baseman's mitt a couple of steps in front of the runner. At the plate I watched Bobo Kelly, for at that time I had never seen anyone hit a softball as far or get around the bases as fast as he could. When I first saw him in the batter's box, I couldn't understand why the outfielders were moving back. He stood there in his army cap, the remains of a cigar clamped between his teeth, and holding his bat in a relaxed, upright position parallel to the buttons on his shirt, as if he had no intention of swinging it. When the pitch came in, however, he somehow managed to get both back and around on it in some terrific blasts to straight away center and right center, and his power coupled with his base running speed gave him many home runs and enabled him to stretch almost any hit into extra bases. But the player whom I continue to see most clearly is Roy Wardwell. In my recollection, he seems to have been everywhere, in his catcher's mask behind the plate, playing the outfield, rounding the bases, urging his teammates on with a steady stream of chatter. His great energy and enthusiasm for the game have always represented for me the spirit of softball as it was played back then. It was such a good evening's entertainment to go out and stand behind the bench or sit on the bank for a softball game in those days that by the time of the last out when the dusk had begun to draw down over Vail Field and the mist to rise from the Kedron, I still wouldn't have had my fill. And as the players stood around in small groups for a few moments before heading home or maybe down to the fire station or to the Pine Room at the Woodstock Inn or up to the pull-off by the trash barrel on Rose Hill for a few beers and some post-game talk, I would always be pretty reluctant to call it a night and head home myself.

Vail Field's great annual summer event, which was as exciting to me as all the baseball and softball watched or played there, was

the Rotary Carnival. For three nights, often in early August, the
northern end of the field was completely transformed into something magical. Offering none of the enticements of amusement
parks or large fairs, such as Ferris wheels and merry-go-rounds,
the Rotary Carnival still completely captured the imagination and
had us crossing off the days until it opened. It was organized and
carried out each year by the Woodstock Rotary Club as a way of
raising money for local community projects and causes such as the
construction of the Rec Center swimming pools and the creation
and continuation of scholarship funds for students graduating from
Woodstock High School.

The approach of carnival time was signaled by the arrival on
Vail Field of the trucks bringing the lumber that was stored each
year in the basement of the courthouse. During our baseball practices, we could hear the ring of hammers and see the Rotarians
putting up the frames of the game booths and closing them in with
heavy building paper stapled to the uprights and cross pieces. Then
we would see the men of the Woodstock Electric Company working off step ladders to set up the public address system and all the
lights by which the booths and the grounds would be illuminated.
The dirt roadway that extended from the stone entrance piers to
the east end of the grandstand served as the midway for the carnival. Most of the booths were set up in a loop of two rows on the
grass between the midway and the fence of the property at 26 South
Street. The exceptions were the food booth, which was always
located near the base of the grandstand stairs, and sometimes a
ring-toss booth and a ring-the-bell-with-a-hammer, which were
closer to the back of the bandstand. One booth — I remember it as
Roll-A-Ball — usually stood by itself behind the grandstand. Beyond that the old tennis court was sometimes roped off and used
for pony rides.

From the moment the trucks arrived and the activity of construction began until the closing of the carnival with the fireworks display and the drawing of the grand prize at the end of the third night, I found it difficult to be very far from Vail Field. I have often wondered what, if anything, could have dissuaded me from leaping on my bike and racing from Pleasant Street out there the moment my parents had released me from the supper table; or, once I had reached A&B Motors and actually heard the music and caught my first glimpse, what sum or guarantee, what promise of future wealth or greatness could have turned me around and sent me away thinking it worthwhile simply to stay home that year. For my first view of the carnival from South Street beckoned me with its own future. In the indecisive light of early evening, the sky over Mt. Peg maintained its blue as though the day intended to go on forever. But out beyond the bandstand and farther out along the pines, the shadows were gathering and showing that darkness, as though working from the ground up, had already begun its slow advance. And strung out across the middle distance where the two times seemed to merge, the pale lights of the booths and of the midway, set against the arrival of evening, promised their own time of endless possibility. I always stopped to look. Then, checking the dollar in my pocket and thinking about the three hours or so ahead of me, I rode my bike between the stone uprights and parked it by the bandstand.

Vail Field really did seem to have undergone a transformation, even since the afternoon when I had watched the final preparations for opening night being made. For one thing, there were the smells — first of popcorn from Ray Houghton's popcorn stand; then as you advanced down the midway, you'd pick up the smell of fried onions and hamburgers from the food booth, and farther along by the old tennis court, looking strangely unlike itself under the bright lights set up for the pony rides, the smell of horse manure and hay and leather as the small children were being led around the roped off area among a murmur of voices and the creaking of saddles. And the Rotarians themselves would have changed from the people we knew them to be into barkers, some of them wearing derby hats and tilted boaters and shouting out their particular games to attract the notice of the growing crowds.

Although at the time I would have welcomed more than my allotted sum of a dollar a night, it now seems to me to have been just the right amount. A great deal more might have made me as inattentive and jaded as the two summer boys from New Jersey whom we used to see standing at the dart booth spending untold sums throwing darts at the folded-up dollar bill taped to the board. Much less would have made the carnival simply a spectator sport for me since each game cost a dime to play. My dollar pretty much matched what my pals had to spend, and that meant we were in sync as we roamed around the carnival. Besides, I could usually coax an extra quarter or so out of my father, who worked in the food booth along with Ed Lord and John Bancroft and others, which was good for a hamburger and a Coke, especially if I could show him that I had some of my own money left. I would spend a good deal of time deciding how to parcel out my dimes and stretch them over the evening by watching other boys trying their luck or skill, and such observation in itself was enjoyable as well as instructive. The Hit-the-Cat booth in the far northwest corner of the grounds was always a must. Fred Doubleday, who at that time ran the Wood-stock Taxi Service, often managed that booth with the assistance of Elwin Young or some other high school boy. A natural show-man, Fred wore a huge light green cap with big white polka dots and sometimes sang right along with *Bye Bye Blackbird* or *Take Me Out to the Ball Game* or *I'm Looking Over a Four Leaf Clover* and other songs that would alternate with announcements over the PA system. His booth, where you stood and threw baseballs at weighted, standing canvas cats to knock them over, had its own

141

kind of he-man appeal and offered the consolation to a loser of at least having shown off his arm and his best fastball. Roll-A-Ball was also pretty irresistible because, with the exception of the dart booth with its folded up dollar, it was the one game at which you could actually win money. You selected a color or colors from a row of colored squares painted on the oilcloth on the counter in front of you, some of which said 2 to 1 or 3 to 1 or 5 to 1, and the one silver one said 10 to 1. Then, when the bets were made, at a table in the center of the booth, a softball sized rubber ball was rolled down an inclined plain onto a board of indented, colored squares fenced in on four sides by tautly stretched rubber bands that kept the ball bouncing in from the sides until it came to rest in one of the colored squares. Even a couple of wins on Roll-A-Ball could greatly increase my possibilities for the rest of the evening. I usually had a try at the various ring-toss games such as Hoop-La, in which various prizes were set on square blocks on a low table in the middle of the booth, and contestants attempted to toss wooden hoops of some eight inches in diameter down over the blocks to win the prize. Larry Angwin was quite often in charge of this booth. He was a short, portly man who had once posed for a *Saturday Evening Post* cover by Norman Rockwell of a traveling salesman sitting on the edge of a bed in a rooming house (it happened at Louise Brownell's house at 48 Pleasant Street) in his striped pajamas and playing solitaire on his suitcase and smoking a cigar. In his booth Larry was to be seen with straw hat and ever-present cigar and a cane encircled with hoops, and to be heard calling out "Hoop-La, Hoop-La, a dime for five, five for a dime." At another booth where the object was to toss smaller rings over the heads of canes, I could usually come away a winner but never of the coveted cane with the globular head covered with silver spangles.

Among the prizes, which were purchased every year from the Whippen Novelty Company in Westfield Massachusetts by a delegation of Rotarians who traveled there for that purpose, were a number of alluring items. Some of the ones to be won on the wheel of fortune games especially caught my eye. One of these wheels was usually run by veterinarian Jim Roberts. He too was seldom seen without a cigar. With his loud voice and flashing eyes and overall expansive personality, Doc, as my father called him, was easy to hear as he spun the wheel and called out from a cloud of cigar smoke, "...and where she stops nobody knows." He had the look of a person who, as my father put it approvingly, "liked to raise a little hell." And Doc and dentist Benton Pinney and some of their fellow Rotarians and my father usually did just that to cel-ebrate the closing of another carnival on the last night after the crowds had gone home. Exactly what they did in the small hours of the morning there on the littered grounds of Vail Field among the empty booths remains a secret. But my father tended to rise somewhat later than usual on those Sunday mornings and to chuckle about some huge fireworks, "old hellers" he called them, that Doc brought out on those occasions and touched off to keep the town awake.

I liked watching Jim Roberts in action at his wheel, and I cov-eted some of the prizes there. So much so that it was worth gam-bling a certain percentage of my nightly dollar on the chance that the wheel would stop at my number. In one year on two nights in succession, it did just that. The first time, I chose the western style cap pistol and holster set, and the second time I went for the deco-rative copper horse. I can still experience some of the incredulity and excitement I was feeling when Jim asked me what I would choose for my prize and, my heart racing, I said, "the horse." And he took it down from the display shelf next to the wheel and, with a wide-eyed expression that let me know he shared some of what I was feeling, handed it to me.

My short string of luck, however, was nothing compared to my sister Jane's run at Roll-A-Ball when she was eight or nine years old and going to the carnival with my father. Placing her nickels and dimes on various colors, she won, and she won, and she continued to win. Her streak lasted long enough to attract some notice and to convince a couple of my friends to start betting on her colors, and they won right along with her. Of all the photos and the stories and the memories of my father, nothing brings him before me more immediately and completely than my recollection of the delight he expressed throughout the years when any one of us would recall Jane's luck and excitement at winning all those games of Roll-A-Ball.

The story of those three nights is not to be conveyed simply by any tally of winnings and prizes, for much of the thrill of it all came from the chance to stay up late and to be among the crowds which were always on hand for the Rotary Carnivals. My friends and I spent much of our time there simply wandering around watching people. Sometimes word would spread that someone with great strength was wielding the hammer in such a way as to ring the bell on just about every try or that someone was mowing down whole rows of cats with blinding fastballs, and we would rush over to watch one of the older boys victoriously handing his girlfriend a stuffed animal or draping yet another paper lei around her neck. Or one of us would produce a firecracker from his pocket, one that promised to carry a tremendous charge, and we'd search out a place to set it off. Out there beyond the carnival lights where the rest of Vail Field seemed plunged in darkness, danger lurked and romance beckoned. Even from the shadows in front of the grandstand, which was about as far as some of us dared to stray, a young high school couple might be seen hand in hand disappearing into the night in the direction of the footbridge, and the shapes of older boys would be suddenly lit up by the flashes of the M-80s and cherry bombs they would be tossing around on the baseball diamond.

These explosions from out beyond the midway anticipated the fireworks display, which was set up on the third night at the far south end of the field in front of the pine trees. We looked forward to it and dreaded it simultaneously since it was grand but it signaled the end of the carnival for another year. Cars parked along the bank on South Street and poured onto Vail Field for the prime parking spots along the edges of the diamond, and the grandstand and bandstand would fill with spectators. Then the PA system would announce that the fireworks were about to begin, and the lucky pyrotechnicians, like strange, visiting gods, would be seen moving about out there in the darkness with their flares. Then the first rockets would go up and send forth their umbrellas of color and explosive flashes that would light up the whole field like summer lightning so that we could see even the houses along Maple Street and South Street. We wanted the fireworks to last forever, except that we were always waiting for the final barrage and the ground display of the American flag burning bravely and then the pause followed by the King Kong of rockets. It would leave the ground with a thud and rise end over end into the dark sky and produce one flash that would turn the field to daylight, and then a second later would come the great, once-a-year explosion that would bounce off Mt. Peg and Linden Hill and go rumbling up and down the Kedron Valley. Then the sounding of the horns and the starting of the car engines and the smoke rolling over the field and the flashlights of the auxiliary police directing traffic would mean the end of it all.

For some time after the carnival and the removal of its booths, Vail Field would wear a kind of stunned look and would seem pretty quiet. Things would be the same as they had been, but, stripped of the guise in which familiarity clothes the ordinary, different somehow. In the afternoon stillness the bright sunlight would be slanting in at a different angle, and the grandstand and bandstand would appear to rediscover each other across the suddenly widened distance between them and to settle into their accustomed repose. From the porch of the Lewises' house at 37 South Street would drift the sounds of conversation and laughter of Joe and Eva and Ozie Derr and James Thomas and Alva Hazard and other members of Woodstock's African-American community, who gathered there on their weekly afternoon off, and they would sometimes cheer us on in our practices and pickup games. But whether it was in the rose tint of the long grass along the bank or in the glimpse of the green turning to yellow on the leaves of the small elm trees along the fence by the sandbox and the slide, autumn had begun to announce itself, and we'd play all the harder to stave off thoughts of school, still, we'd remind ourselves, nearly a whole month away.

I was away from Woodstock and not greatly concerned at the time with the great changes which swept away the bandstand and the grandstand and so radically altered the look of Vail Field. If the alterations have produced a field which is less exclusively designed for baseball and better suited to a wider variety of sports and recreational activities, they have done so at a great cost in aesthetic appeal. The view out over the greensward has been brutally interrupted and obstructed by a number of ostensibly useful but distinctly unsightly structures. With no intended disrespect for Wendell Cameron, who did so much for athletics in Woodstock, the pavilion that bears his name was sprawling and unattractive when first erected and has long since taken on a haggard and delinquent look. Worse looking is the whole sagging wooden enclosure for the hockey rink. Beyond these disfigurations, the view of the grass-filled and unkempt diamond, damned with faint praise by Ken Miner as merely "playable," is spoiled by a recently erected chain-link fence running between the team benches and the baselines. By comparison to these features, there was something positively stately and classic about the old bandstand and grandstand, even in the state of disrepair which evidently spelled their doom. If the bandstand had once, in fact, stood in the park or on the old Woodstock Fairgrounds, as some suspect, that longevity alone ought to have established its claim as a historic building and to have protected it. However, it did not. A similar case might have been made for the grandstand, which had stood since before the turn of the century.

The master plan for Vail Field renovations was written up in 1967 by then Rec Center Director Ron Packard, who lived in Woodstock for some five years. In it Packard said, "As people drive by Vail Field, it is easy to spot the old grandstand looking the same as it has for years and years." Presumably that was the intention of its designers and builders. He went on to say that "it has become an eyesore and a health hazard to the many people who use the field." That it was, in fact, dangerous in its last days can be verified by the testimony of parents who worried about their children playing in and around it. Marge Vail, whose daughter Laurel received a nasty cut from an exposed nail, was relieved when the grandstand was finally razed. However, buildings that are neglected do have a way, eventually, of displaying that neglect and becoming hazardous. At the conclusion of his report, which to any native with a place in his heart for Vail Field, ironically argues more strongly for the preservation than for the destruction of the grandstand, Packard assured the people of the village that its demolition would present no problem, for "the Woodstock Area Jaycees...are ready and willing to do this immediately." Thus, late in 1967, the old grandstand, which Benton Dryden spoke of as having "withstood the ravages of time, except when the 1938 hurricane moved it two feet," was finally not strong enough to withstand the enthusiasm of a group of civic-minded Jaycees. And down it came. There was little public opposition. The committee for the renovation of Vail Field was already busily debating what sort of structure would take its place. Among their priorities was the specification that it "be as nearly vandal-proof as possible." Indeed, in reducing the Vail Field grandstand to a pile of rubble, they may have felt a dim awareness of having set a dangerous precedent, and their concern about vandalism was probably well-advised.

At the time that all these changes were being made, I was, it seems to me now, strangely unmoved. Not until some twenty years later did I share some of my father's sadness and dismay over the loss of those two historic buildings and the disappearance of the old Vail Field. It happened on a spring afternoon in the late 1980s in Middlebury, Connecticut, when my son Jonathan asked me if I would hit him some pop flies so he could get in some practice before the opening of the little league season. I picked up a bat and three or four baseballs that were floating around in our sports closet, and we walked down to the playing fields of Westover School. At first it didn't go so well. I couldn't get the right angle with the bat and kept hitting him grounders and line drives. Then when they started rising, Jon began to experience the difficulty of judging a fly ball. I talked to him and sympathized with him, and gradually he began to get the hang of it. Then I experienced one of those uncanny moments of transference which are so well known to sons who in their turn have become fathers. Suddenly it seemed to me as though I was my father and that my son out there punching his glove and waiting for the next one was I myself, and I was speaking words of advice and encouragement in my father's voice and gripping the bat with my father's hands. But not just my father's, for as we continued working at it and I cheered him on and tried serving up the ball to myself with my opposite hand, other men of my father's generation — Ed Potwin and Chick Wells, but particularly Ken Miner — began getting their hands and voices into it as well. I was feeling my identity strangely parceled out and very much enlarged in my being simultaneously my father and my coaches on the one hand and my son on the other. And even though I was in Connecticut, I began to sense the old Vail Field assuming a kind of illusory presence around us, the grandstand at my back as Poppa and I and my coaches hit flies, the grandstand out there in front of me behind the plate as Jon and I made the catches and threw the ball back in.

Since that day I have often found it difficult to realize that Vail Field as my father and brother and sister knew and loved it back then now exists only in memory. Nothing brings it back more fully and lights up those days more vividly than the faces and the words of baseball players of that time. Up at the high school in West Woodstock on Alumni Day of 1997, I was watching with Morgan Vail a sort of pickup game between some members of the high school team and a team made up of a group of their predecessors. As we were talking about the old days on Vail Field, we noticed among the alumni players a tall man in shorts who had been hitting the ball solidly but whose somewhat labored base-running suggested that he was of a somewhat earlier vintage than most of his twenty to thirty-year-old teammates. Thinking against all logic that he might be someone of my generation, I walked down to the bench to investigate and was stunned to see that it was a remarkably fit and youthful looking Tom Flower, Morgan's teammate who had caught both games in Wichita in 1950. Later that day I found him in the park, and shortly after that, I visited him at his home in Enfield, Connecticut. During the course of the afternoon that we spent reminiscing and going back over it all, Tom recalled with great fondness Vail Field as it used to be and spoke of missing the old bandstand and grandstand when he went back to Woodstock. A healthy septuagenarian with a lovely wife and five sons, he is forward-looking man with few regrets. Still, just as I was leaving, he re-vealed something that seemed to have always been on his mind: "I've had a good life," he said, "but when I think back to Wichita, I think that maybe I should have delayed college and just gone to Florida and tried out everywhere. If Bernie [Carr] could make it, I could have too." I told him that I could recall my father saying that he was a much better catcher than Bernie. He nodded his head slowly with a sort of faraway look in his eyes and then told me that he had enjoyed our talk. On my way home as I was thinking over our conversation, I was reminded of a morning in the summer of 1993 that I spent with George Goodrow, who pitched for the legion team in the 1940s and acted as the manager for the team that went to Wichita. It was the day after his 81st birthday, and we had been sitting in the basement of the Historical Society, going through photographs of old Woodstock and talking baseball. As we left by the back door to go to lunch, we stood there for a moment looking out over the back lawn to the banks of the Ottauquechee and to Mt. Tom. Thinking back to what we had covered that morning and no doubt to much more besides, George, it seems to me, spoke for a great many people when he said, "That was a long time ago, but those were great days. I wouldn't trade the memory of them for anything."

Neither would I.

Pember Inn

Memory is the sense of loss,
and pulls us after it.
MARILYNNE ROBINSON

The large brick house which sits behind the white fence at 11 Church Street used to identify itself by a small sign hanging over the front porch as Pember Inn. It was owned and operated by Anna Brockway Pember (1884-1969), a short, white-haired lady in her sixties who was the widow of Karl Pember, former Windsor County Clerk. Mrs. Pember let three rooms on the second floor on a more or less long-term basis to respectable people who had seasonal employment in Woodstock or who were retired and wished to live for a time in what was then a quiet village, and she served one meal a day, a very good home-cooked dinner. She drew her clientele from places in and outside the village. In fact, the variety of people seated there at her tables for dinner was a tribute to her culinary skills. The diminutive and proper Mrs. Winslow, a neighbor at 6 College Hill, and her boarder Miss Evelyn Hunt, an artist and somewhat of a poet who taught French and English at the high school, regularly dined there, as did other members of the Woodstock High School faculty such as long time history teacher Dorothy Cook and her boarder Earl Beaudette, a young biology teacher and ski enthusiast; and Kenneth Liggett, a lantern-jawed, white-haired industrial arts teacher who always looked somewhat incomplete to me, seated at the table without his shop apron on. Mrs. Lola Renton, retired kindergarten teacher, and Bea Vincent, an equestrian who taught riding at Ferguson's Stables, were often there; and, for a time, the regular attendance of massive, bull-chested Nicholas Hashey, who taught science and coached football at the high school, attested to the quantity as well as the quality of Mrs. Pember's evening fare. A gregarious young man who wore bright red vests, drove a yellow and red '53 Buick convertible, Flashy Hashey, as he became known, gained great popularity with his gym classes for introducing them to a ridiculously rough and chaotic outdoor game (no doubt of his own creation) called Miami Beach Murder. During his brief time in Woodstock, he added considerable vivacity and color to the dining room at Pember Inn. Also, a number of students from John Doscher's Country School of Photography in South Woodstock took their dinner there. These included Barbara Larsen, who went on to run and then to own the school, and George Hutchins, a quirky and oddly brilliant gentleman who boarded for a time at Pember Inn and was discouraged from performing the music of his favorite composers on the front room piano because his bursts of inspiration produced nothing but fortissimo.

Memory has its own time which is not to be reckoned by the adding up of years. I estimate my association with Pember Inn to have lasted about twelve years from roughly 1951, when I was nine years old, until 1963, when I was twenty-one; but in my experience the number of those years means nothing because they were endless and because I have continued to dwell in them all of my life. I came to know Mrs. Pember and her house through her grandson, George Pearsons. We were classmates from first grade through our second year at the University of Vermont and close friends throughout these years until his untimely death in an automobile accident on 24 December 1962.

George lived much of the time with his grandmother, and he made his spending money waiting on table at the evening meals that she prepared and issued from her old-fashioned kitchen. They called this job "serving," and over the years George had to cut short many after-school activities — such as bowling or playing basketball at the Rec Center or, later on, "backroading" in his black '53 Chevy or listening to our favorite 45 rpm records — to go and serve. That obligation entailed setting several tables in the dining room of Pember Inn, after which there was usually a short time for him to practice the piano or for us to play catch or to wrestle on the side lawn or just to sit around and talk before it was time for me to go home to supper and for him to change into his dark pants and white shirt in preparation for his duties when Mrs. Pember's dinner guests arrived. I would often be back before the end of dinner, and over the years I spent a good deal of time waiting for George to finish serving. Sometimes I would occupy that time in the attic, which consisted of two rooms, the small front one where George slept at the top of the narrow staircase, and a larger one that functioned as a storeroom, although its double bed meant that it could be used as a bedroom. It had a palladian window looking westward and a back window that afforded a splendid northward view of Mt. Tom. This room and the closet between the two rooms were filled with boxes and trunks and garments long since out of fashion and hats and parasols and picture frames. The single permanent inhabitant of the attic was an old-fashioned clothing store manikin named Lil, who for years was the object of our derision. I recall her being most impressively attired on an occasion when, unbeknownst to Mrs. Pember, we took her out for a ride in George's car. She occupied the space between us in the front seat, stretched like a plank, her heals touching the floor, her neck resting on the back of the seat, in her permanent state of rigor mortis, her dumb stare fixed on the car's ceiling. We drove around town entreating her to relax, reminding her that she was not in a dentist's chair, and comparing her to some of our most unsuccessful dates.

More often my times at Pember Inn were spent in the large front room, which was the parlor or sitting room. It was a beautiful room in its way, one of the great interiors which continue to occupy an intimate and unfading place in my memory. It was entered through glass-paneled doors off the front hall with its banistered staircase and landing. The single, most memorable furnishing of this front room was its immense, antique, gilt-framed mirror, which gave back at various angles, the piano, the paintings, the mantelpiece, the couch and the stuffed furniture, the coffee table, and the bookcases. In a slightly clouded fashion it seemed to affirm the room's air of civilized hospitality and its suggestion of slightly faded grandeur, especially when the warm circles of lamplight and the shadows in the corners gave the room a Rembrandt look of brown and burnished gold.

The house's cultured, antique atmosphere was, I suppose, partly inherited and partly created by Mrs. Pember, or "Gram," as George fondly called her. A graduate of Mt. Holyoke College, she maintained an interest in the arts and carried on a life-long love of classical music. Although her high-pitched voice crackled somewhat and suggested no musical timbre, she was an avid listener and, like my father, a silent whistler. I often saw her on her rounds in her dining room or plodding from her kitchen to her small first floor bedroom, her white hair drawn back into its perennial bun, her dark eyes attentive to her tasks, and her lips slightly parted and pursed as though whistling some silent melody. In the late afternoon and in the evening after dinner, she sat in the front room in a chair drawn up before her large high fidelity radio-record player, listening to her favorite programs of recorded music. She preferred the romantic composers, as I recall, and she very much encouraged George in his musical inclinations, requiring that he dutifully practice her piano in preparation for his lessons.

Her grandson and my friend George Pearsons was, I suppose,

very much influenced by his grandmother and her house. From my first experiences with him, I think I sensed that he was extraordinary in his way, and, looking back now, I realize that he was unique. So much so that in the forty-odd years since his death, I have found substitutes for him but never a replacement, and the deepest friendships I have enjoyed seem curious offshoots of my friendship with George. His grade school teachers and we, his classmates, recognized his intelligence in his mathematical ability, his talent in spelling bees, his musical ability and his overall quickness and retention in all subjects, which eventually resulted in his graduating salutatorian of our high school class, the class of 1960. He even had a penchant for comic verse which blossomed in response to an assignment made by Guy Musetti, our eighth grade English teacher. Mr. Musetti asked each of us to write a poem, however brief, to assist us in our study of poetry. The results, which were compiled and printed in mimeograph copies under the title *Poems by Eighth Grade 1956*, were distinguished by brevity, by innumerable cliches, and by a startling lack of originality, and eleven out of the thirty were titled "Autumn Sunrise." With some reluctance, I offer my own efforts as an example.

The Graveyard

Sullen and cold lies the graveyard,
Weird shadows, strange objects lie within.
The playground of the dead grows darker,
All is quiet but the sound of the wind.

Pretty dreadful. Among those that Musetti selected to read in class, the favorite was George's:

Never Put a Frog in Auntie's Bed

You can come to the table
As dirty as you please,
Or lock the family car all up
And go and lose the keys.

You can choke your sister's favorite cat
Until he is half dead,
But never! Just never put
A frog in Auntie's bed!

You can push your sissy cousin
Into a muddy brook,
Or lock your room and stay up
All night reading comic books.

You can run across the village square
When you know the light is red,
But please! Don't ever
Put a frog in Auntie's bed!

You can put the table salt
Into the sugar bowl
Or smash the baby carriage
Into a telephone pole.

You can drop your mother's antique vase
Onto your father's head,
But never, never, never put
A frog in Auntie's bed!

For if you do this deed, my friends,
This will happen to you:
Ma'll thrash you and Pa'll thrash you
Until your face is blue,

And you'll have to hit the sack that
Night without being fed.
So you see you shouldn't ever put
A frog in Auntie's bed!

Such doggerel was very much the envy and the delight of us lesser lights, and I remember that we asked for several encores.

Among the rest of us in the class, many of whom must have seemed plodders next to him, George was not stigmatized by his success in school as he might have been had he been a different sort of person. From first grade on, he was as rough and tumble as the rest of us. He rode his 18-inch bike with the right sort of recklessness, and even though he was prone to prolonged nosebleeds, he never shied from coming in low for tackles in our pickup games of football. He was one of the best gymnasts in our class because he had some natural ability at "tumbling," as we used to call it, but also because he was not afraid of getting hurt. Thinking of George as he was even in grade school, I recognize in his character that kind of fearlessness which is the essence of true courage. Pacifistic by nature, he was not afraid to avoid a fight, but if it was unavoidable, he waded directly in, no matter what the odds. He showed the same fearlessness in his friendships. In our first years in grade school our teachers would sometimes ask us, as either a written or an oral exercise or both, to name and describe our best friend. I was always surprised not so much by the number as by the variety of my classmates, popular or unpopular, shy or outgoing, who wrote down "Georgie Pearsons." This was not wishful thinking on their part as much as it was their acknowledgment of the courage and generosity of spirit which permitted him to spend time with some of the more isolated members of our class and to find the goodness in them. And he was resourceful. Whereas I had ongoing childhood dreams of building a soapbox and entering it in a derby and of constructing a raft like Huck's and Jim's and living on it and floating down the Ottauquechee, but never got much past the dreaming stage with these, George decided that he wanted a doodlebug, so he made one. He built it out of scrap wood and carriage wheels and powered it with a lawn mower engine attached to the rear wheels. It had an accelerator and a brake and a steering mechanism, and best of all, he let his friends drive it. I remember having my first go in the driveway of Pember Inn and of George's driving it on the sidewalks all the way down to our house on Pleasant Street one spring night. We took it down to Frost's Mill and drove it around the front yard in a circular track around the telephone pole until it was nearly dark and we had used up all but the amount of gasoline he estimated he would need to get home. Years later the same resourcefulness helped George and Bob Summers get through a hopeless weekend evening. Stuck at Pember Inn without a car, without dates, and without any prospect of entertainment, and bored as only teenagers can be bored in such circumstances, they decided to see whether they could stretch a worn out t-shirt of George's from the front of Pember Inn to the Town Hall. They somehow made appropriate measurements and were astonished by the distance. Then they spent hours carefully and methodically tearing up the tee shirt into tinier and tinier strips and tied them together and then ran their long strand of tattered white cotton threads down the sidewalk past the Universalist Church, and I think they just might have made it.

We were especially impressed with George's musical ability. By the age of eight, George played the piano so well that our third grade teacher, Mrs. Stinson, who had a piano in her classroom, enjoyed hearing him perform as much as we did. Occasionally, on days when we had finished our lessons early, she would give ear to our requests that George be allowed to play, if he was agreeable, which he sometimes was not, or at least he pretended that he was not. One of his objections was that our requests — from everyone in unison before he had even begun to adjust the piano stool — were always the same: "The Indian War Dance." After keeping us waiting through a piece that he had just learned, he would usually accede, and we would once again thrill to the strains of "The Indian War Dance," a piece that Mrs. Stinson worked into our social studies unit on the American Indian and made the occasion of a public performance at the old Woodstock Inn. I remember her resolutely leading our group of timid third-graders up South Street during lunch hour to perform for the Rotary Club our circular war dance on the carpet in the lobby of the inn. George was at his best on the piano, and he was backed by Don Eaton, sitting cross-legged and playing a tom-tom made at Camp Kitchigamink and wearing a long feathered headdress that was the envy of all of us who sported single feathers and shuffled and pranced a most pacific and stage-frightened preparation for massacre. During George's classroom performances and practice sessions, we were always asking him to "play flat." He would respond by adopting a very serious expression and dignified carriage at the piano and playing a few bars, and then somehow when we least expected it, he would begin hitting occasional notes and chords out of key and accompanying them by appropriately pained expressions on his face until we were hysterical or until Mrs. Stinson indulgently put a stop to this nonsense. The song that I was most eager to hear him play was "La Paloma," The Dove. Of the melodies that continually drift back into my consciousness and bring with them entire lost vistas of rooms and streets and times of day and people, that one is perhaps the most evocative. Under its spell I am once again in our third grade class room in the front, northeast corner of the first floor of the grade school on South Street under the stern but benevolent eye of Mrs. Stinson, listening with rapt attention to George's hands doing different things — his left playing the continuo, his right playing the melody of "La Paloma." In later years during high school and college, George's interest in music led him to play at times with Chick Wells' orchestra and to join up with Pete Wells, on drums, and Jim Raymond, on trumpet, in a combo that played dinner time or dance music around the Woodstock area. They made what was perhaps their most memorable appearance in the 1961 Alumni Day parade. The theme that year was cities, and our class decided to do a float depicting Newport, Rhode Island, by staging our own miniature jazz festival. We put the combo on the back of a flatbed truck and dressed in beatnik fashion as their audience, accompanying them on assorted bongo and congo drums. I can still hear the cheering crowds and see George bent over the piano as we drew into the square, his tan hat with the front brim turned up tilted down over his eyes, his hands flying over the keys, and Jim leaning back blowing his brains out to keep up with Pete's furious tempo and to make themselves heard over his pounding drum rolls.

Mrs. Pember showed a partiality toward musicians and often attended concerts given locally at the high school gym or at the Woodstock Inn. In the early 1950s in the summer season, the Woodstock Inn Trio gave weekly concerts in the ballroom of the inn. The windows of the room were left open for purposes of ventilation and for the enjoyment of the guests sitting on the porch, and I remember riding my bike or walking home from Vail Field with my father on long summer evenings and hearing strains of Brahms and Mozart and Boccherini drifting out over the green. Mrs. Pember sometimes asked George to accompany her to these concerts, and he sometimes talked me into going along. Unlike her two nine-

year-old companions squirming in their nearly identical green cor-
duroy sport coats, Mrs. Pember attended these evenings out of interest but also, I suspect, out of a sense of obligation to the musicians, one of which, Josephine Treml, was George's piano teacher.
Miss Treml for a time occupied an apartment on the top floor of
the old Tracy Block, which was destroyed by fire in May of 1971.
She was a short, bright-eyed, round-faced woman who radiated energy and spoke English with a Hungarian accent. Her apartment
left a deep impression on me. It was, as I realized many years
later, the first loft apartment I had ever seen, and it had the first
skylight I had ever seen, and that skylight was open to the summer
air and to an evening view of yellow and orange sky over Mt. Tom.
I am reminded of my first view of that apartment by stage sets for
La Boheme, for as well as being a musician of some accomplish-
ment, Miss Treml was a painter of sorts. Scattered about in the
large space around her baby grand piano were a number of easels
with half finished canvasses of both representational and abstract
composition, and several palettes and brushes and paintings caught
the western light that poured into the room. The music that by
curious patterns of association brings back to me both this room
and the front room of Pember Inn, one sometimes superimposed
on the other, is the theme from the movie *Moulin Rouge*, the story
of the life of the French painter Toulouse-Lautrec, and the movie
posters from the Town Hall enter that picture too. I only saw Miss
Treml's apartment before George's lessons since she advised me to
wait outside until they were finished. Given our capacity for foolishness, this was a wise decision on her part. As a result, I passed
the lesson time sitting on the front steps of the Tracy Block watching the nighthawks climb the air behind the Woodstock National
Bank and then dive toward the roofs of the shops on that side of
Central Street with a strange whooshing, air-splitting sound.

  In the Woodstock Inn Trio Miss Treml was accompanied by

violinist Beatrice Griffin, an austere looking woman with pale skin and very black hair who lived for a time in the back apartment at 10 Court Street, and by cellist Willem Durieux. Mr. Durieux, or "Mr. D" or, as he was more popularly known among most school children, "The Mouse Man," was very much the object of our attention wherever he happened to be. I think he lived in New York City in the winter, and he spent his summers in Woodstock, usually renting a room for at least part of the season at Pember Inn. He spoke English with a pronounced Dutch accent, and he was an extraordinary looking man who we used to think looked like George Washington. With his bristling mane of receding, white hair swept back from his forehead and his prominent hook nose and his twinkling eyes, he looked every inch the maestro, bearing a resemblance to both Stokowski and Toscanini. From his craggy face and his hair he might have been a man in his seventies, but from his enthusiasm and vitality he was youthful, ageless. He wore loose fitting summer suits of seersucker or linen and short-sleeved white shirts without a tie, and he usually carried an umbrella. His brisk constitutionals around the village from early summer on often brought him by the grade school playground, where he was instantly recognized and greeted by flocks of adoring children: "It's the Mouse Man!" He gained this nickname from a trick with which my father used to entertain my brother and me, but with which most children were unfamiliar. He would take out a clean, folded pocket handkerchief and, by rapidly rolling and tucking, fashion it into a mouse which he would hold in his hand and pat and stroke and then encourage the children to do the same, and always when they least expected it, he would make the mouse jump toward them, startling them and provoking delighted squeals of surprise and laughter. On summer mornings he would often appear at playground on Vail Field, where he would join our games of four-square or challenge the best tetherball players like Jane Barnard or Bing Watson in strenuous matches in which he showed a great competitive spirit and demonstrated considerable quickness and agility. He loved children and enjoyed himself thoroughly around them in his old world manner without losing a bit of his dignity.

We heard Mr. D occasionally practicing the cello in his upstairs room at Pember Inn, and knowing him as we did made performances of the Woodstock Inn Trio somewhat more interesting. I say "somewhat" because George and I faced those musical evenings with an odd mixture of dismay and expectation. In spite of our fascination at being in the Woodstock Inn, of entering and passing through its magnificent lobby and down along the corridor to the ballroom, we were certain to become bored with the performance, I more quickly than George. In that certainty lay our tacit hope of becoming silly and yet of being able to stifle our hilarity in such a way that Mrs. Pember would not notice the ridiculous faces that we were flashing at each other. She was, in a way, our straight man. Mrs. Pember's presence and her disapproval of our nonsense were both a temptation and a risk, and we were prey to both. Not that she herself did not have a sense of humor; very much the reverse. In fact, it was her inability to become as annoyed with us as she might have liked and thus the possibility of cracking her composure and compromising her authority that often egged us on.

George had a gift for the comic, and some of his best moments came out of that peculiar combination of forgetfulness and impulsiveness which is the essence of slapstick humor. I remember him asking me once, completely apropos of nothing, "Did you know that it is the impurities in black pepper that make you sneeze?" One summer day during our college years when George and I were working for Paul and Paul, Painters, we were given the task of painting the porch ceiling of what was at that time the Hedley house on Cloudland Road. It was a great high ceiling, and I watched in disbelief as George, his mind altogether elsewhere, came walking around the house carrying a three-foot stepladder, his brush, and a bucket of paint. He stepped onto the porch, set up the ladder, walked up its three steps, dipped his brush, and *then* looked up... to find that even his longest reach would leave him some six feet short of the ceiling. In somewhat the same manner, he once managed to run out of gas twice in one day. I remember George's telling me of Ralph Tracy's surprise when he pulled into Tracy's Esso and asked him for 25 cents' worth of regular before setting out for White River. And I remember something about his thumbing a ride and getting a gallon can and enough gas to get back to Woodstock. Once back, he looked me up, and we came up with 50 cents. We took it down to the somewhat bewildered but still good-natured Mr. Tracy. Secure in the knowledge that he was purchasing twice as much as before, and now smart enough not to set out on a long trip, George was cruising around town when suddenly, to his astonishment, his car chugged to a stop on River Street, out of gas again.

In some ways, George was curiously wise beyond his years. He was the first person I knew who hated television, and he refused, on principle, to watch it. Unlike the rest of us, he was never one to squander money on soda pop and candy bars and what has come to be known as junk food. In fact, he once gave me a lecture on how foolish it was to go around making repeated stops to purchase things to eat when better food could be gotten for nothing three times a day at home. Since he was not one to snack and he preferred his grandmother's cooking to anything else, he always had a hard time in diners and snack bars. For some reason, whether he felt compelled to order or he simply allowed himself to forget that he really didn't want anything, he would study the menu with great indecision and still be studying it after the rest of us had placed our orders, and sometimes we would be half way through our meal by the time he made some choice. When it arrived, more often than not he would regard it with some surprise, and, realizing that it was something that he had no interest in eating or drinking, he would sample it and then rely on one of us to finish it for him. Without at all intending to be, George was often at his funniest during some of these moments. A typical one occurred on the way back from one of our frequent trips to Hanover when we were in high school. We liked to drive there primarily to listen to records in the listening booth at the Dartmouth Music Store and to treat ourselves to a sundae at Eastman's Drugstore. But we also seldom left Hanover without stopping at the Dartmouth Smoke Shop for a few Puerto Rican crooks — particularly noxious rippled cigars that had been dipped in rum and cost a nickel. They gave off an acrid smell and left a cloying, sweet taste on the lips and in the throat, but since they were for some reason essential to our image at that time, we smoked them, often. On this particular day, we had forgone Eastman's in favor of a quart of Pepsi and a large bag of potato chips, each. We lit up the crooks, opened the Pepsis and the two bags of chips, arranged everything on the front seat of George's Chevy, and happily headed home. George's small hat was perched squarely on his head very much like Art Carney's in *The Honeymooners*. Halfway down the long hill on Route 120 out of Hanover, the combination of the salt from the chips and the rum from the crook hit him. When a long swig of Pepsi, which wasn't particularly cold, complicated rather than alleviated the situation, he turned to me with a look of revulsion and shock (why had he purchased any one of these items, let alone all three?), expressed his displeasure with a long gagging sound, and pitched the chips and cigar out the car window. Then he turned the entire quart upside down and let it stream out behind us along the road.

In thirty years of walks through the village, I have seldom passed Pember Inn without at least slowing my step to look and to remember. And my gaze is always directed upward from the fence to the windows of the front room of the attic. One afternoon when Mrs. Pember was taking a nap, we somehow ran her garden hose straight up the front of the house from the spigot to one of those third floor windows, and for a half hour or so we gave free car washes, whether they were wanted or not, to all the cars that passed in the street below. We were having a great time until we hit Byron Kelly in his convertible, top down, and soon afterwards received a surprise visit from policeman Elio Paglia. When we saw the cruiser pull up, we dropped the hose, slammed the window, and after some terrified confusion during which we realized that his knocking, if it were allowed to go on, might arouse Mrs. Pember, George answered the front door to greet him while we cowered at the top of the stairs. "Pag," who was never more than one step behind us and often, as we would discover to our chagrin, several steps ahead of us, simply regarded him for a moment and said, "It looks like your grandmother has a leak in her hose." When George, gazing in feigned amazement at the dripping front porch, the sodden lawn, the drenched strip of sidewalk, and the stream running from the middle of Route 4 to the front steps, began trying to express some innocent surprise and concern, Pag far less casually cut him off with, "FIX IT!" George's rejoinder was the only one possible in these circumstances — a sudden coming clean and a nervously muttered "Yes, sir."

Anyone fortunate enough to have known George Pearsons as a child and a youth and a young man would certainly have remembered him for his warm and generous and inclusive sense of humor, for that was a constant and continuing element in his character and his life. But those of us who knew him best loved him for other of his qualities as well: for example, his lack of any sort of affectation. He was simply no good at pretence, as some of us found out when we tried to teach him to fake laughter in order to help himself into the good graces of a girlfriend's father who continually cracked corny jokes. We coached George, but he simply could not bring it off. His attempts were appalling — they looked ridiculous and sounded worse. I went along with him once to pick up his date and sat on the side steps on the other side of the father, and at each bad punch line found myself having to do double duty to cover George's stony silence. I went into prolonged spasms of loud, raucous laughter until my jaws ached from the strain, all the while pleading with my eyes for help from George, but to no avail. He said later that he envied my capacities, but he just could not do it. And, reluctant as I was to admit it, he couldn't.

George was as deep as he was true, and because of what was perhaps his most remarkable quality, his openness, his depths were clear and visible, and his friends opened up to him. I remember his bounding down the stairs from his piano lesson at Miss Treml's early one fall evening and meeting me where he had left me on the front steps of the Tracy Block, tossing a football up and catching it. We were in the third or fourth grade at the time. I said, "If I had one wish, I think I would wish that football was a year-round sport." He smiled and said, "I know what you mean." I asked him what his would be. He looked at me self-consciously and then looked away and muttered, "World peace, I guess." There it was. He didn't want to upstage me or to expose himself with a non sequitur, but he couldn't speak less than the truth. I felt momentarily abashed, but because it was George, I thought a great deal about what a fine answer it was and may have even felt better for the reminder that there was a world out there.

George had a speculative mind and both the fearlessness to speak straight from the heart and the warmth to encourage others to do the same. On weekend nights when I would sometimes sleep over in his room up in the attic of Pember Inn, two floors above Mrs. Pember's bedroom, we could carry on pretty much as we were inclined, especially when there were no boarders in the front room beneath us. We would wrestle and sneak downstairs to search for doughnuts and explore the spare room and sometimes consult Lil or encourage her to strike poses in front of the window, and we would talk. We talked late into the night about everything — about movies, for we went often to the Town Hall Theatre; about girls; about sports; about music, particularly after we had been swept up by the first wave of rock and roll; about space travel; about life and death, and we wondered out loud about time and God and the dimensions of the universe. Sometimes I think I could divide up all the people I know into two groups — the vast majority who outgrow, pretty early, the fascination of these sorts of discussions, and a minority who, heaven be praised, never outgrow it. Most of us when we are young have these sorts of talks, sleeping out in a field with a friend, maybe, looking up at the stars, before those social personas which come along around age twelve begin to control us and shrink our thoughts and make us wary of exposure. Because George and I had known each other since we were six, the social factor was never of much importance between us. We trusted each other. In one another's company we could always open the floodgate so that throughout the years from childhood into college we kept up a sometimes punctuated but never fully interrupted flow in which candor was the norm and silence was never awkward. These conversations cost us innumerable hours of sleep in Pember Inn and, later, in our apartment in Burlington when we were at UVM, but they were well worth it. They were, in fact, milestones, and they have remained directives in the life which it has been my lot to lead.

My last clear images of George come from the late summer and autumn of the last year of his life. One of our close friends,

168

Ron Hively, had decided to take a leave from the University of Vermont and spend his junior year studying at the Sorbonne in Paris. On his last night in Woodstock, we all went up to his house to say goodbye to him, and then, unbeknownst to him, we assembled at Pember Inn to prepare a surprise for him. We made a huge sign which said something like "Good Luck, Hively" and stretched it between two long poles, and we packed a box of supplies for him which included several packs of American cigarettes, a couple of quarts of Pepsi, some candy bars, potato chips, etc. We tipped off his parents, who would be driving him to New York to catch the boat, and found out what time we could intercept them on their way out of Woodstock the next morning. Since Ronnie had been part of a similar sendoff two years earlier when Bob Summers had left to join the Navy, and therefore might be anticipating a repeat performance, we decided to set up our surprise down in Taftsville. We assumed that by the time he had gotten that far from town he would have given up on us if he had been expecting anything. We assembled everything by the gas pumps at the Taftsville Store, posted a watch, and then, when we saw the car approaching, rushed into the middle of Route 4. My brother and Bob Summers stretched the sign across the road, and George and I cavorted and danced beneath it. The surprise was complete. Carl Hively pulled the car over to the side of the road; we presented Ronnie with the gifts and wished him well in Paris, and that was that. There was no camera to capture anything of this, as it turned out to be, last meeting of five friends, but my memory, oddly, carries something like two different cinematic "takes" of the sequence. The first is recorded, as it were, by a hand-held camera from the point of view of one of us in the midst of our activity and gives a series of closeups that preserve the immediacy of it all — the surprise and gratitude on Ronnie's face; the amusement on the faces of his parents, Carl and Cecile Hively; the sort of embarrassed excitement of each of us there along the side of the road. And there is a slightly longer still shot of hands, particularly George's and Ronnie's, joined in fare-well handshakes through the open window of the car. But the second take, which did not begin to assume a shape in my mind until a year or so after the event, offers a kind of aerial view as though shot from a helicopter hovering over Route 4 where the small stream runs into the Ottauquechee just west of the center of Taftsville. In it, the morning mist has just risen from the river, and there is no traffic on the road. A green Ford approaches Taftsville from the west, and a small group suddenly appears from the front of the Daniel Taft, Jr. House and scurries into the road. There is a brief flurry of activity; then the Ford pulls over, and the group follows it to the side of the road for a moment. Then it pulls away to resume its journey. The group packs its mummery into another car and passes under the camera on its way back to Woodstock, and the road is empty once gain, and the town is quiet. From such a height it was hard to identify anyone specifically and impossible to hear anything of what was said. Except for the way in which one death reduces us all and makes us aware of the small, uncertain place we occupy in the final scheme of things, I have no explanation for this second sequence, shot, as it were, from such a height.

It was later that autumn that George and I spent our last full day together. We had both dropped out of college after two years, with the intention of somehow going to Europe for a spell before returning to our studies and finishing up our degrees. I was spend-ing the fall painting rooms in the old Woodstock Inn in its off-season, and George was living with his sister, Bev, and her hus-band in Bridgeport, Connecticut, and working for Sikorsky Air-craft. Hoping to book passage on a tramp steamer for some mid-winter or early spring sailing, we got together in late October, just two months or so before his death, and drove to Montreal to talk to steamship companies along the docks of the St. Lawrence. They were not encouraging because of the labor unions, and throughout a long and disappointing day we walked and drove for miles around the city before more or less giving up and heading home to review our options. The long drive back was made longer by our taking a wrong turn and going nearly 90 miles northwest out of Montreal before discovering our mistake. Fatigued, we switched drivers repeatedly on the way home on Route 7, and when necessary relied on plenty of lunacy and nonsense to stay awake. Prior to that day we had not seen each other for two months, and from the beginning of the trip to the end, we talked nonstop about everything. Somewhere outside of Brandon — I can still recognize the place — we pulled over to stretch and light up a couple of Pall Malls. I had been spending evenings in September and October plowing through Dostoevsky, and George, somewhat disillusioned at least with the engineering side of mathematics in his work at Sikorsky, had been working on Melville in his spare time. Our conversation had turned toward what was becoming to us the fascinating problem of literary symbolism. Though it must have been nighttime by then, I picture us standing outside George's Plymouth in the cold, late autumn twilight air, looking out across a flat, rocky pasture at a darkening bank of clouds piling up in the western sky. George was talking about *Moby Dick* and pondering the biblical significance of the moment when the Pequod meets the whaling ship Rachel, which has been rammed by the great white whale and is wandering in search of her lost children of the sea. That day we had run the full range of what we had been up to for years, from hilarity to this moment beside the road, which must have lasted nearly an hour and which I think was one of our finest, and I remember thinking, "Here is truly a man for all seasons."

I don't remember when I last saw Mrs. Pember, but I know that I never saw her after she sold Pember Inn and moved into the Homestead, where she spent the last years of her life. Two incidents comprise my final recollections of her. Several months after George's death, she told my father that she would like to see me when I was home from college. On the first opportunity, I went up to Pember Inn one spring afternoon and found Mrs. Pember looking a good deal like her old self. The expression that I had seen in her forehead and in her dark eyes on the day of George's death, a look of bewildered anguish that altered her whole countenance, had passed. We talked in the sunlit dining room. I recall her sitting straight up in a chair pulled aside from one of the tables as she always sat when she was listening to her programs of recorded music. She asked me about my studies and my academic interests, and we talked of George. She asked me if I had dreamed of him, and told me that after her husband's death she had made some inquiry into spiritualism, without much satisfaction. She said that George had not yet appeared in any of her dreams. This struck me as very much the sort of conversation he and I had had on many occasions, and I was flattered by her interest. George had, as I told Mrs. Pember, appeared in my dreams, and the pattern was always the same: I'd have come to Pember Inn to see him for the first time in a long while, and I was unsure of where he had been. I would always have to wait a few minutes for him to come down from upstairs or outdoors, and when he came into the room, he was the same in some ways but different in others. For one thing, he was there for only a short stay and was unwilling or unable to tell me where he had been or where he was going. I felt shy and inadequate around him and reluctant to ask him some half-formed question which seemed dreadfully important but which I could not articulate. And nothing in his face or manner encouraged me to find the words, for he was peculiarly reticent and closed — the absolute opposite of what I had always known him to be. Mrs. Pember told me that the important thing was our memories of him as he had been. I agreed, and had I known then what I have subsequently come to realize, I'd have told her that I find a great difference between the ongoing presence of the dead in our lives and their occasional appearances in our dreams. When they come to us in dreams, they sometimes carry a strangeness about them that reminds me that whatever death may be said to be, it is not life; it is the antithesis of life, and dreams are one of the ways in which the otherness of death assays to communicate itself to us. Our true relations with the dead are carried in moments of full, waking consciousness when, in the midst of the activities and details of common life — reading or drying the dishes or just looking out a window — they are suddenly felt to be with us, and those moments always seem to carry with them a kind of blessing, which may be received as grace.

I remember seeing Mrs. Pember for what was perhaps the last time sometime later in my college years. We met by chance early one afternoon on the sidewalk between the A&P, where she had been shopping, and Nalibow's Drug Store. I saw her first and greeted her. She was wearing a dark skirt and light colored blouse and carrying her shopping bag full of groceries. We stood very close so as not too take up too much space on the sidewalk, and I remember realizing how short she was or how tall I had grown from the way I looked down and she looked up while we were talking. I was glad to see her, and I knew right away for some reason that she was glad to see me. As I recall, she asked me about my activities and my future plans and inquired after some of George's other friends. It was, I think, a moment in which words were incidental to something that I sensed passing between us. Whatever information and pleasantries we exchanged were, for me, submerged in the sense of respect and affection I felt for her. I remember her hair drawn back in its bun, her upper lip tight across her teeth, and in her dark eyes I saw something at once searching and warm and approving, something that accepted my unspoken gratitude for so many times with her and George along what even then had begun to seem the long path stretching back to childhood.

One June morning a few years ago, I was walking on Elm Street and dropped into the Historical Society for a look at the gallery. On my way out, thinking that I had seen all there was to see, I was suddenly stopped dead in my tracks by a small white sign with black letters attached to the wall above the doorway through which I was passing. It said simply "Pember Inn", and it was the very sign, splendidly unrefurbished, that had hung over the front porch of Pember Inn all those years. It was one of those moments in which we feel an old pulling at the heart and simply surrender to the tide of memories and associations that come washing over us. As with all such scraps and fragments of time gone by, that sign asserted its place in a kind of continuance and at the same time situated itself in a past world that seemed all the more inaccessible by my sudden, intense yearning to have it all back, just as it was, once again.

It's different with the old house at 11 Church Street, which, even without its sign, will for me always carry its name. I've never as much as caught a glimpse of its interior since Mrs. Pember left. Although it has, I hear, been made into apartments, and the white rail fence is a sorry replacement for the old picket fence, the exterior of the house has changed so little that I can imagine its remaining for the rest of my life a kind of symbol and reminder of the way it used to be and of the life which it contained when Mrs. Pember and her grandson George Pearsons lived there. So I seldom pass by without catching a glimpse in the mind's eye of things just as they were: the antique four-poster beds standing in repose in the guest rooms upstairs, the tables of the dining room set for dinner, the great mirror gazing eastward across the front room, the staircase and banister arranging their patterns of afternoon light and shadows in the front hall — all strangely preserved in images that the years have not been able to erase.

Basketball

Basketball was my first love.
Or perhaps it was my religion, if religion
can be defined as that which governs your life.
STEPHEN DUNN

One morning in July, not many years before the old high school building on South Street was razed, I decided to accept the invitation of its wide open doors and to reacquaint myself with its rooms and corridors. I took the familiar walk up past the memorial column with its eagle, and where the sidewalk divided at the great pine tree and the flagpole, I went left and in under the archway of what in my parents' time had been the girls' entrance but to me was the door to the junior high. Inside, the hallways and wooden staircases in their vacancy seemed to have long since exhaled their traffic of students and to have settled into that peculiar stillness that occupies all school buildings in the summer time. I wandered along past rooms where, as a freshman in 1956-57, I had had classes and sat in study halls for a year before being moved to the new union high school in West Woodstock. As I ascended the creaking staircases through shafts of light falling through the eastern windows, I realized that I was looking for two rooms in particular, the only two at the top of the building. The one at the front, the old typing room, was the most eccentric space in the school. It had the distinction of being the smallest classroom and the only one on the eastern side of the building, and since one reached it by going up a small staircase from the top floor, it was also the highest class-room. In both its size and its elevation, it always seemed to me to be something like the school's crow's nest, and it offered a broad view of the rooftops of the southern end of the village. My real destination, however, was the old assembly hall, which occupied all the rest of the space at the top of the building. During my father's school days in the 1920s, this large room was the gymnasium, and he played his high school basketball there. In my school years it had served as a combination art and music room, the music classes being held at the southern end and the art classes at the northern end, with no dividers but rather a kind of no man's land cleared of desks and chairs in between. With its history as a basketball court and with its lofty ceiling and bank of westward windows looking out onto the fire escape landing above the parking lot, this room was one of the school's most engaging interiors. I was walking around it on that summer morning, absorbed in recollections of music class with Mr. Harris, during which, instead of singing, I spent most of my time turning around to watch Mr. Gyra's art classes busy at their easels, when suddenly I spotted a faded red cloth on the floor next to a desk. It was something that had apparently been used as a dust rag and then left there. Picking it up and unfolding it, I saw a white number on it and realized it was a small basketball jersey, and I heard myself uttering the first word I had spoken since entering the building: "Warriors." And I sensed a door opening onto winter Saturday mornings in the old high school gym far be-low me and my introduction to the game of basketball.

The Woodstock midget and junior league basketball program was begun in the winter of 1951-52. It was the brainchild of Wendell Cameron, a basketball and baseball coach and long time Wood-stock sports enthusiast, and a group of men who listed the follow-ing concerns as their purpose in founding the leagues: "to give the youngsters...an opportunity to play competitive basketball; to bring grownups and children into closer relationship and to create an inspiration for teamwork, sportsmanship, and good citizenship; and to create a 'feeder' system for Woodstock High School varsity teams in the future." Not long after it was begun, the success of at least one of these objectives was clearly realized in the number of league, district, and even state titles won by some of the high school teams made up of boys who had completed the five year midget and junior program. The plan was simple: all the boys between grades four and six who signed up were divided up among four midget league teams, and all the boys from grades seven and eight who signed up were divided up among four junior league teams. The midget teams were named after Ivy League colleges, and the juniors were named after NBA teams. The uniforms, which were provided through an arrangement with Sterling's Sporting Goods, consisted of white cotton shorts and different colored, numbered jerseys for all the teams: Cornell — maroon, Dartmouth — navy blue, Princeton — black, and Yale — orange; Lakers — blue, Celtics — green, Bullets — yellow, and Warriors — red. In the beginning, the teams were coached by men of my father and mother's generation who had played high school basketball in their day, and they were assisted by high school boys, some of whom went on to become junior league coaches. The season, which was some eight weeks long, opened with a practice session, and all the games were played on Saturday mornings except for the postseason tournament, which was played at night.

My experience in these leagues was unforgettable, and it began what was for me a kind of obsession with the game of basketball. As I discovered in my first practice session as a fourth grader, I was not a natural basketball player. But since my class would be the first to complete the full five-year program, there was plenty of time to work at improving. During that practice, which was preliminary to any selection of teams and was held in the basketball

179

court above the Town Hall Theatre, I was taught by coach Hal Maynes how to shoot a two-hand set shot and what was then called a step shot, the old name for a lay-up. I remember on my first attempt at a foul shot holding the ball with my elbows spread wide and the fingers of both hands pointing directly at each other (as though I were about to propel myself toward the basket by swimming the breast stroke) and sending up, or rather out, a cannon shot that brushed the bottom of the net on its way out of bounds. The step shot went rather better, as it seemed natural to bank the ball off the backboard. But my lack of everything — skills, confidence, and experience — made me a bench warmer for coach Fred Doubleday's Princeton team throughout my first midget league season. I played very little, had to be reminded a few times that I wasn't supposed to be sticking to my man when I was playing offense, and got the ball in my hands during a game only once all season. I held it for an indecisive two or three seconds, paralyzed by worry that I might travel or double dribble, and then I passed, or rather handed, it to sixth grader Wilfred Drury, the toughest boy in the school, because he seemed to want it very badly and because I was afraid of him. The next year, playing for Roger Stearns' Yale team, I saw limited action, scored a total of one foul shot all season, but was told that I was much improved.

If, by my third season, I had finally caught up with some of my more athletic classmates, it was because of my love for the game, because of my determination to become better at it and because of my father's contributions. Part of my determination came from a conversation with my father at the end of my second midget league season. We had just come home from watching the league championships and were sitting up later than usual, discussing the games and the players and the season. My father was particularly impressed with the play of Fred Bradley, the best athlete in our class, and he foresaw a bright future for him in basketball. Without in any way intending his praise to be construed as a criticism of my meager contributions as a player, he nevertheless managed to make me feel pretty jealous of Fred. I lay awake a long time that night and made a vow to myself that I would do all I could to turn my father's attention to me and to earn that sort of admiration for myself from that time on. My father helped my brother and me in any way he could. Sharing our interest in basketball at all levels, he began taking us to Dartmouth College games. We were astonished at the size of the court and the size and speed of some of the players. And in watching such All-Americans as Columbia's Chet Forte, Pennsylvania's Ernie Beck, and Yale's Johnny Lee, we saw the game played as we had never imagined it. More importantly, my father bought us something that really began to make us into basketball players. Howard and I had made up a game in the entryway to our kitchen in which we shot a tennis ball into a stovepipe hole in the wall up near the ceiling. It gave us good dribbling and jumping practice, but for shooting it was useless since the hole was flat in the wall and thus faced out rather than down. In sympathy with us and our interest in the game, my father bought us a small basket and inflatable rubber basketball, somewhat larger than a softball, and mounted the basket on the wall over a doorway in the living room. That was it. From then on we had a distinct advantage over boys in families who rated interior decoration higher than good fun. We played "horse" and "21" and tremendously competitive games of one-on-one and, when friends were over, two-on-two. Sometimes, on otherwise quiet evenings, we even coaxed my mother and father into playing with us. The upshot of the new basket was that at the cost of some badly smudged wallpaper, a worn rug, and a few damaged household items my brother and I very much surprised the coaches in our last midget league season by exhibiting skills we had not begun to master by the end of the previous season. Many times over the years I heard my father chuckle over the installation of that basket, and when my son, in his time, became so obsessed with the game of basketball that he made his own rim out of a coat hanger and put it over a doorway in his room, I found him the same sort of miniature backboard and basket, hooked it over a closet door at one end of our living room, and watched his game go up several notches in a very short time.

Not that living room basketball by itself was the answer, for we supplemented everything we did there with hours of practice and pickup games at various places around town. There were only two outdoor courts, one at Vail Field and one at the Rec Center. At the north end of Vail Field, as part of the playground, two backboards and baskets had been fixed to telephone poles about twenty yards apart. We sometimes shot baskets there, but we rarely did more than that because of the bent rims and the tattered nets and the uneven grass surface. In fact, the only evidence of their use was a worn dirt place beneath the basket nearest the sandbox and the teeter-totter. The old Rec Center court, in spite of its eccentricities, was much more to our liking. It was located where the Olympic-sized swimming pool is now situated, and it was even shorter and narrower than the high school court in the gym on South Street. Its surface was cement, and it was bordered on one and a half sides by a three-foot stonewall topped by a high playground fence. The western end of the court terminated abruptly in a huge cement wall, to which one of the baskets was affixed. A blue stripe running from top to bottom of its north side suggested that this wall had been intended to serve as a tennis backboard, but I remember seeing it used as such only a few times. The basket at the opposite end was set in a good metal backboard fixed to an upright girder anchored where the cement ended and dropped the height of a curbstone into the gravel of a playground area. This open end and the unenclosed space from there to center court on one side were the only out of bounds areas, and this was the end of the court for fast breaks. Any momentum generated by the team shooting at the cement wall basket had to be slowed down quickly in order to avoid collision, and the player going in for the lay-up had to angle sharply his path to the basket or take the shot from a standstill or actually use the wall itself for the last step, as outfielders used to do to increase their elevation in reaching for fly balls. The baskets were pretty much even in height, and the chain link nets were good for all weather and seldom became tangled. The dangers on that court were the loose dirt from the gravel driveway that bordered it and the deadly gap that widened each year between the wall and edge of the court as they settled toward the river. I never saw anyone step into this crack, but to have done so could have meant a broken ankle or worse. Besides this potential danger, the worst effect of the court's settling was the inconvenience of having to give an extra few inches to any shot taken from the sagging southeast corner.

The other liabilities of play on this court were the uneven illumination for night games — the wall end was lit up, and the backboard end was in deep shadow — and the proximity of the Ottauquechee River. Exceptionally long shots had a way of bouncing off the rim, clearing the high fence, taking another bounce off the stones in the retaining wall, and landing in the water. Most of the shots that went astray in this way were, admittedly, those two handed bombs or baseball throws (now known as "buzzer beaters" but we called them "desperation heaves") which often go along with the end of a long afternoon's play when attention becomes unfocused and weariness sets in. Once we saw the Rec Center's basketball on its way to the river, we would be off on the dead run across the back lot and down the steps by the big brick fireplace to the water's edge. There we would break branches off the nearest willow and try to reach the ball with them or use the strategy of throwing the biggest stones we could find out beyond the ball to make waves that would wash it in to shore. Rarely, and only in desperation when the water was low, someone would wade out after it. In the spring, all we could do was watch the ball go bobbing along on the fast, icy currents toward Taftsville and begin discussing how to break the news to Rec Center directors Frank Riley or Chris Knowlton or to assistants Bud Smith or Milt Watson that we had lost yet another ball in the river. After some passing around of the blame, we'd usually opt for going up to the office in a pack and confessing. In answer to the expected accusation that it wouldn't have happened if we hadn't been fooling around, we always offered the standard excuse: We had just been shooting from the number 5 spot, the most distant of the nine numbered circles painted on the court for the game of around-the-world, and the ball had just bounced over the fence, and we had tried everything imaginable to retrieve it. And the narrative of our riverside determination and resourcefulness would lengthen and expand as we pleaded our case. The Rec Center staff members were usually quite understanding, especially considering that we never owned up to any sort of irresponsibility unless they had actually been looking out the window and witnessed the whole thing.

The Rec Center sponsored no organized league play on that old court. The only games we played there were pickup games, and in the summer when baseball and softball were in full swing, sometimes about the best one could do was some one-on-one or just some practice in dribbling and shooting. Of course, we styled our play on that of the players we had seen in Dartmouth games and in high school varsity games. We worked on different kinds of layup shots, our favorite being something that for a while we called the "smittie," after varsity forward Fred Smith. A new boy in town and a stranger to us, Fred appeared one summer afternoon at the Rec Center court. He was lanky and wore thick glasses, and it was obvious to us that he didn't lack confidence and that he was out to

184

make a certain impression on us younger boys. We deferentially tossed him the ball when he clapped his hands for it, and he proceeded to put on a show. He was "cool," as we were starting to say then, and he had a spectacular, if not very accurate, underhand layup. He would begin his drive from half court and go up from out beyond the foul circle to attempt in midair all sorts of feints and fakes and double pumps, his elbows flapping like the wings of some great, awkward bird attempting in panic to get off the ground. Sometimes he brought the ball all the way around like a softball pitcher and released it in a scoop before he landed, and he had a way of prefacing his moves with dedicatory remarks such as "This one's for my own true love Betty Lou." It was quite an exhibition, and from then on, much to our own and to each other's amusement, we worked at making "smitties" part of our basketball repertoire.

I spent many solo hours there at the old Rec Center court, trying to perfect different sorts of shots — the hook, the reverse layup, and especially the jump shot, which was just beginning to revolutionize the game of basketball. I imitated the turnaround jump shot of varsity center Bob Fleming and the fade-away jump shot of Pennsylvania's Ernie Beck and Oklahoma's Arnold Short. To keep up my concentration when I began to tire, I doubled as both player and announcer, performing last minute heroics in imagined state and even national championships to my own imitation of the voice of Marty Glickman. Time was always running out in those fancied moments, and I'd fill the silence of my solitary play with the imagined roar of the capacity crowds as my last second shots poured through the basket. Except for the murmur of my announcer's voice, the only sounds would be the ball bouncing against the pavement and hitting the rim or swishing through the chain nets; and, in the background, giving a kind of immediacy and a sense of possibility to my dreams of glory, the rushing of the Ottauquechee.

Besides the Rec Center court, there were some other hoops

where we sometimes got together to play. Fred Doubleday put up a good backboard and basket on a pole in his back yard on Maple Street, and Max Spaulding set one up on his garage on Pleasant Street. Fred Bradley had a low rim on his grandfather's barn on North Street, but the ball, once it began to roll down the sloped lawn, didn't stop until it had reached River Street at the bottom of the hill. We used to ride our bikes up to Willow Vale to Don Eaton's and play in our bathing suits at the basket his father had set up on the side of his garage until we were hot and sweaty, and then we'd cool off in the brook behind their house. The Hackett boys' father had a new basket installed in one of the barns at the Billings Farm, and I remember practicing there by myself on winter afternoons after school before the junior league championship game in my eighth grade year. So obsessed were we that we made use of any space that could function as a basketball court. We stumbled around in a dimly lit garage on Central Street and gathered in hordes around an extraordinary contraption in the middle of the grade school play-ground. It looked something like an iron bucket with its sides cut out welded to the end of an iron pole. It had no backboard and no net, so it could be shot at from anywhere. When the ball dropped in, it bounced around before making up its mind which of the three openings it would roll out. Games played here at recess or lunch time were chaos since there was no limit to how many could play and no out of bounds, just packs of kids arguing and shoving and running all over the playground and shouting for the ball.

Too much space was certainly not the problem in the court we set up in the Amsdens' garage. It was a dark, cramped, narrow rectangle with a dirt floor at the back of their house at 42 Central Street. We played there on rainy days and in the winter, and even with the doors left open for light, the rim set on the back wall was barely visible before our eyes adjusted to the gloom. Since more than two people in that space constituted a crowd, our games of three on three were brutal. The main difficulty was trying to stop Lyman Amsden, a tall, rawboned boy with painfully sharp elbows, and trying to get off a shot that he couldn't block under that low ceiling. Resorting to football and hockey tactics to create enough space to maneuver with the ball, we were always crashing into and bouncing off the garage walls. On the other side of the end wall to which the basket was fixed was an apartment, and our games created a dreadful disturbance for its occupant, Miss Bernice McKee. She would put up with it as long as she could, and then she would emerge to tell us that our noise had become quite unendurable and to ask us to stop playing for a while. And, smudged and battered, we'd reluctantly wander out into full daylight in search of something else to do.

Places of this sort were about the best we could come up with if we wanted to play pickup basketball in the winter. We sometimes went so far as to use snow shovels to clear a small space on the Rec Center court, and we'd play there until our clothes were wet and our hands were freezing. Given the easy accessibility of the two school courts today, it seems to me somewhat of a mystery and certainly a shame that we could not more often gain permission to use the indoor courts back then. Except for the Saturday morning midget and junior league program, the high school gym, under supervision of custodian Charlie Raymond, was absolutely off-limits. No one could go in there to practice. We had somewhat better luck with Eddie Potwin, custodian of the Town Hall, especially if we were accompanied by an adult, who usually turned out to be my father.

The room that housed the old Town Hall basketball court was one of Woodstock's great interiors. In its day it served many purposes. It was a movie theatre in the 1920s, and it was the basketball court for the Woodstock High School teams of the 1930s. The Woodstock Country School, when it was located on Church Hill, played ball there, and in 1955 after the school had moved to South Woodstock, it served as their home court for a season. It was also the scene of hunt suppers sponsored by the Sportsmen's League and, in the 1940s and 50s, the place where the annual Firemen's Ball was held. It even served as a clinic once, as recalled by my mother, who had had her tonsils removed there sometime in the 1920s. In my memory, it was, as a basketball court, more beautiful than functional. Its great vaulted, beamed ceiling, similar in design to that of the Norman Williams Public Library, soared overhead, giving the hall a kind of cathedral look, and it had very good natural illumination. Unlike most of today's gyms, which slumber behind heavy Plexiglas windows in semidarkness until the overhead lights are turned on, the Town Hall gym looked like a gallery. Light poured in through the clear glass of its arched windows, which lined the east and west walls, so that even on a winter afternoon, it was possible to play basketball there without turning the lights on. Its floor of light colored wood had not been varnished in years and was, I'm sure, better for dancing than for playing basketball. Even with a good pair of sneakers, we could take a running start and simply slide along its surface. The backboards at both ends of the hall were constructed out of planks lined up horizontally and clamped together and painted white. By some miscalculation, the court was off center lengthwise, with a very large out-of-bounds area on the south end and virtually no out-of-bounds on the north end, but instead just a line crossing the floor some six inches at most from the wall. I remember that in trying to see whether we could fit behind that line we'd put our feet one behind the other and stand perpendicular to the court and twist our bodies around long enough to toss the ball in bounds. Still, since our experience at the Rec Center court had familiarized us with walls, we adapted to this peculiarity and could even appreciate the minimal slowing or stopping space provided by the backboard's extension. The walls were hung with netting that extended down from the ceiling to protect the windows from the ball, and the sidelines were crowded with long, light green colored benches with armrests at each end, which we would sometimes struggle to push or carry away from the court's edge. The backboards in that old hall were dead, the rims extremely kind, and the foul lanes, which remained six feet wide even after the game had officially expanded them to twelve feet in 1955, gave the court an antiquated look that reminded us of our first years of playing basketball as midget leaguers.

For four years, beginning in 1953, the Town Hall court was the home of a girls' midget and junior league basketball program. This program was begun and supervised by Eddie Potwin, a fine athlete in his day and one of the boys' midget league coaches, and his wife Geneva, who had played high school basketball in nearby West Lebanon, New Hampshire. The parents of five daughters, they formed the leagues in response to the prevailing sense among many of the grade school and junior high school girls that girls deserved the same sort of opportunity as the boys. In each of its first three years, more than eighty girls from grades five through eight were enrolled in this program, and in 1956 it was expanded to include fourth grade girls. The game they played was the old girls' game with six instead of five players on a side — three defenders on one end of the court and three offensive players on the other with the half court line dividing the two fields of action. The idea, long since proved fallacious, was that young ladies did not have the strength and the stamina to play the boys' game, which would require them to run up and down the whole court. But though the girls' game as they played it in those leagues may seem sadly outdated to us today, it did have the progressive feature of alternating throw-ins instead of jump balls.

The girls' season began with a few practice sessions designed to enable Eddie and Geneva to assess the talent; then the girls were divided up into twelve-member teams which gave themselves such names as The Galloping Goofs, The Dangerous Demons, The Golden Fillies, and The Crazy, Mixed-up Mudhens. Games were played on Tuesday and Friday afternoons. As with the boys' leagues, a number of Woodstock people pitched in to make the program a success. Many local women, including the mothers of some of the players, donated their time as coaches and timers. To raise money for the uniforms, a benefit showing of the movie *Good Morning Miss Dove* was given at the Town Hall Theatre, and a food sale was organized. The Rotary Club made a donation, and *Vermont Standard* photographer Larry Godsill took team pictures and sold them for twenty-five cents each at Sterling's Drug Store. Though I found the girls' game of basketball less interesting than the boys', I often went to watch the girls play and always became involved in the action. In fact, quite a number of boys regularly attended those games, and some even helped out with the program, working as scorekeepers and timers. My brother was one of the full time referees, calling the games with Eddie and Geneva and occasionally with Wendell Cameron. As the skills of the girls increased, a sort of all-star team made up of the best eighth graders played teams from Springfield and Lebanon, and well-known Twin State League referees Fred Legere and Bromo Scelza donated their time on those occasions. As with the boys' program, the beneficial results of this league included the improved play of the varsity and junior varsity teams when the girls came to play high school basketball.

Those days when both the boys' and girls' leagues were flourishing were, I suppose, the beginning of basketball's bid to rival baseball and football as spectator sports in Woodstock. Though many of my friends and classmates stayed equally involved in all three sports, I could have played basketball all year without missing the other two. My passion for the game and my concentration on it through hours of practice and improvised play gave a tremen-

dous excitement to times when I could actually play organized basketball on a genuine indoor court. In fact, every aspect of midget
and junior league play was charged with significance for me. I
remember my brother and me practically running from Pleasant
Street to South Street and getting to the gym just about as the doors
were being opened on Saturday morning. When the time came, we
couldn't undress fast enough in the locker room to put on the white
shorts and the jerseys with our numbers on the back. This was my
first experience with a sports uniform, and as I began to grow
enough so that it didn't hang on me, I became captivated by its
mystique. For instance, I always wondered why the Dartmouth
midget team had jerseys with sleeves and all the other teams had
the standard basketball tops, and why the junior league's Lakers
team had tops made of the same heavy, glossy material as the varsity uniforms instead of the light, tee shirt cotton of the other teams'
uniforms. We argued endlessly in school over which team was best
and discussed which team had the best uniforms, and each of us
was proud to receive at the end of each season a white felt patch
which could be sown onto a warmup jacket. Each year, it was a
different shape and design — that of a basketball or a shield or a
hexagon — and it had the name of the league and the year of play
printed on it in green and, for the lucky ones, the word "champions" across the middle.

I was a gym rat back then, spending most winter afternoons
watching the high school team practice. My hope was to get in a
few shots at the end of their sessions while the players were show-
ering and before Coach Dailey locked up the balls in the cage.
Sitting there in the bleachers by myself or with a friend, I took in
everything from shooting and passing techniques to how the boys
dressed for practice. The long basketball shorts that have become
the standard today would have looked pretty strange back then when
short shorts were so much the fashion that the varsity team shorts

even had elastic around the legs. They looked more like men's briefs or the sorts of bathing suits the men of my father's generation wore than like the shorts now worn by basketball players. As midget and junior players, we wanted to grab the right shorts when the coach brought the box of uniforms down into the locker room and to avoid getting stuck with a pair that looked like "bloomers," as we used to say. Since the high school teams wore white high-top sneakers and elastic kneepads, naturally these became the rage among the midget and junior league players. I think I was in the sixth grade before I finally wore out my last pair of black sneakers and replaced them with white ones. That same year I got kneepads for Christmas, just in time for my last midget league season when I had finally mastered some basketball skills. Though I'd like to forget the vanity of it all, I remember as clearly as I can recall anything else about that time just what it felt like to dress up my white shorts and black Princeton jersey with new white athletic socks and white sneakers and a kneepad worn on one of my shins. I didn't feel overdone, as I might have a season earlier, but rather as though, in all my efforts to improve my game and to become a basketball player, these were the stripes I had earned.

Today there is nothing left of those basketball courts where we played. The school gym on South Street remained basically the same until the summer of 1996, at which time it began to undergo extensive renovations. But on the morning when I discovered the small red jersey lying on the floor of the old assembly room and made my way from there down through what had been the high school and junior high school buildings, I found the old gym very much unchanged. It just seemed to have shrunk and to be too small a space for all that had taken place there. And I was astonished at its silence. It had been anything but quiet on those mornings of midget and junior league play, and the noise came as much from the court as from the sidelines and the bleachers where the fans —

a few parents and a great many players who had already finished their games or were waiting to play — cheered on their favorite teams. The action of the midget league games in particular resembled that of a swarm of bees. All ten players moved up and down the court in a pack around the person with the ball, whose teammates would be shouting for it while their opponents would be crowded in among them, trying to "stay with their man" and hoping for a steal. Since games were often decided by no more than one or two baskets, the excitement mounted as the game wore on, finally to show a score of 8 to 6 if it was a close one or 12 to 5 if it was one-sided.

The locker room, too, was much as I had left it many years before. The air of that dark, damp basement cave was still redolent of wet towels, sweat, and sneakers. Walking from its inner recesses to the end where the faint light filtered in from the playground through frosted windows and then climbing the stairs that gave back the sound of my feet in the same old way was to feel again the excitement of approaching the arena. I went up and took a seat in the old built-in bleachers which rose as so many wooden steps along the whole south side of the gym. To sit there for a while in the stillness was to be ambushed by memory — to begin to recover all that was there and to recall what was missing. Gone were the heavy rows of attached, wooden slatted chairs which lined one side of the floor as the team benches and seats for the timers and scorers, and the other side as a single row for spectators. And the old wooden scoreboard, which displayed all of its small, carved number-shaped spaces at once and indicated the score by which ones were lit up, had disappeared from its place beneath the northeast windows, along with its triangular bench of controls which were lowered from the wall in the corner. But that row of windows still looked out over the school's front lawn with its pine tree and flagpole.

THE LONG LIGHT OF THOSE DAYS

Up there in the bleachers by myself, I began to sense once again what it had all been like — how high the baskets had seemed and how large the ball and how far away the foul line — and to fill the silence with its old sounds and the empty space with its missing people. It was always a packed house when Coach Ken Dyer brought in Woodstock's archrival Hartford High School Indians. The sidelines and bleachers were full, as was the stage, where the students always sat for games. Even the entryways, including the one to the junior high where the Future Farmers of America had its concession stand for orange soda and chocolate milk, were jammed, and out in the front hall beyond the double doors, the fans stood in rows three deep. And whether Woodstock won or lost those hard fought contests, Hartford, with guard Ray Brooks' terrific speed and dribbling skills and the great shooting touch of the Sacco twins, Harry and Jerry, was always exciting to watch. At half time we used to tag along with my father when he went down to the janitor's room in the basement of the grade school to have a cigarette and join the other men in a discussion of the game. My brother and I would stand there in the thick smoke of that tightly packed space and listen to their analysis and commentary and imbibe their serious enthusiasm and then go back up for the second half to watch the action with a more critical eye.

With these recollections, the old gym began to come back into focus and to wear the look of other occasions from those years. I could remember how welcoming it seemed on mornings in gym class when we were choosing up sides for our favorite game of "attack," and how threatening it became when I would see the mats spread out for gymnastic exercises. I recalled how light and open it appeared on the last day of the school year in June during the late morning assembly after we had returned from playing on Vail Field and were glimpsing the summer vacation in everything we saw. And I remembered how very much it seemed to refer to times

194

gone by on the Wednesday evening of graduation week when, at the end of Class Night, we watched our high school heroes walk out of the gym for the last time, our sadness lightened only by the feeling that we were that much closer to stepping into their place.

When our time to play high school basketball finally came, we were only a year in the South Street gym before we moved up to the new Woodstock Union High School. With the full five years of midget and junior league play behind us, we went on to put together what was up to that time the best basketball team Woodstock had ever produced. Once we had become accustomed to our new, official-sized court, which at first seemed unmanageably large, its predecessors began to look pretty dated. Still, it seemed necessary to look in on them from time time. When I was home from college, I would sometimes climb up one of the fire escapes at the Town Hall to peer in through the glass at the old basketball court and be assured that it was unchanged. I had no idea then that it would not be around forever, but in October of 1964 its doom was spelled by the Selectmen's approval of the proposal to remodel that great old hall to accommodate the offices of the agricultural agency. Competing front page headlines in *The Vermont Standard* of March 3, 1965, announce, on one side, the beginning of those renovations and, on the other, the tournament victories of the Four Horsemen and Co., who would be the first Woodstock team to capture two successive state crowns. Thus, by one of those accidents of history, just as one of the express purposes of the boys' midget and junior league program — to create quality varsity teams — was achieving its greatest fulfillment, the place where it had all begun, that is, the court on which the very first practice session was held in 1952 and on which the league's founders had in their time played their high school basketball, was about to disappear and to become the stuff of memory.

All of us, I suppose, have heard from our fathers stories about some of the strange places in which the game of basketball was played in their day, and in turn have told our children of the places where we used to play. Recently, my son came back very excited from visiting a friend at a boarding school in Vermont. He had discovered there, he said, "the best basketball court I have ever seen. It's way out on this hilltop in the top of a barn, and it's got windows of clear glass that look right off to the mountains and a kind of cathedral ceiling with birds' nests up there and bird droppings on the floor, and you should see it, Dad." I readily agreed that we'd have to have a look at it the next time we were up that way together, and I was pleased that he counted on me to understand what was so great about such a place. In these days when the individual character and integrity of so many things are threatened by uniformity, basketball courts have a way of looking pretty much all the same to me. They are, admittedly, vastly improved facilities compared to the places where we played our first games and some of our "away" junior varsity games, just as those, in turn, were less eccentric than courts my father recalled — second story lofts with dangerous barn doors and blazing wood stoves. Still, the cracker boxes we played in at Pittsford and Brandon in 1957 had their own personality and were, each in its own way, unforgettable. Such courts have by now, I suppose, long since been superseded by others of regulation size in newly equipped union high schools, but I like to think that some of them, or at least traces of them, linger on in a kind of somnolence in old schools and armories and public buildings in the center of towns all over Vermont. I'd like to go looking for them, as I went looking for some trace of the old Town Hall court in Woodstock a couple of years ago. In talking with former town clerk and former midget league coach Fred Doubleday one day, I was surprised to hear that up above the space that had housed the basketball court, the Town Hall still had its old balcony, where audiences had sat for movies and, later, for

196

high school basketball games. Escorted by Fred on my way up to have a look, I stopped briefly on the second floor and found that there was nothing whatsoever in its warren of offices with their desks and computers and copy machines to suggest that basketball games had once taken place in the space they occupy. Then Fred walked into the middle of a partitioned space and, standing next to a file cabinet, turned a 45 degree angle toward me and mimed a two-hand set shot. "I used to let 'em go from about here," he said. At that moment, I realized that we were standing somewhere just beyond what had been the top of the key. Back in the hallway, following Fred's directions, I ducked around a corner and down a hall and found a door at the end that opened to the bottom of a long stairway. Climbing it, I felt memory begin to kick in. At the top was the old balcony just as it had been when we used to take time out from our pickup games to sneak up there for a look. Through wide gaps in a partition at its edge, I could look down onto the makeshift ceiling of those offices and out into the top part of the old hall absolutely unchanged from the way I remembered it. The upper halves of the arched windows still let light into this encapsulated space unanchored by any floor. And above them were the corbels from which the five great hammer arches sprang to span the ceiling with its same lights, some of them still wearing their protective wire mesh covering. It was uncanny. Down under the office ceiling, which seemed suspended in the air of the old hall, the business of the present was being efficiently transacted, while up above, sealed off by everything except that long, dark staircase, this place of the past floated like a thought cloud or dream or like some memory retained by the Town Hall itself of the way it used to be before the changes were made.

Basketball, for anyone as captivated by it as I was back then, can become so absorbing that for the duration of a game the court becomes the world. One's whole attention becomes so fixed and concentrated and one's decisions are so completely determined and made within the parameters of the game in that bounded space in which it is played that while the contest lasts there is nothing else, and there is nowhere else. So much is this the case that the aftermath of the games sometimes includes a kind of reorientation to the world into which we exit from the gym. During those moments of re-emergence and adjustment when we are, at least subconsciously, settling back into the common round of our lives, the details of what is familiar have a slightly different look as though they were tilted just a bit or spaced a little differently or as though we were seeing them from a slightly different angle or from eyes with sharpened vision. If we trust to the wisdom of words for some light on the matter, the word "recreation" might satisfy in its suggestion that one of the primary functions of the interval which recreation itself provides is to "re-create" the world for us in however fleeting a way or to rejuvenate us by renewing our capacity to see the world in its novelty, that is, as fresh and new. Though I was unaware of the nature of this process at the time, it is to one such experience that both my brother and I owe one of our most vivid recollections of Woodstock in those years when to us basketball was everything. We left the South Street gym at the end of a morning of midget league play and began our walk home, absorbed in an excited discussion of our games. Just where South Street ends at the Green, as we were crossing from the Martin House to the Woodstock Inn, we really noticed for the first time that what had been a cloudy winter morning when we entered the gym had turned into a glorious day of January thaw. The sunlight on the snow was almost blinding, and the wet streets glistened. The gold eagle on the porch roof of the inn blazed in the midday sun, and above it the inn tower lifted into a sky of dazzling blue. We slowed our walk, and as we looked down the Green toward the center of the village, everything — the street, the sidewalk, the buildings and snowbanks and even the park fence — looked washed and refreshed. We've spoken of that experience many times since and of the way we seemed to be seeing it all for the first time. And I know that as we walked along, swinging our duffel bags, it never occurred to us that the courts to which we owed such visions or the village as it was showing itself to us then would ever be any different, and we never guessed that the brilliance of that moment would remain with us down through all the years that succeeded it.

Mount Tom

Because the realness of his inward being
lives at his back, the man of words...
will turn back, to the place of necessary,
beloved shadows.

GEORGE STEINER

On my return trips to Woodstock, I most often approach the town from the east. And I am always a bit relieved when, after negotiating the dips and turns of Route 4, I can see the narrow valley of the Ottauquechee quite suddenly opening out, the hills moving off to the north and south and their steep, wooded slopes becoming more gradual and giving way in places to upland meadows. I find myself waiting for that place approximately two miles outside the village where the road, keeping to its elevation along the southern side of the valley, offers a more distant but more reassuring view of the river. Instead of looking down into it over guardrails, I can catch sight of it as an occasional flash of silver where it runs through the fields of the flood plain. And I can look beyond that to where the pastoral hillsides of Cloudland veer off northward to become the eastern ridges of the Pomfret valley, or follow the river's course to where all the landscape to the west is lifting into prominence. There, just as some of the gables and rooftops and church steeples of Woodstock become visible, the pattern of woods giving way to open land is interrupted by the two curved tops and massive shoulders of a long wooded eminence. This is what I've been watching for; this is Mt. Tom, and I'm home again.

The name Mt. Tom, though I grew up speaking it, used to make me wonder who Tom was. I never got an answer, and as far as I know, the origin of the name is rather a mystery. But since it has been around at least from the time of its appearance in deeds drawn up as early as 1772, Woodstock natives simply take it for granted. Then too, the name may seem something of a misnomer since Mt. Tom's elevation of 1,340 feet raises questions about its right to be called a mountain at all. However, from certain perspectives in the village, it does seem to deserve its title. Seen from Pleasant Street, for example, which points straight toward it, or from the junction of Routes 4 and 106, where it looms over the Green, Mt. Tom may appear to be higher than it really is. And to look across the Ottauquechee at it from the back lawns along Elm Street is to appreciate a description of it that appeared in the *Boston Evening Transcript* in 1911: "Mt. Tom, which looks down upon the town from across the river, rears its head perhaps fifteen hundred feet above the bed of the stream in mighty precipices." From a number of vantage points, it is indeed impressive. But to me, and to many natives of Woodstock, it is more than that, and its name, as well as specifying a place, suggests a state of mind and evokes a memory and carries with it an assurance and a kind of sustaining vision.

Although I recently talked with a man who grew up in Woodstock and has lived in its vicinity all of his life without ever going to the top of Mt. Tom, such people are, I hope, rare. During my childhood and youth, all the young people whom I knew had at least some familiarity with some part of "the mountain," as we called it. I was introduced to it early in life by my parents, who used to take my brother and me for walks there in the spring and summer and autumn. So early, in fact, was my introduction that I have little memory of my first outings there, and I date my acquaintance with Mt. Tom to April 12, 1945, when I was three years old. It was a Thursday, and my father had some time off because all the stores in Woodstock were closed on Thursday afternoons back then. As I am told, we were returning home from the mountain along our usual route when we were approached by Mamie Clough, the great granddaughter of Republican Senator Jacob Collamer (1791-1865), who was a confidant of Lincoln's during the Civil War. She stopped us outside the family home at 40 Elm Street and exclaimed to my parents, in a distraught manner, "Oh, our president is dead, and now we will have to put up with that awful man!" So I have always found it convenient to date the beginning of my life-long relationship with Mt. Tom to this day on which F. D. R. died and was succeeded by Harry Truman.

From where we lived on Pleasant Street, the shortest route to the top of the mountain was the Old Trail, and the shortest route to the beginning of the Old Trail was straight through the property of the Billings mansion. By virtue of its extraordinary series of owners, this imposing house has earned a place in history. From the time of its construction in 1806 until 1825, the Marsh house, as it was then called, was the home of George Perkins Marsh (1801-1882), who is now recognized as the prophet of the conservation movement in America. As the scene of Marsh's boyhood, the Marsh house and its farm were the center of his early excursions into the natural world, in which he climbed Mt. Tom, explored the landscape around Woodstock, and became familiar with the geography of the Green Mountains. In these wanderings he began to develop his powers of observation and to discover the interrelations of man and nature that would lead to the writing of his great work, *Man and Nature*, one of the most important and influential books of the nineteenth century. As biographer David Lowenthal has shown, it is to Marsh and to the revolution in thought that his work inspired that America and even Europe owe their understanding of "the problem of conservation as one of interdependent social and environmental relationships." *Man and Nature* was "the first book to recognize the full significance of man as an environmental agent, the first to realize the appalling losses caused by the destruction of forests and other resources and the first to propose a remedy for the future." The sort of stewardship which Marsh espoused was exercised by Frederick Billings (1823-1890), a railroad magnate and native of Woodstock who returned to his hometown to purchase the Marsh farm in 1867. Billings rebuilt the Marsh house and began the work which, according to Lowenthal, would earn him the reputation of a conservationist and "pioneer in reforestation." Beginning in the 1880s, he planted fifteen to twenty thousand Norwegian spruce, European larch and white ash on the slopes of Mt. Tom. By 1911 the Billings estate was famous as "the most interesting example of forestry in the state." This tradition of responsible forestry management and land use was carried on by the late Laurance Rockefeller and then passed on to be preserved by the Billings Farm and Museum and the Marsh-Billings-Rockefeller National Historical Park.

From the time of my first walks on Mt. Tom via the Billings property, I understood that the extensive and beautifully maintained grounds of the mansion were closed to the public but that it was all right for us to enjoy them as though they were parkland. Only during the Rockefellers' ownership when the property understandably, become more strictly private, did it occur to me to wonder about my family's simple assumption that it was quite permissible to wander respectfully about the grounds of the Billings mansion on our way to the start of the trail. As I have recently learned, it may have originated with my Grandmother Coffin, who, as my brother recalls, actually walked up onto the porch of the mansion itself, knocked on the front door, and requested and received from Mrs. French her permission to stroll around her property. Having succeeded in her mission, as she usually did, she noticed my brother's look of consternation and said to him forcefully, "Remember, it never does any harm to ask!" Thus, from my earliest association were the buildings and grounds of the mansion considered by me to be simply a part of Mt. Tom.

Among my earliest memories are my brother's and my fascination with what we called "the little houses" at the southern edge of the Billings property. Built in rustic Victorian style and constructed from willow split and applied to a wooden frame, these two summerhouses were connected by a beautifully raked and manicured, curved dirt path. They were sufficiently alike and different to absorb us completely, and they had features which came to have for us a peculiar sort of childhood significance. Just as I always crossed the wooden sidewalk on the west side of Billings' Bridge in great eagerness to glimpse on the cement wall at the far end a small orange spot of paint looking vaguely like a sunburst, so Howard and I approached the lower summer house in anticipation of finding among the stumps and shoots that had been cut away from the willow branches forming the walls, one particular stump that we called "the little nub." Sometimes, when our object was not a hike, my parents simply took us there, and we climbed repeatedly in and out of the low window openings and played games on the steps and benches of these summerhouses.

Above these summerhouses, we would idle along the paths and roadways of the mansion property, climbing the stone steps that led from one level of the terraced lawns and gardens and stopping at the marble fountain that stood at the crossing of two garden paths. On a level between this garden and the large cottage with its swimming pool and greenhouses stood a pediment topped with what appeared to be a model of the Billings mansion. It was a dollhouse-sized mansion painted the same gray color as its prototype, and it was situated at the end of a long path between hedges so that as one approached it, it seemed to invite comparison with the mansion, which had just risen into view over the lawns and gardens. On the other side of the drive that bisected the Billings property from North Street to Route 12, we would walk up the broad mown way through the trees to what we called "the little pond." This extraordinary place and its surroundings seemed to have been conjured out of myth or fairy tale. Perhaps the size of a small swimming pool, this pond was fed by a spring that bubbled out of the ground among mosses and pine needles. Its clear water spilled some ten or fifteen yards down a shady, crooked channel, passing beneath two stone slabs serving as bridges for a winding path that rose from the water's edge. On one of the curves in this path, a stone bench among ferns offered a perspective of the pond and a place to sit and listen to the quiet rushing of the stream, the sighing of the great pines overhead, and the occasional croak of a frog among the cattails and lily pads. The surrounding glades, carpeted with moss, offered many varieties of plants and flowers identified by small zinc markers stuck in the ground, and we would search these out until we made our way past the bungalow and across the field with its large vegetable garden and then crossed the mountain road to the woods where the Old Trail began.

My adventures among the acres of land that formed the grounds of the Billings mansion were not confined to these early outings with my parents. Throughout my years in grade school, one of my best friends, Fred Bradley, lived on North Street on property that adjoined that of the mansion, and we spent most of our afternoons after school up there in the woods. According to our inclinations, on these excursions we might play on the rope swing that Fred's grandfather had fixed to the high branch of a large maple at the edge of a field or hew small saplings for the huts and forts that we were always in the process of constructing, or we might find a stand of small pine trees and each climb to the top of one and sway back and forth and play a kind of absurd aerial jousting in which we tried to bump or pull each other out of our separate crows-nests to the ground below. Sometimes in the spring we ranged as far as the woods behind the River Street cemetery gathering mosses and wild flowers for terrariums. But mostly we spent our time exploring and playing games of cowboys or Robin Hood, and since these games required an adversary, the caretaker for the mansion, Carl Bergstrom, and his grounds crew were imagined to fill that role. We did a great deal of sneaking around and spying on them, and we imagined that they were hostile. Every time they were seen traveling anywhere in their truck, we knew they were after us, and if they refused to cooperate by seeming altogether oblivious to our presence, we made use of some of our homemade grenades — a firecracker in a wild cucumber — to wake them up and, hopefully, to set them in pursuit.

Nor did the onset of winter keep us away from the Billings property. On the contrary, it was our premier ski area. My brother and I would carry our skis up through the lower of the two summer-houses, put them on there, and trek over the lawns past the green-houses to meet Fred in the open fields near the base of the Old Trail. Whatever slopes we chose, we had to prepare them by labo-riously sidestepping up them to pack them out. Sometimes we chose what we called "the gradual place," where the mountain road sud-denly emerges from the woods and skirts a large field. Skiing here, we gained the confidence necessary to tackle "the breakneck," the first open field bordering the drive from North Street to the man-sion, and so named because of its relative steepness and the neces-sity of stopping abruptly before the drop into the roadway. And sometimes we packed out runs on the main lawn of the mansion and glided down and practiced schussing to a stop before the hedges. Many times I would ski these slopes by myself, staying up there until my fingers and toes were numb and it was nearly dark. Al-though in the village of Woodstock there were other places such as the golf course that offered longer and more open slopes and the prospect of better runs, I seldom made use of them. For the grounds of the great gray mansion in winter — the buildings closed up, the swimming pool drained, the fountain quiet in the gardens with their vacant look, empty of all but snow, the little pond sealed in ice, and everywhere evergreens bowing their snow-laden branches toward un-cleared paths and walkways in the deep stillness, to all of which I was the solitary witness — made a deep and lasting impression on me.

As fascinating as the Billings property was in itself, it no doubt derived some of its enchantment from its location at the base of Mt. Tom and from its association with the possibilities for adventure which Mt. Tom afforded. Of all the ways to the top of the mountain, the Old Trail was the most rugged and most precipitous. A narrow, one-person track that cut a diagonal across the face, it was, as its name suggests, the older, more time-honored of the two trails up the face of the mountain. It had none of the tame, ambulatory appearance of the wider Faulkner Paths, with their well-raked and manicured surface and green benches, and it offered the names and initials of generations of hikers in the bark of the great beech trees through which it threaded its way. Part of the experience of walking its lower reaches included climbing over or crawling under the trunks of trees that had toppled and lay across it, their exposed roots wearing a wild and demented look, like gorgons, where they had been torn out of the earth. But the more rugged terrain and the greater chances for adventure were to be found on the trail's upper reaches. Once we had gained the elevation where the woods drop away on the south side and rise steeply on the north to reveal stacks of boulders and sheer rock faces and the trail ascends in places with the help of what appear to be steps hacked into the rock, we would pick up the pace in anticipation of exploring once again the region of the caves. We knew we had reached this region when we arrived at the enormous, moss-covered boulder that we recognized as its gateway, and we would always make our ritual entry by crawling through the narrow, tunnel-like crack that ran along its base and coming out under its impressive overhang to rejoin the trail and to begin our excavations. In the days when we first explored this area, the number of caves seemed endless, for we were small enough to be able to squeeze into all sorts of holes in the ground and crevices in the rocks. The most spacious and impressive and perhaps the only one really to merit the name of cave is still safe and accessible to grownups as well as children. One simply steps off the trail, descends a few steps to an open space in the rock wall and then, still standing, edges along a six or eight foot crack and up a step into what a flashlight or candle will show to be a tall and surprisingly spacious room with a sloping floor.

The day on which my brother and I and some of our friends discovered for ourselves this and some of the other caves was one of our most exciting times on the mountain. In the afternoon when we came down off the Old Trail, feeling ourselves to be the Lewises and Clarks of Vermont, our first stop was the Woodstock Electric Company to tell my father the exciting news. Very much to his credit, and to our life-long appreciation, he reacted with genuine surprise and amazement, asking us how we had made the discovery and wanting to know exactly where the caves were. His excitement fed ours, and it was not until many years later, when we wondered how he could have walked that trail for so many years without knowing about the caves, that Howard and I cajoled him into something like an admission that he in his youth had made the same discovery.

My sense of claustrophobia, which always prevented me from becoming any sort of intrepid spelunker, also excluded me from one of the not-so-fortunate adventures in Mt. Tom's caves. Howard and Fred Bradley and Sandy Morse decided to explore a grim looking, large opening at the base of a cliff below the trail. Hacking through dense undergrowth, they advanced into the yawning mouth and from there, with the help of flashlights, wriggled and crawled back into a number of tunnels and passages which they had not even guessed were there. I was quite envious of their stories of the experience and was feeling sadly excluded until Barbara Bradley called my mother to report an alarming discovery — odd looking little bugs embedded in Fred's skin. My mother promptly checked Howard and made the same discovery and the same phone call to Lois Morse, who found the same on Sandy. All of the boys had ticks. The treatment was a bath followed by the simple solution of holding a lighted match close enough to the red, swollen area to make the little monsters back their way out, probably much in the same fashion as the boys had exited some of the tightest caves.

As adventurous as we were in the region of the caves, there were areas which we left pretty much to themselves. One such area begins just beyond the caves. Here, where the trail crosses from the north to the south side of the mountain and traverses the lower part of the valley between the two peaks, it edges along the top of a cliff and then makes a momentary northward turn as though it would enter the mountain itself. The footing in places along this section of the trail is made uncertain by the wetness of the rocks, and the damp, cool air, freighted with the scent of wet moss and rotting vegetation, seems to issue from underground. Mists linger about this place, and the sunlight seems cut off not so much by the dense foliage as by the forbidding expression of the haggard rock faces looming ominously above. Of all the places on Mt. Tom, this valley, with its cliffs and its chaos of scattered boulders and fallen trees, is the most inhuman, the most primeval. It is as though some remnants of the cataclysmic forces that heaved the two peaks into place on either side of it had somehow not completed their work and were lurking about, brooding over the next catastrophe. Even at our most adventurous, we simply hurried along the trail through this alien landscape without pausing for as much as a look-around, and we never gave any thought to exploring it.

Another reason not to linger there in what my brother and I called "the valley of the mists" was our eagerness to reach the great cliff. Here, where the trail actually crosses the base of the precipice with the help of a line of steel plates wedged at an angle into the rock and a section of hand railing, we'd stop to gaze dizzily up the sixty-foot face and fantasize about someday scaling it. None of us, to my knowledge, ever attempted it. In fact, it was not until the early 1990s that I actually saw people out on the cliff, and then my daughter and I only caught the last part of their ascent. For fifteen minutes or so that seemed much longer, we firmly grasped the railing and somewhat reluctantly raised our heads to watch two novices, coached from above by an expert climber, find the necessary handholds and footholds to reach the top without rope. Fortunately, as boys we were cautious enough not to try anything foolhardy, and we were always so eager to follow the trail up its last steep, winding pitch to the top of the cliff that we seldom stopped long enough at the base to ponder any feats of mountaineering. Carrying our bag lunches and whatever accessories were appropriate to our day's activities on the mountain, we would clamber up the last few yards of path in competition for the two seats carved in the rock of the cliff's overlook. Here we would stop to eat lunch and to test the height of the cliff by throwing over its edge just about anything we could lay our hands on. Sticks, branches, tufts of moss, rocks, pine cones, and eventually sandwich crusts, lunch bags and maybe even a water bottle or two would, in turn, sail out into the empty air, and we would listen for their landing far below. And somehow, even within easy reach of the top of the mountain, we tended to linger at this spot beyond our purposes. The top of the cliff has always exercised that sort of appeal. Looking out over the great basin of the mountain immediately below us, we would gaze down into Woodstock like conquerors and watch the miniature cars creeping through the streets, and we'd begin locating particular places such as our own streets and houses and the churches and commercial buildings in the center of the village. We'd trace the course of the Ottauquechee under the Middle Bridge, down along River Street and under Billings' Bridge and straight eastward only to break its long curves where it runs through the Billings Farm fields and, visible over the chimneys of the mansion, winds down along the valley to disappear into a perspective of distant hills backed by the gray lines of mountains. And, as always happens at some point there on top of the cliff, conversation would slow, exclamations would cease, and as the eye took it all in, words would give way to thoughts and dreams and a longing simply to stay there watching the seasons change and the years succeed one another through decades and generations. In countless times there over the years, I have uttered and heard spoken by people of all ages and places very much the same words expressing the same sentiments — most memorably, perhaps, by a friend of my daughter's, an eleven-year-old English girl, in 1987. Although she lived at the base of the Malvern Hills, and was accustomed to some of the most magnificent vistas in all of Britain, she had very much the standard response on her first hike up Mt. Tom. Reaching the top of the cliff and getting her bearings, she looked off toward Blake Hill and, after some moments of silence, said, as though to herself, "Oh, I could stay here forever!"

As reluctant as we always were to leave this spot, it was the promise of even more wide-ranging views that urged us to ascend the final thirty yards or so to the summit. It never occurred to me back then to wonder why the top of the south peak, which is, according to one source, actually the lower of the two peaks by some 105 feet, is designated the top of Mt. Tom. Henry Swan Dana, in his *History of Woodstock, Vermont 1761-1886,* tells us that "the south peak is 537.03 feet, and the north peak 641.82 feet above the base of the town hall," and seen from the east, the north peak is obviously higher and appears to be greater in land mass as well. However, seen as most people in the village see them — from the south and southwest, for example, from the Green or from River Street or Elm Street or Church Hill or Linden Hill — the two peaks look to be nearly equal in height. For whatever reason, history has favored the south peak so that even now, at a time when trails have finally been cleared onto the north peak, the markers distinguish them as "north peak" and "the summit of Mt. Tom" respectively. In contrast to the more densely wooded north peak, the south peak as the official top of Mt. Tom has for years been maintained almost as parkland. It is the place to which the Old Trail and the Faulkner Paths and the mountain road all lead. Years ago the road that was extended to encircle it was leveled and shored up by stone work so as to accommodate horse drawn carriages as well as adventurers making the climb on foot or on horseback, and, more recently, a hewn log bench for picnickers and hikers has been placed at a vantage point that looks directly down on the center of the village. In addition, the star and the cross which are lighted each year at Christmas and Easter show signs of recent structural improvements, and the trees and brush have been cleared so as to offer splendid views of Woodstock set in its range of hills and vistas of the Green Mountains off to the west. In fact, with these points of interest there is little to suggest to anyone standing on the summit that it is really not the point of highest elevation on Mt. Tom. To hikers stepping onto the top from the Faulkner Paths and walking around the circular road, the oaks and evergreens block the view to the north and thus make the north peak invisible. Anyone ascending from the backside of the mountain sees it simply as a ridge paralleling the road for a short distance before the road dips and turns away to rise to the south peak. Only from the Old Trail is the north peak visible, and it is last seen from the top of the cliff, where it can be glimpsed looming just on the edge of vision like something always to be only half-consciously realized. During the Christmas and Easter seasons in particular, when attention is drawn to the star and cross blazing at the edge of the night sky above the village, one is vaguely aware of the north peak's curious, shadowy otherness. Only partially illuminated by reflected light, it appears to glance down over its great shoulder with a benighted look, like something unredeemed, something from out of myth brooding with a sort of pagan skepticism over the light which was brought into the world. Even as boys eager to explore uncharted regions, we left it pretty much alone. We ventured onto it years before trails led up to it, made our exciting discovery of its great white rock, and realized to our amazement that we had gained an elevation higher than that of the mountain's summit. And then we turned away from it and left it to itself once again.

For we had more important things to attend to at the summit. My brother and I would sometimes challenge our companions to a distance vision contest simply by asking them what time it was according to the hands of the clock on the steeple of the Congregational Church. The comparatively nearsighted among them would think we were joking until someone would produce a watch and confirm our accurate reading. Then too we would always spend a few moments at the base of the cross and star, staring up its supporting telephone poles and wishing that the central ladder began close enough to the ground to permit us to retrace the steps of the lucky man from the Woodstock Electric Company whose job it was to change the light bulbs and make the necessary repairs. And without making it known to the others, I would, at least in passing, perform some ritual gestures at the old, green, iron hitching posts where horses used to be tethered. Lifting one of their iron rings, I'd let it drop just to hear once again in the dull, clinking sound some of the earliest music of my childhood walks with my parents, and I would look for the peculiar, decorative lion faces gazing north, south, east, and west along their base. For some years I have identified their appearance from beneath the snow as the end of their hibernation and one of the first signs of spring.

But often times our reaching the summit would signal a time to rest from a long morning of warfare. The place where our mock battles were waged was the south face of the mountain, the peak of which was our Mt. Serabachi, our Monte Cassino. We played endless games of war on Saturday mornings in the fall and spring and throughout the summers of our grade school years. It was quite natural for us to do so since we grew up on war stories and war movies and the pictures of war in *Life* magazine and *Look* magazine and in family scrapbooks and comic books. As small children we had pushed toy tanks around in sandboxes and in the dirt at the edge of the garden and sailed toy destroyers and aircraft carriers around in the bathtub and marched around in the house in our father's and uncles' soldier's and sailor's caps, carrying toy guns. We had seen all the veterans in uniform in the great, solemn Memorial Day parades and heard the deep silence in River Street Cemetery and at the war memorial by the court house shattered by the firing of guns in salute to the war dead. In fact, we were every bit as excited about war games as we were about sports. Although even the smallest back yard, as long as it offered some cover and room for maneuver, would serve as a place to sneak around and hide and shoot at each other, our greatest campaigns were fought on Mt. Tom. For weapons, we used rifles and machine guns made from pieces of scrap wood picked up at Frost's Mill and nailed together. Once in a while someone would be carrying one of the very highly prized wooden Lugers or Thompson machine-guns which Jim Brownell fashioned with a jigsaw and could sometimes be persuaded to part with in a trade or a sale. We would divide up into two teams, one of which would be given a head start to hide and secure its positions against the invaders. By agreement, anyone who was shot would remain stationary until he was tagged alive by a still living member of his team. Bursts of pistol, rifle, and machine gun fire came from the vocal chords, followed by "gotcha Ronnie" or "gotcha Tom." The defending force offered particularly stiff resistance once they were dug in among the rocks just beneath the top of the mountain.

When we started these games, as we often did, from the Leonard twins' house at the bottom of Rose Hill, our campaigns took us through what we called "the Chinese Gardens." The official name of this place was Togo Hill. It was the result of an extraordinary landscape project carried out around the turn of the century by Dr. Charles L. Dana, a grandson of the man who built the house that is now the Woodstock Historical Society. With a great deal of vision and the help of what his son, John Cotton Dana, describes as "men, oxen, and blasting powder," Dana succeeded in turning several acres of pasture and woodland around his summer cottage into gardens and bowers displaying artifacts and replicas from various ancient cultures around the world. The men employed by Dana to carry out this project included local artisans Tink Day and Ernest Rennie, who did much of the intricate woodwork, and English-born, decorative painter Tom Phillips. As a child, I had often heard of this place, which by then belonged to Mrs. William Taft Barlow, Dr. Dana's daughter, and showed only traces of its former glory. Nevertheless, when my parents first showed me the great front gates in one of our walks on Rose Hill, the view which they offered suggested enchantment. Looking through them, we could see a raked dirt driveway winding past a small pool set among rocks and moss and guarded by a stone figure of an oriental god and then disappearing as the woods opened into a large mown area bordered by trees. It was not until some years later when we were ranging all over the southwestern part of the mountain with Rodney and Ron Leonard and Tom Brownell that my brother and I were able to satisfy our curiosity about what lay beyond those gates. Though Togo Hill was by then in a sad state of disarray, when coming on it, we would always interrupt our games of guns to trace its pathways among the ruins of what had once been Persian gardens, Japanese gardens, Chinese gardens, and Roman gardens, and we could sit among some of the still brightly colored remnants of the Chinese memorial gate and cross the wooden Greek bridge over a shallow ravine and admire the stone bas reliefs, reproductions of those at the Parthenon, which sat among the leaves at the base of a cliff on which they had once been mounted. We would examine the great decorative urns that were taller than we were and search out among the remaining antiquities two figures in particular. One was a large and fierce looking marble dog which, unbeknownst, to us, was Togo, a five-hundred year old Japanese statue meant to keep off spirits. The other was an imposing stone bust of the Greek god Zeus situated on a stone column at the end of a natural, open air temple among evergreens and glowering toward the north. As boys we were much in awe of these figures and used to imagine how scary it would be to be lost on Mt. Tom at night and to come upon them without warning. Togo Hill, or the "Chinese Gardens," has seemed to me to be a curious complement to the grounds of the Billings mansion, as though the south peak, not to be outdone by the north, had decided to create its own splendid gateway and, in its statuary, its own resident spirits requiring propitiatory gestures from travelers seeking entrance to the mountain fastnesses above.

As Rose Hill was slightly far to the west of our main route to the top of the mountain, our games of guns did not often take us through Togo Hill. That main route was the Faulkner Paths, and it was better than the Old Trail because the paths were more wide open and they offered more room for maneuver. No doubt simulated warfare was hardly what Mrs. Faulkner had envisioned in creating these paths and overseeing their design and construction from the spring of 1936 until the late fall of 1937. In fact, the idea for them came from Baden-Baden, a spa town in southern Germany which had built mountain paths for those who came there to take the cure. The Faulkner Paths do have about them a kind of geriatric look. They wander up the south peak in twenty-four tightening loops until they end at a small plateau just beneath the rocky ledges rising to the summit. This design makes them ideal for such family outings as those which first took me there as a child when my parents and brother and I would amble along, collecting acorns and looking for puffballs, those round, dried out mushrooms that when squeezed or stepped on emit a curious brown smoke. However, in our boyhood excursions and games, the Faulkner Paths, especially where their parallel loops are nearly contiguous and seem merely to wander back and forth without ascending, were simply too slow, and we would take the vertical shortcuts that have been made and followed by generations of less patient, more energetic hikers. More to our liking then was the final ascent, the short trail that began where the paths ended and led straight up over the ledges to the top. Traces of this trail can still be seen to the west of the new trail that cuts a diagonal across the rocks to come out somewhat nearer to the cross and star.

Back then, the Faulkner Paths started just where they do today, but in place of what is now Faulkner Park stood a meadow, which was fenced in from Mountain Avenue and from the path. One entered the Faulkner Paths by passing from the sidewalk of raked, crushed stone through a turnstile and walking between the fence bordering the meadow and the low, wide stone wall enclosing the grounds of what was then known as the Faulkner mansion. On any of our outings we would stop and gaze across the wall at the lawns and flower gardens, which were maintained by Roy Campbell, Fred

Bradley's grandfather, and especially at the little man-made pond which he kept stocked with speckled trout. It was also his job to keep the paths themselves cleared and raked and to keep their green wooden benches repaired and in good order.

In some of my earliest walks on the Faulkner Paths with my parents, our destination would be the little stone bridge. There my brother and I would take turns sneaking down into the shallow gully to play troll, and we liked to imagine sheltering there in a rain or hiding there to spy and eavesdrop on unsuspecting walkers. This bridge and another location a few levels below it never fail to bring back those and other memories, including my one and only experience in playing spin the bottle. Six of us, three boys and three girls, began the game sitting around in a circle across from each other in the middle of the path where, on the fourth level, it passes behind a boulder with two trees growing out of it. The couple at whom the ends of the Pepsi bottle pointed when it stopped spinning simply stepped around to the privacy of the other side of the rock and kissed, no peeking allowed. After a few rounds on that level, we went up to the stone bridge and played by the same rules. The problem was that when the couples made their way to the designated private place beneath the bridge, the boys were fine, but two of the girls were too tall to stand in the stone archway without bumping their heads.

Down the years, I have never thought of that morning without huge enjoyment. Just to recall it on my walks up the mountain — the furtive, anxious jockeying for position on the circle around the bottle; the nervous, silly giggling; the peeking; the inevitable cheating; the painful meeting of nose to nose, then learning to tilt the head; the enduring, innocent, breathtaking business of lips meeting; the lightheadedness for the rest of the day that left me so restless and disoriented that I walked out of a Saturday matinee at the Town Hall Theatre half way through the movie — brings on laughter of the best kind, welling up from the heart and spilling over in tears. Thus did the Faulkner Paths in the days of our youth prove equal to our earliest imagined exploits in matters of love as well as war.

In retrospect, the greatest thing about either of those enterprises was that it got us onto Mt. Tom and made us familiar with so much of what it has to offer. Whatever may be said today about allowing children to play war games and to handle weapons, toy or real, I'm sure that I owe to all of the pretend guns I nailed together much of my love of woodlands and hills in general and of Mt. Tom in particular. Not only did our long games of guns give us days on the mountain, but they also caused us to roam all over it, taking measure of its escarpments, keeping a vigilant watch for the enemy along its ridges and hollows, and, for long periods of time, simply lying in wait in something like perfect silence. In such moments, though largely absorbed in the competitive spirit of the game, we were taking in much of which we were hardly conscious — the speckled patterns of light and shadow where the sun penetrated the foliage, the calls of birds in the stillness, the distant tidal sound of wind in the treetops, the fresh, damp fragrance of earth and decayed leaves right beneath our noses — and we were no doubt gaining some lasting impression of longevity and permanence from our contact with the trees around us, some of which were nearly four hundred years old.

It was perhaps in the spirit of those scarcely realized moments of intimacy with our surroundings that we rarely extended our games beyond midday and began our slow descent of the backside of the mountain. Or it may have had something to do with the nature and configuration of our chosen routes home that we decamped our armies at the summit and simply wandered along together, casually exploring and talking about the morning's campaigns. For whatever reason, back then and in innumerable hikes on Mt. Tom over the years since, I have never made the transition from its rocky face, which fronts Woodstock, to its mountain roads, which slope northward away from the village, without feeling as though I were moving from action to contemplation and setting forth into quite another world.

That world was, of course, largely the creation of conservationist Frederick Billings. Along with the natural beauty of the landscape, enhanced by the various forestry projects which were carried out under his guidance, the most impressive part of what Dana refers to as "Mr. Frederick Billings' mountain domain" was "the network of roads, five miles or more in extent, and furnishing delightful drives and walks through the forest." What it took to complete this project, which was begun in 1886 and occupied a large work force for several years, is immediately apparent to the hiker within the first one hundred yards or so of his descent from the summit where the road is carried across the ravine between the south and north peaks by an impressive stone causeway. This was usually our first stop. We would pause there long enough to gaze down into the black water of the shallow pool below and to throw a few stones, and we would imagine ourselves mountain climbers able to scale the steep side of the north peak looming in front of us. And then, over that part of the road that points directly west and for some distance actually rises in its descent of the mountain, we would carry on, disputing over the morning's battles, recalling and imitating moments from such World War II movies as *The Sands of Iwo Jima*, *Back to Bataan*, *The Halls of Montezuma*, and *Breakthrough,* or arguing over the prowess of the Yankees and the Dodgers and talking about baseball cards. I can see us now, as though from the height of the ridge beneath which the road passes, toiling along, challenging each other, laughing, wrestling, then suddenly, impulsively, joining a straggler who is testing his strength against a standing dead tree or trying to dislodge a boulder so as to send it

221

toppling through the woods on the downhill side of the road. The crashing of the tree or rock, as we listen breathlessly, suddenly gives way to the woods' stillness, and the trunks of oak and beech seem momentarily to be regarding us, and the rock face above us to be wearing a frown.

Such oddly sobering moments would make us attentive to the woods and to the terrain in their own right, and we would find that we had reached that elevation where the road levels and our steps are softened by the carpet of needles shed by the great pines extending back on both sides and towering over us. These are some of Mt. Tom's largest trees. As though the land had risen to them, they occupy this eminence "like temples," as Thoreau saw the pines of Concord Woods, or "like masts outfitted to catch the wind as though they would cast anchor and set forth into the sky in pursuit of drifting clouds." We sometimes gazed up into their tops and listened. Taller and more massive and aloof today, they are still making much the same sound which I and my friends heard back then. On even the stillest of summer days when the leaves on the smaller deciduous trees growing around their base are unruffled, there can be heard up in their highest reaches a continuous soft, rushing, as of distant migrations. Rooted there on that height along the back side of the mountain where even the sounds of the village's noisiest parades are inaudible and the celebrations of the most long-awaited armistice have always been but faint rumors, these pines carry on their unchanging commerce with wind and sky, untroubled by the fleeting voices of walkers below and by the occasional drowsy clacking of mowing machines in the meadows toward which the road descends.

In spite of all of my years on Mt. Tom, the sight of these meadows has always come as something of a surprise. As boys, from the moment we caught our first glimpse through the pines of bright sunlight on field grass, we approached them with a kind or excitement and relief, as though we had somehow doubted they might still be there. When the road has negotiated its series of curves through the pines and emerged from the obscurity of the woods into the open, it seems, in fact, to be approaching some settlement or, at least, perhaps a farm. But the nearest building, the John French house at the top of Rose Hill, is largely hidden by its location and its design under the brow of a field, and that field's last traces of an old barn foundation were uprooted and plowed under years ago. For me this area, known to natives of Woodstock as Hill Top, has for years had its own peculiar significance. In the spring of my fifth grade year, four boys — Tom Brownell, Gil Emery, Bruce Johnson, and I — went up the mountain one afternoon after school and so much lost track of the time that, much to our parents' consternation, we didn't get home until seven o'clock. We talked all afternoon as we walked along, and at precisely that point in the road where Hill Top drops away to the southwest to offer an impressive view of the hills along the far side of the Ottauquechee Valley, we were brought to a halt by the discovery that some thought or feeling which until that moment each one of us had always assumed was private and incommunicable was, in fact, common to us all and could be shared. Whether it was some experience such as deja vu or some sense of the altered look of things since early childhood, I have long since forgotten, but that particular spot on the mountain road has, since that moment, always resonated with a feeling of unity and accord. In somewhat the same way, Hill Top, the field itself, as both a name and a place, has always been charged with its own sort of meaning. For it was a place where my mother and father often had picnics with their friends in the years before they were married. And, as is so often the case, the places of one's parents' courtship seem, even in name only, to be invested with a kind of glory.

Bordering Hill Top are the other two fields which complete this large area of open land largely enclosed by forest. Instead of following the mountain road where it veers around in an arc to bisect these fields, we would sometimes take a shortcut through the first field, racing as though just liberated, down over its northward slope to join up with the road at the edge of the woods. But more often we would keep to the road so as to wander in the largest and the loveliest of Mt. Tom's fields, which rises to the west and then rolls off toward the most distant wooded ridges along the backside of the mountain. In my mind's eye, this wide meadow has always had a great deal to do with sunset and the gathering light of many homeward treks. For years one of its most impressive features was its single, massive elm tree, which rivaled in size and magnificence some of the greatest elms to be seen in the village. Even after its slow death from Dutch elm disease, it stood a towering ruin, mocking my unfulfilled boyhood dream of someday whiling away an entire summer afternoon in the shade at its base. Then it slowly lost its branches and limbs until nothing stood but the huge column of its trunk, and finally that fell and was cut up and disposed of so that today, where its low stump was visible for a time, barely a trace remains to be seen.

There is something Arcadian, something golden, about these meadows. Because one enters them from the shade of the woods and is thus dazzled by their expanse of sunlight and by the surprise of their being there at all, or perhaps because they offer such a harmonious variety of slopes and rises, they seem to have been created simply to be admired and to inspire wonder. Still maintained, as they always have been, by the Billings Farm, they show no trace of the cows that grazed there when I was a boy and little sign of the men who keep them mowed to prevent the incursion of the surrounding woods. They appear to take care of themselves, or, better still, to require no care. Unfenced, they allow the walker to wander where he will and, where he would once have heard the clacking chime of cowbells and the lowing of the herd, they now invite him to accustom his ear to the quick, decisive chirp of the redwing blackbird and the agitation of distant crows. Whether their expanse is glistening with snow or their pasture grasses are sprinkled with buttercups and daisies or tinted purple and riffled by autumn breezes, or one finds them cropped and stubbly, they appear undefiled, and they offer a vision of light that seems to emanate as much from the earth itself as from the sky that suddenly widens above them.

Where the road leaves these fields and reenters the woods, we would cross a low stone causeway fording a small stream and stop at the stone drinking trough near the place where a number of branches of the mountain road meet. Here we would splash each other with the water that bubbled up into the trough and wonder whether it was safe to drink, which it probably was, but we didn't. Farther down the mountain road at another intersection, we would find the other drinking trough and then veer off to the north on a road that skirted a field to come out at the top of the old Mt. Tom Skiway. At the far edge of this field, very near the spot occupied today by the new cross-country warming hut, sat the only dwelling of any sort on Mt. Tom. It was a small cabin, very much like a hunting camp, with four bunk beds and a wood stove, and we had discovered it quite by chance in our wanderings. We knew it as Brownell's Cabin because Jim Brownell, a high school boy, had built it along with some of his friends including David Corkum, whose father, Harold Corkum, was manager of the Billings Farm. Although Jim's younger brother Tom had passed the message down to us that we were not supposed to be in or around the cabin, the temptation was simply too great, and I think that for several years we made as much use of it as did its owners. It was particularly useful in the winter when we would be skiing along the mountain road and wanted to get out of the wind for a while. In a freshly painted and improved condition, it now serves as a garden shed at the Corkum house on River Road.

Our main winter activity on that part of Mt. Tom, however, was sliding. Back then the only winter traffic on the mountain road was the tractors that went up from the Billings Farm and, in the process, packed the snow so that it was perfect for our runner sleds. On Saturday mornings a great number of us would trudge up the road, well mittened and scarved against the cold, pulling our Speedaways and Flexible Flyers by the ropes until we came to the place where it leveled off. Then, with a great running start, we would attack the slope in waves and go racing down the hard packed road, crowding each other, skidding around corners, and in some cases going off the road into snowbanks, flipping over, and even, as I did once, crashing into trees. Fortunately I slid backwards and partially off the sled before it plowed into a beech tree and pretty well folded up, embedding its front rim deeply enough in the bark to leave a mark which my brother pointed out to me on a recent walk on the mountain. If we stayed on course without much slowing down, our speed could take us down to the big pine tree near the entryway to the old sawmill. Over the years as I have watched my children slide straight down open fields on flying saucers and plastic sleds, I have wished that they could experience the thrill of steering a runner sled down a long, winding road of hard packed snow. I have often told them the stories of our sliding adventures, just as my father used to entertain us with stories of the great travois rides down Church Hill and Hartland Hill in the early days of the century when the streets were rolled instead of plowed and automobiles were few.

More often than not, however, when we boys, walking on the mountain road, left the meadows and came to that first intersection, we would ignore our parents' admonitions and turn left and go the short distance to the fifteen-acre pond called Pogue Hole, or

226

the Pogue, as it is known locally. Of the two main approaches to the Pogue offered by the network of mountain roads, this one from the south is much more dramatic. Instead of offering the preliminary glimpses through the trees of sunlight flashing on water which greet the eyes of anyone coming in along the backside of the pond from Prosper or West Woodstock, this approach from the Woodstock side discloses nothing until you are all at once standing practically at the water's edge. Following along the short distance of road that rises toward a great opening in the surrounding forest, I have always waited for the moment when the road crests that raised section of the south shore which is the pond's dam and outlet and suddenly reveals the entire pond in its woodland setting. In all the years of my visits there, my rising anticipation has never diminished in the least the peculiar force of that sight in all its detail of calm water stretching out under the sky to points along its varying shores. I have always simply stood there for a while, oddly astonished in spite of the familiarity of what I have seen so many times and in spite of the similarity of this moment to all such moments at this spot.

Pogue Hole is a natural pond which nevertheless owes some of its character to human enterprise and to legend. In the last decades of the nineteenth century, Frederick Billings included in his project for Mt. Tom the enlargement and improvement of the pond as it then stood, and since then, the Pogue has been maintained by the Billings Farm, which has kept up its encircling road, and by the Woodstock Aqueduct Company, which has used it as an alternative water supply in times of drought. In light of this stewardship, its name has for years seemed something of a misnomer, better suited to the pond as it appeared to the first settlers in this area and as it was described in accounts praising the work carried out by Mr. Billings. *The Vermont Standard* in June of 1891 celebrates the removal of "muck, sedge, and other matter that filled and occupied the surface" on the east side of the pond, which "used to be a regular quagmire covered with cat tails and brush, frightful to look at and absolutely dangerous to any step" and suggests that with the disappearance of the pond's "familiar ugliness ...the next step is to change its name."

Perhaps it was in response to these improvements and this suggestion that Pogue Hole began to be referred to as "the Pogue," as it has most often been called for as long as I can remember. However, in my earliest recollections and throughout my childhood, although the name had been softened, the pond itself retained something of its older character. Stories we had heard from our parents, which no doubt they in turn had heard from their parents, encouraged us to stay away from it in our explorations of Mt. Tom. We knew it to be bottomless, and we had heard that a team of oxen and their driver, while engaged in ice-cutting operations, had fallen through the ice and their bodies were never found. Earlier accounts speak of it as "most fearsome to the youth of [the nineteenth century]. It was a quaking bog and swamp hole of untold depth which swallowed everything that come within its reach without remorse, and never gave a hope of rescue." We had heard that the Pogue was the crater of an extinct volcano, and we knew that even the best of swimmers, were they to fall in, would not stand a chance because of quicksand. So entrenched were our superstitions that even skeptics such as distant cousins or new boys in town, to whom the Pogue on introduction seemed innocent enough, soon began to share our wariness. At first they posed really quite unanswerable objections — "Bottomless? You mean it goes through to the other side of the world? Then it would just drain out like a bathroom sink, and all the water would come out in China." But then we would speak of the volcano and the hapless oxen and driver, and they would tend to fall silent and to stay away from the steepest shores and to stand back a ways from the water, as we always did, in our stone-skipping contests.

Even today some story or event will occasionally make me remember momentarily the darkened look the pond used to wear as a result of these legends. For example, Dana tells us that "Connected with the early memories of Pogue Hole is one sad tale: here being the spot where Moses Samson was accidentally shot and killed by Nathan Tinkham, June 15, 1781, while the two were deer hunting together along the edge of the pond." Something like this incident or the recollection of an apparent suicide drowning that occurred there in the late 1970s or the closing scenes of the movie *Ghost Story* (shot in Woodstock during the winter of 1980-81), in which a model T Ford containing a dead body is pulled out of the Pogue, tend to bring back temporarily the old shadows. And I confess to having felt very uneasy one night as I watched my son warily swim out into the darkened water to untangle his fishing line from a clump of weeds in what at that moment looked much more like a quaking bog and swamp hole than it did the Pogue. However, my times there with my family and friends and my solitary wanderings there over many years have done much to scatter the mists of superstition and to give the Pogue a kind of brightness in all weathers and seasons.

Gazing across the water, I can still see the north side of the pond with some of the wonder of childhood. This most distant ridge, covered with beech and larch and maples and crowned with Norway spruce and stands of white pine, still suggests parkland and still beckons to me like some far off country. And it invariably awakens in me some barely remembered times when I went along with my grandfather Jillson and some of my uncles and aunts to fish for hornpout there at night. Walking northward counterclockwise around the Pogue, I always pause to converse with the mountain itself at that point of land where the road turns from its westerly direction sharply north. Here where my brother and my son and daughter have so often fished for bass and where, only a few years ago, I took my first Pogue swim, I can never resist breaking the stillness by shouting across the water at the north ridge, a wooded hillside that rises steeply from the pond's edge to what survey maps identify as the highest point on Mt. Tom. And in the echo that answers me, the north ridge returns my shout enriched by some barely discernible inflection of its own, the contribution of its rocks and trees, just as it returned our chorus of treble shouts, uncensored, when as boys we tested its fidelity with all sorts of exclamations.

But the Pogue, set in its rim of hills which shut out sound from all directions, favors a quieter approach. Sometimes, stealing upon it in the fall, I have seen Canada geese or a great blue heron lifting off from its surface. In early May on a morning walk around the pond, I've watched turtles of all sizes sunning themselves on fallen logs before shyly slipping into the water, and at the close of a summer day, I've heard the call of the hermit thrush in the stillness of the woods along its shores. Once, on a rainy Sunday evening in the autumn, where a section of the mountain road leading from the Pogue to the top of the old Mt. Tom Skiway skirts a small swamp, an owl with fully extended, perfectly motionless wings glided over my brother and me and disappeared into the dusk among the tree trunks without making a sound. That peculiar silence to which the Pogue seems bonded is most profound in the dead of winter when the pond is sealed in ice and snow and the only sounds are the muffled gurgling of water trickling into the bottom of the spillway and the occasional onslaughts of the north wind against the highest encircling ridges. Then, in the fading purple light, is the north ridge a study in black and white, where dark, vertical lines of tree trunks and barren branches rise against a backdrop of unmarked snow, and the sky over the great stands of pine on the pond's north side is a wash of emerald and deepening blue.

Over the years, some changes have taken place at the Pogue, but they have been few and gradual. A boat house once stood on a point of land just west of the dam, but the rotting remains of it which I saw sagging toward the water in the early 1950s have long since disappeared. The dam has been raised little by little, and a new cement spillway built to replace the old, slatted, wooden one. Through the tradition of forestry preservation initiated by Frederick Billings and carried on by Laurance Rockefeller, the surrounding woods have been thinned of brush to encourage growth and to let in more light and offer longer perspectives. And the log bench recently placed at the intersection of the circular road and the road coming in from Prosper blends well with the landscape and is no doubt a welcome sight to footsore walkers. However, despite these alterations, the Pogue still presents very much the same scene which I first beheld half a century ago, and its legends still stir the imagination. Bottomless, in a way, it may be, as Walden Pond was reputed to be in the old stories circulating around Concord in Thoreau's time. Just as I used to hear stories of "workers from the Billings farm" who tried unsuccessfully to measure the Pogue's depth, so Thoreau tells us of men who "have gone down [to Walden] from the village with a 'fifty-six' [pound weight] and a wagon load of rope, but have failed to find any bottom, for while the fifty-six was resting by the way, they were paying out the rope in the vain attempt to fathom their truly immeasurable capacity for marvelousness." By such stories and such efforts "the beholder measures the depths of his own nature," and we may rest with Thoreau in his assurance that "while men believe in the infinite, some ponds will be thought to be bottomless." Thus does the Pogue, like Walden Pond, offer itself as an image of the unchanging and the eternal. Trees have come to its shores and grown up and aged and fallen and been replaced by other trees, and successive generations of men in their time have seen themselves and their calmest thoughts reflected in its waters. But the pond itself stays the same. Its face is unaltered, so that on any day in high summer the visitor there will find it wearing its garland of water lilies and see its unwrinkled surface returning the placid gaze of the blue sky just as it did for the people of his parents' and grandparents' generations in their time.

Natural wonder though it surely is, the Pogue owes much of its splendor to its setting, to its residence up there in the great unchanging world of Mt. Tom and to its being part of what this world means to a native of Woodstock. Of all the hills that surround this village in its basin where the two river valleys meet, Mt. Tom is the most dramatic and, ultimately, the most reassuring. Those people who come to us from parts of the country that are less closed in and would contest the mountain's abruptness and the way its sudden, steep ascent cuts off too early the afternoon light, may soon grow accustomed to its great shadow. A woman who moved to Woodstock from Texas, Mrs. DeLette Rowland, once told me that upon first occupying the house at 3 River Street which was to be her home for many years, she experienced, in her words, something like "claustrophobia" every day when the sun dropped behind Mt. Tom. But she had long since become accustomed to it, she said, and felt that the mountain offered a kind of security which she couldn't imagine living without were she to find herself again in the wide open spaces of the southwest. Those who would find its massive walls too much of an obstruction and climb the mountain to gain a view north-northwest to Barnard and Pomfret would be disappointed when they discovered that neither summit opens out in that direction. Still, they may console themselves with the peripheral view westward to Pico and Killington and the relatively long look eastward until they draw in some, lower their expectations, and begin to look down at the village in its setting. And then they may begin to understand that this is the point, that this is why people revisit the summit in all seasons. Whatever may be said for the longer vistas, Mt. Tom belongs to Woodstock and offers us, primarily, a chance to look at ourselves. There is something reflexive in the way its face with its rugged brow is turned inexorably toward rather than away from the village, as though it is brooding on us a little from a perspective immensely older than our oldest houses or trees or roads or human purposes. And that perspective, without eschewing the sense of history, which even a stranger imbibes with the very air of the village, can give all of us who experience it even in a moment's vision, a deeper sense of belonging to this place in this moment in time.

Since returning from my earliest outings on the mountain with my parents, I have found inspiration and reassurance in the knowledge that, however long might be the intervals between my visits, the cliffs and paths, the caves and roads, and the woods and meadows would always be there carrying on their existence in the absence as well as the presence of all hikers and walkers until my return. During my years in Woodstock, I have looked upon its twin peaks from everywhere in the village, just as, in my years away from home I have seen it from afar and, in my mind's eye, gone back there time and again. Whether partly visible through the mists of an overcast day or wearing the first morning rays of sunlight that break over Blake Hill or sharing some secret with the sunset sky over its western shoulder, Mt. Tom down the years has always answered my search for signs of permanence among the changing scenes of village life. And it has become perhaps more valued as so many changes have brought about the disappearance of so much that I knew and valued in Woodstock. The mountain is a great old friend. Now, as it has become a national park, my hope is that it may be allowed to retain its character, that it may be treated with love and respect by those strangers who seek to make its acquaintance, and that it may continuc to inspire and to sustain the people of Woodstock in just the way it has always done.

This book was designed by
Wayne Thompson
and set in
Times New Roman
using Pagemaker
by Wendy Chamberlin
at The Woodstock Historical Society, Inc.
and printed by
Queen City Printers Inc.
Burlington, Vermont
on
and bound by Ace Bindery